NEW
FRONTIERS
IN MIDDLE EAST
SECURITY

Middle East

NEW
FRONTIERS
IN MIDDLE EAST
SECURITY

Edited by Lenore G. Martin

palgrave

First published in hardcover in 1999 by St. Martin's Press
First PALGRAVE™ edition: May 2001
175 Fifth Avenue, New York, N.Y. 10010 and
Houndmills, Basingstoke, Hampshire, England RG21 6XS
Companies and representatives throughout the world.

PALGRAVE is the new global publishing imprint of St. Martin's Press LLC Scholarly and Reference Division and Palgrave Publishers Ltd (formerly Macmillan Press Ltd).

ISBN 0–312–21414–6 hardcover
ISBN 0–312–23992–0 paperback

Library of Congress Cataloging-in-Publication Data
New frontiers in Middle East security / edited by Lenore G. Martin.
    p. cm.
    Includes bibliographical references (p.) and index.
    ISBN 0–312–23992–0
    1. Middle East—Politics and government—1979– 2. Middle East—Economic policy. 3. National security—Middle East. I. Martin, Lenore G.
DS63.1.N46   1998
956.05'3—dc21   98–44039
                                                                       CIP

A catalogue record for this book is available from the British Library.

Designed by Orit Mardkh Tenzer

First paperback edition: May 2001
10 9 8 7 6 5 4 3 2 1

Printed in the United States of America

TO TONY

WHOSE STRENGTH AND LOVE

ARE MY SECURITY

Contents

Part III: Economic Capabilities

Part IV: Natural Resources

Part V: Military Capabilities

Conclusions

Preface

*T*his book is the culmination of a project whose goal has been to create a new approach to the analysis of national security, with particular application to the Middle East. This new approach combines the rigor of international relations theory with the profound understanding of Middle East regional specialists. We hope it will prove useful to scholars and policymakers alike.

Chapter 1 sets out the conceptual framework. The national security paradigm integrates five variables, each of which forms a section of the book. The variables consist of political legitimacy, ethnic and religious tolerance, economic capabilities, availability of essential natural resources, and military capabilities. The contributors to the book illustrate the great value of an interdisciplinary approach to analyzing national security in a regional context. Their work underscores the interrelationships between the variables in the national security paradigm.

Madawi Al-Rasheed, a social anthropologist, examines the implications of the Saudi regime's use of official history to bolster its political legitimacy. The regime, which promotes its religious foundations in Wahhabism, encounters challenges to its legitimacy from both the Shi'i religious minority and the political Islamists. Farhad Kazemi and Augustus Richard Norton, both political scientists, examine the challenges and possibilities of increasing political legitimacy through political reform in the region. Mustapha Kamel Al-Sayyid, also a political scientist, attempts to measure political legitimacy and correlate it to national security.

The two chapters in the section on ethnic and religious tolerance by Sencer Ayata and Ayşe Güneş Ayata, both political sociologists, explore challenges to ethnic and religious tolerance in Turkey. One chapter focuses on the Islamist movement, Alevi-Sunni splits, and secularist revival; the other focuses on the Kurdish issues.

Sohrab Shahabi and Farideh Farhi, political scientists working on economic issues, discuss the structural and other reforms required for the economic development of the states of the region. Roger Owen, an economic historian, considers the potential for regional, subregional and transregional economic groupings as a means to increase the economic capabilities of those states.

Hillel I. Shuval, a water specialist, demonstrates the limitations of employing military capabilities in resolving the inter-state conflicts over Jordan River water, an essential natural resource for both Israel and Syria. He advocates peaceful resolution through conversion of water resources into exportable goods that can be acquired with economic capabilities.

Finally, in the section on military capabilities, Yair Evron, an arms control specialist, analyzes the opportunities for arms control in the region in his discussion of the potential for development of a common security system in the Middle East.

The conclusions of the book draw the chapters together, pointing to the integrated nature of the variables and discussing policy implications and directions for future research in developing a strong theoretical framework for analyzing issues of national security.

Lenore G. Martin
Cambridge, Massachusetts
April, 1998

Acknowledgments

*L*arge numbers of people and institutions have given generously of their time and resources to support this project. First I would like to thank the Maurice Pechet Foundation for its steadfast support over many years and, in particular, for its support of this project from its inception. This support not only enabled me to take a leave of absence in 1993-94 to develop the project, but also helped to support two conferences that brought the participants in the project together. Middle East Technical University in Ankara graciously hosted our first conference in 1995; the Rockefeller Foundation generously invited us to use its Bellagio Study Center for our second conference in 1996. The Center for Middle Eastern Studies at Harvard University has been an intellectually nurturing home for the project. I am especially appreciative of the continual support and wise guidance of its Director, Roger Owen. I am also indebted to him for his perceptive comments on my contributions to this book. His input was tremendously helpful in the preparation of this volume. Emmanuel College provided me with the time to work on the project during my sabbatical in the spring of 1997 and the Center for International Studies at MIT provided me with the place for that work. Furthermore, the Center for International Affairs at Harvard University has made it possible for me to explore developing concepts in international relations theory.

In addition to the contributors to this volume, a number of scholars have participated in the project by giving papers, providing commentary, and reviewing papers. These include Ziad Abu Amr, Ahmed Youssef Ahmed, Shamlan Al-Essa, Said Assaf, Barry Buzan, Massoud Karshenas, John Kolars, Bahgat Korany, Mary Morris, Carol Saivetz, Hossein Seifzadeh, Mohammed Selim, Gary Sick, Nabil Sukkar, Bassam Tibi, Saadia Touval, Masayuki Yamauchi, and Steve Yetiv. Their assistance has had an important impact on the project. I also want to thank Margaret Owen for her especially insightful editing and her wonderful and sustaining sense of humor.

My dear friend, Ayşe Güneş-Ayata, who helped coordinate our meeting in Ankara, proved through her patience and perspicacity that friendship can actually be strengthened by a potentially frustrating long-distance endeavor. Moreover, I remain very grateful to my colleague, Dick Norton, with whom I discussed my ideas of national security in the Middle East many times and who commented on my papers in a number of different formats. I am particularly grateful to him for encouraging me to hold a second conference on "New Frontiers in Middle East Security" and joining in the application for the use of the Bellagio Study Center of the Rockefeller Foundation for that meeting.

Most of all, I join the ranks of so many academic parents and spouses in thanking my children and husband for their support. Actually, my husband Tony's support was more than the usual moral support. He has accompanied me on research trips to the Middle East numerous times, exchanged ideas with me, and read and reread my work. His expansive intellect and generosity of spirit have supported this project and much of our lives together.

Finally, I want to acknowledge my deep appreciation for two of my mentors, Morton Kaplan and the late Albert Wohlstetter. Both of them challenged me to think analytically and theoretically while a graduate student, and I continue to appreciate that challenge so many years later.

List of Contributors

MADAWI AL-RASHEED

Lecturer in Social Anthropology
Department of Theology and Religious Studies
King's College, University of London
London, UK

MUSTAPHA KAMEL AL-SAYYID

Professor of Political Science
Director, Center for the Study of Developing
    Countries
Cairo University
Cairo, Egypt

AYŞE GÜNEŞ-AYATA

Professor and Assistant Dean
Department of Public Administration
Faculty of Economics and Administrative
    Sciences
Middle East Technical University
Ankara, Turkey

SENCER AYATA

Professor of Sociology and Department Chair
Middle East Technical University
Ankara, Turkey

YAIR EVRON

Professor of Political Science
Tel Aviv University
Tel Aviv, Israel

FARIDEH FARHI

Research Associate
Institute for Political and International Studies
Tehran, Iran

FARHAD KAZEMI

Professor of Political Science
New York University
New York, NY, USA

LENORE G. MARTIN

Professor of Political Science
Emmanuel College, Boston
Affiliate in Research, Center for Middle Eastern
 Studies
Harvard University
Associate, Weatherhead Center for International
 Affairs
Harvard University
Cambridge, MA, USA

AUGUSTUS RICHARD NORTON

Professor of Anthropology and
 International Relations
Boston University
Boston, MA, USA

ROGER OWEN

A. J. Meyer Professor of Middle East History
Director of the Center for Middle Eastern
 Studies
Harvard University
Cambridge, MA, USA

SOHRAB SHAHABI

Deputy Secretary-General
Economic Cooperation Organization
Tehran, Iran

HILLEL I. SHUVAL

Linenfeld-Kunin Professor of Environmental
 Health
School of Applied Science and Technology
Hebrew University of Jerusalem, Israel

List of Acronyms

ACC	Arab Cooperation Council
ACRS	Arms Control and Regional Security
CBM	Confidence Building Measures
CDLR	Committee for the Defense of Legitimate Rights
CFE	Conventional Armed Forces in Europe
CSBM	Confidence and Security Building Measures
CSCE	Conference for Security and Cooperation in Europe
EU	European Union
GAP	Günay Anadolu Projesi (Southeastern Anatolia Project)
GATT	General Agreement on Tariffs and Trade
GCC	Gulf Cooperation Council
HADEP	Halkin Demokrasi Partisi (People's Democracy Party)
HMEWP	Harvard Middle East Water Project
IMF	International Monetary Fund
MENA	Middle East and North Africa
MWR	Minimum Water Requirement
MU	Maghrib Union
NAFTA	North American Free Trade Area
NATO	North Atlantic Treaty Organization
OPEC	Organization of Petroleum Exporting Countries
OSCE	Organization for Security and Cooperation in Europe
PKK	Partiye Karkeran Kurdistan (Kurdistan Workers' Party)
PNA	Palestine National Authority
SAP	Structural Adjustment Program
SCP	School for Training Chaplains and Preachers
UAE	United Arab Emirates
UNIDIR	United Nations Institute for Disarmament Research
WMD	Weapons of Mass Destruction
WMDFZ	Weapons of Mass Destruction Free Zone
WP	Welfare Party
VP	Virtue Party

List of Permissions

Map 9.1 "Major Water Projects in the Jordan River Basin," from Stephan Libiszewski, *Water Disputes and Their Role in the Resolution of the Arab-Israeli Conflict*, ENCOP. Occasional Paper No. 13 (Berne: Center for Security Studies and Conflict Research/Swiss Peace Foundation, August 1995), p. 8.

Map 9.2 "International Border between Israel and Syria and the 1949 Truce Line," from *Peace with Security: Israel's Minimum Security Requirements in Negotiations with Syria* by Ze'ev Schiff, Policy Paper No. 34 (Washington, D.C.: The Washington Institute for Near East Policy, 1993), p. 8.

Map 9.3 "Existing Syrian Dams on the Yarmuck River and the Site for Proposed Jordan-Syrian Al-Wahda Dam and the Hydroelectric Station," from Arnon Soffer, "The Relevance of the Johnston Plan to the Reality of 1993 and Beyond," in *Water and Peace in the Middle East,* edited by J. Isaac and H.I. Shuval (Amsterdam: Elsevier Press, 1994), p. 121.

Map 9.4 "Suggested Possible Lines of Israeli Withdrawal from the Golan Heights Based on Water Security Considerations," copyright *Ha'aretz* Daily Newspaper Ltd., October 8, 1993, Part 2.

Map 9.5 "The Jordan River Basin Watershed Boundaries, Tributaries, and Mean Annual Discharges," from Arnon Soffer, "The Relevance of the Johnston Plan to the Reality of 1993 and Beyond," in *Water and Peace in the Middle East,* edited by J. Isaac and H. I. Shuval (Amsterdam: Elsevier Press, 1994), p. 120.

CONCEPTUAL FRAMEWORK

CHAPTER ONE

Towards an Integrated Approach to National Security in the Middle East

LENORE G. MARTIN

INTRODUCTION

*F*or both scholars and statesmen, how a state defines its security is a critical issue in international politics and foreign policy. During the Cold War the superpower competition focused the definition of national security in military terms. However, at the end of the Cold War this focus seems insufficient. Events such as the collapse of the Soviet Union, despite its superior military capabilities, have reinvigorated the debate between realists and liberals over what constitute the true foundations of security. The realist approach emphasizes the military aspects of national security; the liberal approach emphasizes multiple non-military aspects. From a theoretical perspective, the problem with the realist approach is that with only a single factor it can explain too little, and the problem with the liberal approach is that with multiple factors it tries to explain too much.[1]

Some scholars have sought to resolve this academic debate by proposing a third approach which combines a small set of military and non-military aspects of national security into a more comprehensive definition that will work particularly in Third World states.[2] Different proponents of the third approach offer different sets of factors or variables and there is no agreement on the optimum set for explaining national security. I propose in this chapter to increase the explanatory power of this third approach by creating a new paradigm of national security with a small but integrated set of five variables, one military and four non-military. The purpose of this chapter is to demonstrate the logic of this set of variables and how they are integrated.

Throughout the chapter I will use examples from the Middle East to provide quick illustrations of the utility of this novel paradigm as a tool for analysis of national security. In the remainder of the book, well-known area specialists and international relations scholars provide more in-depth analyses of the ways in which the components of this integrated national security paradigm work in the larger, contemporary Middle East. It is hoped that applications of the paradigm to other regions of the globe will further prove the utility of this integrated approach.

THEORETICAL APPROACHES TO THE CONCEPT OF NATIONAL SECURITY

The Academic Debates over the Definition of National Security

At the core of every search for a definition of national security is the concept of threats and every definition calls for answers to three key questions:

1. What is the target of the threat?
2. What is the source of the threat?
3. What is the nature of the threat?

Because multiple answers are possible to this set of questions, the international relations literature has spawned a plethora of definitions of security.[3] The different answers to these questions in international relations literature have coalesced into the two major camps that have dominated the approaches to theory in international relations: realists and liberals, and their progeny, neo-realists and neo-liberals.

The Realist Approach

The emphasis on the primacy of military security is the hallmark of the realist approach to international relations which has ruled the scholarly literature and prevailed in the corridors of power during the Cold War.[4] From the realist perspective, international politics is a struggle for power by sovereign states in an anarchic world. International behavior, wars and alliances, the search for hegemony and the countervailing tendency for a balance of power, could be predicted from the structure of the international system, i.e., the relative power of the contestants. From this perspective states pursue their national interests by maintaining sovereignty and by securing their territorial integrity.

The realist definition of security is very much state-centric. The state is threatener and threatened. The threats are external and predominantly military. Their targets are primarily the territorial integrity and national sovereignty of the state.

For an academic realist as well as for a diplomatic practitioner of realpolitik, the best prescription for a state to achieve national security is to build a powerful military establishment and seek military predominance or at least a balance of military power. During the Cold War, this prescription for achieving security, at least for the global superpowers, meant developing effective strategies of deterrence. Nuclear deterrence was achieved through secure second-strike capabilities, and conventional force deterrence by major force commitments in place on the front lines of Europe and rapid deployment forces ready to reach regional front lines in crisis situations.

The abrupt end to the Cold War created an intellectual crisis for realists whose approach failed to predict the collapse of the Soviet Union and the end of the Cold War, as realist scholars admit and their critics never fail to point out.[5] The problem for realist theory is that it focused on the military balance of power and accepted the status quo of superpower mutual deterrence. It never allowed for the possibility that a superpower could implode and, as a result, radically change global international politics.[6]

The Liberal Approach

The collapse of the Soviet Union revealed in the clearest of terms the relative weakness of the realist approach and the need to look even harder at the contending idealist or liberal approach.[7] Liberal theorists see international politics as more than a struggle for power among nation states. They recognize cooperative behavior both at the state and societal levels; they are optimistic about the prospects for institutionalizing norms for peaceful international conduct and utilizing non-military means to achieve it.

For liberals national security is, accordingly, more than countering military threats and maintaining the integrity of territorial boundaries and regimes in power.[8] Liberals expand the concept of national security to include major threats to human security. Thus for liberals national security is not state-centric. Threats to human security arise both from within national boundaries and across national boundaries and include threats from terrorist movements, as well as economic, environmental, and ideological threats, even natural disasters and diseases.[9] Whenever such threats cross boundaries or are common to more than one state they become transnational issues. It is not just the state that is threatener and threatened. Threats also emanate from transnational actors: groups such as ethnic groups, or movements such as ideological movements, or entities such as multinational corporations.

For liberals there is no simple prescription for achieving national security as there is for realists. There is a clear preference, however, for cooperation at the international level and democratization or political participation at the domestic level. States that reflect open, civil societies and can achieve market economies (though the one does not necessarily presuppose the other) are viewed as more stable and less vulnerable to the inherent threats of social fragmentation and economic collapse.

The problem with the liberal approach is that in avoiding the realist trap of a simple set of factors or variables that explains too little, liberalism falls into the trap of trying to explain too much. Its complex set of variables provides no way for the scholar or the policymaker to decide what are the most important variables for explanation or policy prescription. The liberal becomes a current historian who must consider multiple data sources before fashioning explanations for any current phenomenon. In the search for non-state-centered security, there are too many potential transnational actors, from ideologically motivated political parties to linguistically differentiated ethnic groups to religious communities. There are too many demands upon governments, any one or combination of which could threaten the state: overpopulation, illegal immigration, dysfunctional family units, inefficient educational systems, cultural taboos, and work ethics. And there are too many alternatives to the employment of military means to respond to such demands, from propaganda to modifications of industrial policy.[10] How does the scholar or policymaker prioritize the actors, the actions, and the governmental responses that are relevant to explaining or managing international phenomena in the face of such complexity?

The Third Approach

In sum, the crisis for international relations theory set off by the unpredicted end to the Cold War created an intellectual crossroads that spawned the search for a third road towards new frontiers in security studies.[11] This third approach to defining national security seeks to combine military factors with non-military factors. Much of the focus for applying these new definitions of national security has been in the Third World. Many of the scholars espousing a third approach regard the Cold War security specialists as West-centric. Realist principles work for highly developed industrialized global powers, such as the United States and Western Europe, where the legitimacy of political regimes is not as threatened by fragile economies and demands for greater political participation, and their territorial integrity is not as threatened by secessionist groups.[12] Realist principles do not necessarily work for Third World lesser developed countries who are plagued by internal threats to their stability.[13] The third approach sees underdeveloped economies often lacking critical resources, unstable political regimes, and fragmented societies, as causes of national insecurity per se. Threats to these fragile states emanate not merely from external sources, but more likely from internal and transnational sources.

The Integrated Approach

What distinguishes the various third approaches from each other is their selection of differing non-military factors that, along with military defense, can address the basic needs of national security.[14] Where my own approach departs from other third approaches is that it demands that national security itself be treated as a dependent variable, and that the factors that contribute to the variation in national security be treated as an integrated set of independent variables. I therefore refer to this as an integrated approach. The goal of the integrated approach is to create a paradigm or model of national security in which variations in national security can be explained by the varying interactions of this small set of variables.

How then do I define national security and how does it vary? I define national security as the capability of a state to deter or counter threats to its three components: territory, society, and regime.[15] It is therefore possible to conceive of states as having more security or less security in accordance with the extent of the threats that they face to each of these components and the varying capabilities of the states to counter or deter such threats. At one end of this continuum the very survival of the state is at stake. For example, an extreme form of a highly insecure state is one whose territory is threatened by complete conquest, whose regime is threatened by complete collapse, whose society is threatened by ethno-religious secession or disintegration, and the state has few capabilities to counter such threats. Towards the other end of the continuum, only minor changes to the integrity of the state are threatened. For example, there may be threats to small areas of a state's borders, threats to change a regime that will leave both territory and society intact, or threats of changes in the ethno-religious composition of a society that do not raise threats to the regime or the territory. Indeed at the very end of the continuum, a highly secure state would either face no such threats or, if faced, be quite capable of deterring them. What are the critical variables that provide states with the capabilities to counter or deter such threats? The five independent variables in the national security paradigm are: military capabilities, political legitimacy, ethnic and religious tolerance, economic capabilities, and availability of essential natural resources.

IDENTIFYING THE VARIABLES

How has this integrable set of independent variables been selected? Their selection has been influenced very much by three factors: the theoretical level of analysis; how one defines key terms in the proposed paradigm; and, to some extent, the empirical experience from which the paradigm is drawn or to which it will be applied which, in our instance, is the Middle East region.

The Level of Analysis

In selecting a set of variables in international relations theory, one starting point is to select a level of analysis.[16] The focal choices within the discipline of international relations are global, regional, state, societal, or individual. The boundaries of each choice, however, are never that clear. Global powers act within regions, and regions themselves are notoriously difficult to define. Transnational actors such as militarized ethnic groups (Kurdish guerrillas for example) or organized proponents of global or regional ideologies (communism or political Islam for example) cross societal, national, and even regional boundaries; and international institutions such as the World Bank and the International Monetary Fund, as well as the United Nations and its agencies, interact at various levels. In any event, my approach uses the state as the level of analysis. The state is the most commonly found interacting unit in international relations generally, and within the Middle East region specifically. It is also the focus for policymaking on national security issues. For these reasons it is the state that is the target of threats to national security.

Defining the Key Terms

State

I define the state as an organizing concept composed of the three interrelated components to which I referred earlier: territory, regime, and society.[17] This definition follows the tradition of international relations literature of using the concept of state as an all-encompassing entity, i.e., a unit or actor within an international system, rather than the sociological tradition which refers to the state as a governing or coercive institution within an all-encompassing society.[18]

Territory

That every state has a territorial definition is not disputed. In turn, that territorial definition creates a physical definition for the society within the state. Thus any particular territorial definition circumscribes which ethnic and religious communities are included or excluded from any state, as well as which natural resources, such as water, oil, and arable land are available to support its economy or lie outside of its borders.

Regime

That every state has a regime is also commonly accepted. Regime refers to the political organizing principles or type of government such as democratic and autocratic, republican and monarchical (all of which are found in the contemporary Middle East).[19] One should be careful not to confuse the concept of regime with that of any particular government in power at any moment in time. Changes in governments can well occur without changes in regime. Using Middle East examples, Saddam Hussein formally succeeded Ahmad Hasan al-Bakr as head of government in Iraq in 1979, without a change in the Ba'thist regime. On the other hand, regime changes betoken both changes in organizing principles as well as governments. For example, military autocracies overthrew monarchies in Egypt in 1952 and Iraq in 1958 and, after the British colonial regime left Palestine in 1948, it became an Israeli democracy.

Society

Less easily defined in political discourse is the concept of society.[20] In its most basic form, society refers to the population and all of its interrelations within the defined territory that are subject to a particular regime. In trying to distinguish one society from another it is not unusual to focus on one of the aspects or dimensions of such interrelationships.[21] Thus we could speak of a society in terms of a political community and ascribe to society the same organizing principles as apply to the regimes in power.[22] For example, one can refer to democracies, or civil societies, or tribal monarchies (or more historically, feudal societies or theocracies). We could speak of a society as an economic community which is free market or capitalist, socialist, or collectivist. We could refer to a society in terms of its predominant social strata or ruling class or elite, such as aristocratic or bourgeois or Western-educated. We could also speak of a society in terms of the composition and interrelations of its ethnic and religious communities. Thus we can refer to societies as pluralistic, or relatively homogeneous, or ethnically and/or religiously fractious.

As with the concept of regime, one should not assume that the appropriate label for the society is static. There can be societal changes with or without regime changes. For example, massive immigration or differential population growth rates could change the complex of ethnic and religious communities, as occurred for instance in Lebanon before the civil war of the 1970s. Moreover, when there is a major societal upheaval that changes both the organizing principles of the regime and of the society, we refer to it as a revolution. The Khomeini revolution in Iran, for example, overthrew the Shah's monarchical regime and also created a new theocratic elite; the Ataturk revolution in Turkey overthrew the sultanate and created a new secular elite. Society, in sum, is both multi-dimensional and susceptible to change.

The Independent Variables

By defining the state in terms of its three components of territory, regime, and society, we are guided to the selection of the independent variables of state security by identifying the threats to each of the components. Generally threats to a state can be divided into those that are violent and those that are non-violent. Violent threats target all three components of the state. The sources of violent threats emanate both from outside of the state and within it, and a state requires military capabilities with which to deter and counter such violent threats. What, however, are the non-military sources and targets of threats to the survival and integrity of the territory, regime, and society? These are the four non-military variables: political legitimacy, ethnic and religious tolerance, economic capabilities, and the availability of essential natural resources. Manifested as sources of threats, these variables do not necessarily target all three components of the state. Some targets overlap. Threats to political legitimacy, for example, target the regime and threats to ethnic and religious tolerance target the society. However, threats to economic capabilities may target regime and society, and threats to the availability of essential natural resources can target the territory and also constitute threats to economic capabilities, thereby impacting upon both regime and society. Let us briefly examine each of these variables and how they integrate with each other.

Military Capabilities

A state needs military capabilities to counter external threats of violence as well as internal threats emanating from militarized or armed groups. Such groups include terrorists and guerrillas as well as perpetrators of coups and military insurrections. Clearly a state requires economic capabilities in order to provide for its military capabilities, i.e., to equip armed forces and internal security forces. Furthermore, the need to secure the availability of essential natural resources forms a critical part of defense strategy which in turn dictates the amounts and types of military capabilities a state will require. Saudi Arabia, for example, expends substantial amounts of financial resources on maintaining a sophisticated combat air force comparable in size to that of Iraq and Iran.[23] Such air defense is critical to deter and counter pre-emptive air strikes on its desalination plants so as to secure its water supplies, on its ports and airports so as to secure importation of other vital supplies, as well as on its petroleum facilities so as to safeguard key components of its economy.[24]

Although it is a truism that the greater the state's economic capabilities, the greater the quantity of military forces and equipment it can afford, there is also a qualitative component to military capabilities that cannot be overlooked. Consider the intangible willingness of a population to contribute human resources and to undertake personal sacrifices, i.e., to fight for the regime, the society, and the territory that is imperiled. The extent of this patriotism is affected by the extent of political legitimacy accorded the regime, and ethnic and religious tolerance within the society.

Furthermore, there are foreign and defense policies that a state can pursue to increase or decrease its military capabilities. For example, a state can multiply its military capabilities by forming alliances with other states willing to come to its defense. Alliance strategies, on the other hand, are often constrained by political legitimacy and ethno-religious tolerance variables. The Gulf crisis of 1990-91, for example, which brought hundreds of thousands of Western, non-Muslim forces into Saudi Arabia, stimulated both the Western-educated liberal and Islamist ultra-conservative opposition to the monarchy. On the other hand, the kingdom was constrained by the mutual ideological intolerance between the more conservative monarchical regime in Riyadh, and the more revolutionary Islamic republican regime in Tehran, from forming an alliance that could have helped contain an aggressive Iraq.

Secondly, a state can seek to limit the growth of its military capabilities or decrease them by engaging in arms control efforts with other states. Yet arms control regimes are difficult to implement, as evidenced in the Middle East, when states need military capabilities for internal security as a result of challenges to political legitimacy and ethnic and religious dissension, and when ideological intolerance inhibits the institution of confidence building measures that are precursors for arms control agreements.

Political Legitimacy

Ever since Max Weber's observation, following the sociological tradition, that states claim the monopoly on the legitimate use of violence in a society, social science has acknowledged that those subject to a regime are willing to obey its authority by virtue of the phenomenon known as political legitimacy.[25]

Regimes attempt to reinforce their own political legitimacy in various ways such as through political education and indoctrination, and also by identifying the regime with the state. Therefore, by inculcation of loyalty to the state, i.e., patriotism or nationalism, with symbols such as flags, anthems, and political myths, they also aid in legitimizing the regime.[26] Challenges to the political legitimacy of a regime arise from ideological groups such as communists and nationalists. Regimes that do not tolerate political dissent attempt to delegitimize these groups as disloyal to the state itself.

Political legitimacy enables the regime to mobilize popular support to deter or withstand external military threats. It also enables such mobilization to deter or withstand secessionist threats from dissident ethnic groups, terrorist threats from radical religious groups, or subversive threats to the regime by ideologically opposed factions that threaten coups or large-scale civil disobedience. The greater the political legitimacy of its regime, the more the state has the capability to deter or withstand civil war or revolution, and to maintain the support of its populace in the face of economic crises and deprivation of natural resources.

If the populace does not accept the political legitimacy of the regime, and the state succumbs to internal strife, its military capabilities are weakened or diverted. External enemies can take advantage of internal strife and use the internal enemies of the regime to destabilize the regime, or directly intervene in the state. Civil strife can also spill over and affect the security of surrounding states as rebels seek safe havens and supply routes.

Examples of military intervention and the spillover effect abound in the civil wars and insurrections of recent times in various regions of the world, including the Middle East. Recall, as an example, the Lebanese civil war of the 1970s. When Lebanon's Muslim communities challenged the legitimacy of the Maronite-Sunni power-sharing arrangement and civil war erupted, Syria intervened in 1976 to impose stability; Israel invaded in 1982 to create a security zone in the south; Saddam Hussein supported the brief leadership fight of the Maronite General Michel Aoun; and Iran continues to support Hizbollah, which has fired rockets into Israel from bases in Lebanon.

Ethnic and Religious Tolerance

Ethnic and religious dissension threaten the integrity of the society as well as the legitimacy of the regime. In the Middle East, radical Islamists have directed violence not only against governmental officials but also against religious minorities or the society at large. For example, radical Islamists in Egypt have used violence against the Copts; in Turkey they have used violence against the Alevis; and in Israel Hamas has used violence against Israelis at large. Those societies that have more homogeneous ethnic and religious communities than others may withstand such social shocks because of their relative ethnic and religious cohesion. However, cohesion is not always possible in societies with disparate ideological, religious, and ethnic communities. The political socialization process implemented by regimes to inculcate loyalty to the state and forestall ethnic and religious dissension does not necessarily aim to produce ethnic and religious cohesion. Thus, the general attribute that enables such heterogeneous and potentially fractious ethnic and religious groups to co-exist within the same society is, in my view, tolerance.

Ethnic and religious dissension not only endangers territories, regimes, and societies by threats of separatism and secession; it can also leave the state vulnerable to outside interference. This has been evident in Iranian support for the Iraqi Kurds, Iraqi support for Iranian Kurds, and various transnational Kurdish groups' support for each other. Furthermore, ethnic groups may be concentrated in areas of valuable natural resources for the state and, by engaging in strikes or sabotage, they can adversely impact the state's economic capabilities. More extreme threats of secession could threaten to cut off the state's access to such valuable resources. For example, Iraqi Kurds have been concentrated in the oil producing region of Iraq, leading the regime to attempt to relocate them in 1975.[27] Often ethnic groups may be underprivileged and suffer discrimination in the allocation of welfare or economic benefits, or political participation, thus causing disaffection, such as occurred with the Shi'is of Saudi Arabia and, more recently, the Shi'is of Bahrain. Ethnic and religious groups in the diaspora can sometimes fuel this dissension by providing financial, logistical, and political support from abroad.

Economic Capabilities

Common to both the preservation of regimes and societies is an implicit expectation of the ruled that, in return for granting legitimacy to the rulers, the regime will provide some level of welfare or economic well-being for the society. This might range from small-scale regulation of a market economy to wholesale control of the means of production and distribution. Whatever the organizing principles behind governmental involvement in the economy or reallocation of economic benefits, there is an underlying need for economic capabilities. There can be no debate over guns versus butter unless the state has the economic capabilities to produce or obtain both of them.

A weak economy hinders a state's ability to support its defense establishment either from its indigenous arms industry or through purchase of weapons from global sources. Moreover, a weak economy undermines a state's economic development and its ability to maintain social welfare programs and employment for workers. This feeds back and increases the risks of threats to the legitimacy of the regime, as well as ethnic and religious dissension especially where there is considerable economic disparity between ethnic and religious groups. In Egypt, for example, the extensive welfare services provided by the political Islamists subtly undermine the legitimacy of the Egyptian regime, while the attacks on tourists by the radical Islamists more directly challenge that legitimacy by seeking to deter tourism and thus undermine one of the mainstays of the Egyptian economy.

Furthermore, a state's international opponents can increase its economic vulnerability by imposing boycotts and embargoes, such as the Western embargo against Saddam Hussein after the Kuwait crisis of 1990-91. On the other hand, a strong economy enables a state to strengthen its military, as well as social welfare programs, and can even help the state overcome threats created by limitations of vital natural resources. Thus, for example, desalination plants can be financed to overcome water shortages.

Availability of Essential Natural Resources

Closely linked to a state's economic capabilities are its natural resources such as food, energy, and water, which are critical to the survival of its population. Typically, the territorial definition of the state will circumscribe what natural resources the state has within its boundaries—or must obtain from outside of its boundaries—in order to support its economy. Geography and climate create regional and global variations on this theme: water is more critical in desert areas than tropical areas; energy resources such as oil, gas, and hydro are scarcer in Japan and Europe than in North America, etc. As already noted, a strong economy can compensate for deficits in natural resources by enabling the state to purchase them from others and, on the other hand, plentiful natural resources can help strengthen an economy.

The regime's failure to maintain the supply of essential natural resources creates repercussions ranging from crises such as starvation to retarding economic development. This in turn feeds ideological opposition to the legitimacy of the regime. Foreign suppliers of critical natural resources can threaten to cripple the state's economy, particularly in times of crisis, as evidenced by international concern over "the oil weapon," "water wars," and "food security." Moreover, some natural resources, such as oil and water, straddle state boundaries and provide adjacent states with opportunities to cut them off and create or exacerbate crises. Thus Syria and Iraq view the dams that have been constructed for Turkey's Southeastern Anatolia Project (GAP), for the development of its southeastern economy, as a potential threat to cut off water supplies, from the Euphrates and Tigris rivers, that are vital to the economies of Syria and Iraq.

Excluded Variables

Why not include other variables for the paradigm? Because of the paradigm's focus on the state as the subject of security, this set of five variables excludes other variables that raise issues for human security. Such excluded variables include population growth rates, refugees and migration, as well as environmental hazards, education and communication, and the diffusion of knowledge and technology.[28] While contributing to the pressures that challenge the regime, the society, and even the territory of a state, these human security variables are not independent variables. They do not, by themselves, pose direct threats to the integrity or survivability of the state.[29] Thus, for example, relatively high population growth rates, refugees, and mass migrations put great strains on a state's economic capabilities and natural resources. They can also affect ethnic and religious tolerance within the society. However, they only operate to create threats to state security if one or more of the paradigm's five variables intervene. For example, the influx into Lebanon of large numbers of Muslim Palestinian refugees from Jordan after their expulsion in 1970 exacerbated the tensions within the very divided Lebanese society in which Muslims challenged the legitimacy of the confessional regime. On the other hand, if a regime and society have legitimacy and the state has the economic capabilities, the regime can absorb large waves of refugees, or even erect barriers to overpopulation and immigration, as occurred in Turkey and other regional states with respect to Kurdish refugees, and in the Gulf states with respect to Palestinian immigration. Similarly, although governments attempt to reverse the deleterious effects of environmental hazards or negotiate international agreements to cooperate in combating them, such as agreements over the ozone layer or efforts to address the greenhouse effect, environmental hazards are not viewed as direct threats to the security of the state as a whole.

The Regional Influence on Selection of Variables

As was noted earlier, many progenitors of the third approach to explaining national security reject a realist West-centric analysis that derives from North American and Western European First World experience, and propose security paradigms drawn from the Third World experience. This suggests that the selection of variables that are significant for national security may be regionally influenced, and indeed my own paradigm was created to work first for the Middle East.

Regions, however, defy easy definition.[30] Wherever one draws the regional boundary one always creates issues of inclusion and exclusion. For example, the "core" definition of the Middle East is typically Egypt through Iran, and excludes the Arab states of North Africa and the non-Arab state of Turkey.[31] This work defines the Middle East region as the core states plus Turkey. Why Turkey? Many definitions of the region exclude Turkey, probably because Turkey, since the collapse of the Ottoman Empire, has for the most part excluded itself from traditional Middle East politics. Indeed, republican Turkey traditionally has had a European orientation. This has been partly for ideological reasons, given the Ataturk revolution's desire to break with the Ottoman conventions and secularize the state. The European orientation has also had an economic motive, given modern Turkey's desire to join the European Union. Moreover, Turkey traditionally has viewed its most pressing security issues in military terms and as emanating from across its northern and western boundaries, namely, the Soviet Union/ Russia and Greece.

Yet, Turkey's major internal issues are similar to those of other developing countries of the Middle East. Like most of the core states, Turkey consists of a largely Muslim population and faces similar challenges to legitimacy arising from politically active religious groups, as well as challenges to its territorial integrity arising from an active Kurdish separatist movement. Moreover, Turkey shares and to some extent controls a significant watershed from the

Euphrates and Tigris rivers that threatens vital water resources for Syria and Iraq. Furthermore, Turkish military assistance became strategically vital in Western efforts to respond to Iraq in the Kuwait crisis and to contain Iraq afterwards, particularly in permitting the use of Turkish air bases. And Turkey, itself, has begun to open up more communication channels and trade and investment opportunities with the Middle East core. There are also indications of Turkish willingness to create alignments with Middle East states.[32] For all the foregoing reasons, this work includes Turkey in the national security analysis of the Middle East.

Why, though, select the Middle East region as the first test for a new approach to national security? The contemporary Middle East, with its multiple military threats to security, creates a major challenge to any theoretical approach that seeks to expand the concept of security beyond military threats. During the Cold War period, the realist approach to security in the Middle East mirrored its global perspective, except that instead of the Cold War, there were numerous hot wars between regional rivals: Arabs versus Israelis and Iraq versus Iran. And even today, this region exists in an environment of unrelenting military threats. So why does the realist concept of achieving security by military predominance not make a great deal of sense? The regional arms race, or races, certainly appear to reflect the primacy of military considerations in the search for national security by policymakers in the area. Major military powers in the Middle East, such as Israel, Iraq, and Iran, seek or have nuclear weapons capabilities. All major regional powers spend substantial percentages of their gross national product and governmental budgets on defense. All seek to acquire the most technologically advanced weapons systems that they can either develop or purchase: medium-range ballistic missiles, fighter-bombers, and anti-ballistic missile defense systems.

Yet, a focus on the military defense policies of the Middle East states will obscure other significant security concerns in the region today. This is a time when the political legitimacy of the regimes in the Middle East is being questioned, sometimes by diametrically opposed ideological forces, some interested in democratization, others in Islamization. Ethnic and religious conflict could threaten the continued existence of a number of states within their current boundaries. The economies of some Middle East states face severe strains, contributing to ideological conflict and encouraging political radicalization. There are increasing demands on the region's limited supply of water, which raises the specter of potential conflict. Interestingly, few of these threats to security within the Middle East region are confined within the boundaries of separate states: political Islam is a regional phenomenon; ethnic dissension spans a number of Middle East states; scarce water resources flow across and under national boundaries; and economic trade routes cross borders while trade barriers stimulate the search for collective solutions. Nevertheless, these transnational issues affect the security of the Middle East states and challenge state policymakers throughout the region to respond to them.

In sum, empirical observations about the security concerns of the states in any region, and particularly one such as the Middle East which is highly charged with security threats, also suggest, subject to more rigorous testing, that the military variable, together with the four non-military variables selected, will be the most significant for the national security paradigm.

CONCLUSIONS: RESEARCH ISSUES FOR THE PARADIGM OF NATIONAL SECURITY

Testing the validity of the integrated approach can take the form of trying to apply the paradigm on a state by state basis to analyze the national security of individual states within a region, such as the Middle East, during specific periods of time. It can also be applied across the region to compare how different states respond to similar challenges to each of the variables at the same period of time. Ultimately, the integrated approach to creating a paradigm of national security should also be tested by application to all regions of the world, and indeed to global international politics. Accordingly, to apply effectively an integrated approach to the concept of national security in the Middle East, and indeed in any region, calls for interdisciplinary skills beyond the expertise of any individual area studies specialist or expert in international relations.

Application of the paradigm outside of the Middle East, however, might lead to a need to refine the paradigm. For example, as noted earlier, a researcher might conclude that political legitimacy and economic capabilities have less priority or weight as variables in the more politically stable and industrially developed region of Western Europe. In regions outside of the Middle East the researcher may discover that other variables have an independent role in explaining national security of a particular region and need to be integrable in the paradigm.

In addition, more research is needed on how we can measure threats to national security.[33] The concept of threat was used in this chapter in the objective sense of an expression or situation that indicates both to the parties involved, as well as to an independent observer, an impending danger. There is also a subjective component to the concept that involves the perceptions of the parties involved.[34] For example, general perceptions of their national security by Israelis are quite different from such perceptions by Palestinians or even Egyptians. Because of this subjectivity, threats are susceptible to misperceptions and manipulation. Diplomats and military strategists, like poker players, expend great efforts to develop their skills in creating misperceptions and manipulating opponents. They often succeed because threats are notoriously susceptible to overestimation and underestimation, and intelligence information required for assessing those threats is faulty or misinterpreted. For example, the United States State Department has been accused of underestimating the threat of Saddam Hussein to invade Kuwait. Likewise the United States Defense Department has been accused of overestimating the power of Saddam's army prior to Desert Storm. Similarly, both sides in the Iran-Iraq war of 1980-88 overestimated the amount of disaffection with their opponents' regimes from religious and ethnic affinity groups: Saddam Hussein looked to the Iranian Arabs to support his invasion, while the Ayatollah Khomeini looked to the Iraqi Shi'is to engage in subversion behind the lines, and both sides were sorely disappointed.

Ultimately, application of the national security paradigm should provide both area specialists and international relations experts with testable generalizations on how states respond to integrated sets of military and non-military threats. Even though area specialists may focus their research on domestic policy choices, they should be more mindful of their foreign and defense policy implications, as should international relations experts be more mindful of the domestic policy determinants of foreign policy choices.[35] For example, from the realist perspective, emphasizing the military variable, it was natural for the Shah of Iran to build up his arsenal of weapons to counter external military threats from Iraq. Moreover, the United States encouraged the military build-up of Iran as part of its policy of containment of communism in the Gulf. Yet American policymakers were quite surprised when the Ayatollah Khomeini's revolution toppled the regime from within. From the liberal perspective, the Khomeini revolution should have been less of a surprise because the Shah had been pursuing policies which alienated religious and economic interests constituting large segments of the Iranian population. An integrated approach would have looked for an assessment of how the Shah's policies had impacted each of the military and non-military variables in the national security paradigm, so as not to fail to anticipate their interactions.

Confirming the validity of the paradigm, it is hoped, will also demonstrate its value to policymakers. As this work on the Middle East will demonstrate to policymakers rooted in the realist, Cold War tradition, it is no longer sufficient to analyze defense policy—such as arms development, acquisition decisions, deployment strategies—to develop policy prescriptions for national security. The security analyst must take into account critical domestic policies that affect political legitimacy, ethnic and religious tolerance, economic capabilities, and availability of essential natural resources.

NOTES

1. As Kenneth Waltz succinctly put it in describing theories generally: "The trick, obviously is to link theoretical concepts with a few variables in order to contrive explanations from which hypotheses can then be inferred and tested." Kenneth N. Waltz, *Theory of International Politics* (Reading, U.K.: Addison-Wesley, 1979), 17.

2. Exemplars of this third approach include Barry Buzan, *People, States, and Fear: An Agenda for International Security Studies in the Post-Cold War Era*, 2d. ed. (Boulder, Colo.: Lynne Rienner, 1991); Edward E. Azar and Chung-in Moon, eds., *National Security in the Third World: The Management of Internal and External Threats* (Aldershot, U.K.: Edward Elgar, 1988); Bahgat Korany, Paul Noble, and Rex Brynen, eds., *The Many Faces of National Security in the Arab World* (London: Macmillan, 1993); and Mohammed Ayoob, *The Third World Security Predicament: State Making, Regional Conflict and the International System* (Boulder, Colo.: Lynne Rienner, 1995). An earlier approach to combining realist and liberal perspectives, focusing on non-violent interstate relations, and not Third World issues, is represented by Robert O. Keohane and Joseph S. Nye, *Power and Interdependence*, 1st ed. (Boston: Little, Brown, 1977); 2d ed. (New York: Harper Collins, 1989).

3. Exposure of this confusion of definitions is generally credited to Arnold Wolfers, "National Security as an Ambiguous Symbol," in *Discord and Collaboration* (Baltimore: Johns Hopkins University Press, 1962), chap. 10; and Buzan expands the analysis in *People, States, and Fear: An Agenda*, 3-17.

4. The formative developers of realism are the "classical" realists such as Hans J. Morgenthau, *Politics among Nations: The Struggle for Power and Peace* (New York: Alfred Knopf, 1948 and other editions to 1985) and E. H. Carr, *The Twenty Years' Crisis, 1919-1939: An Introduction to the Study of International Relations* (London: Macmillan, 1939), and the neorealists or structural realists such as Waltz, *Theory of International Politics*. For critical selections of this literature see Robert O. Keohane, ed., *Neorealism and Its Critics* (New York: Columbia University Press, 1986); and for what the authors call the reconstruction of this theoretical approach see Barry Buzan, Charles Jones, and Richard Little, *The Logic of Anarchy: Neorealism to Structural Realism* (New York: Columbia University Press, 1993).

5. See Kenneth Waltz, "The Emerging Structure of International Politics," *International Security* 18, no. 2 (1993): 44-45. Historians have criticized realism and international relations theory generally for its lack of predictive power. See Paul Schroeder, "Historical Reality and Neo-Realist Theory," *International Security* 19, no. 1 (1994): 108-48 and John Lewis Gaddis, "International Relations Theory and the End of the Cold War," *International Security* 17, no. 3 (1992-93): 5-58.

6. Some realists, as a result, have been trying to link domestic political behavior and international structures. See Michael Mastanduno, David A. Lake, and G. John Ikenberry, "Toward a Realist Theory of State Action," *International Studies Quarterly* 33 (1989): 457-74. In this study these authors added to the essential concept of international security a recognition that governments seek to control resources and preserve the legitimacy of their regimes.

7. The idealist label appears for the most part to have been designed by its opponents to criticize an unrealistic utopianism, but is often accepted by its progenitors. See generally for a good summary of the contrasting tenets of realism or neo-realism and liberalism and neoliberalism, Charles W. Kegley, Jr., ed., *Controversies in International Relations Theory: Realism and the Neoliberal Challenge* (New York: St. Martin's Press, 1995), 4-5, 32. A typology of modern liberalism is offered by Mark W. Zacher and Richard A. Matthew, "Liberal International Theory: Common Threads, Divergent Strands," in ibid., 107-150. For representative selections of idealist or liberal approaches to security studies see Richard K.

Betts, ed., *Conflict After the Cold War: Arguments on Causes of War and Peace* (New York: Macmillan, 1994), pt. 3.

8. See Edward A. Kolodziej, "Renaissance in Security Studies? Caveat Lector," *International Security Studies* 36 (1992): 421-38; Dietrich Fischer, *Nonmilitary Aspects of Security: A Systems Approach* (Brookfield, Vt.: Dartmouth Publishing, 1993).

9. See Richard H. Ullman, "Redefining Security," *International Security* 8, no. 1 (summer 1983): 129-53; Ken Booth and Peter Vale, "Security in Southern Africa: After Apartheid, Beyond Realism," *International Affairs* 71, no. 2 (1995): 285-304.

10. See Ullman, "Redefining Security"; Fischer, *Nonmilitary Aspects;* Jessica Tuchman Mathews, "Redefining Security," *Foreign Affairs* (spring 1989): 162-77.

11. See note 1 above for some of the well-known progenitors of the third approach. In the third approach adopted by Joseph S. Nye, Jr. in *Understanding International Conflicts* (New York: Harper Collins, 1993), he sees international politics as politics of "complex interdependence" in which states pursue security with military means but states and "transnational actors" (such as multinational corporations) also pursue welfare goals with non-military means, such as by wielding economic power and using international institutions. Another third approach is offered by Helga Haftendorn, "The Security Puzzle: Theory-Building and Discipline-Building in International Security," *International Studies* 35 (1991): 3-17, who explicates the political/philosophical roots of the security debate, as between those who follow Hobbesian principles versus those who follow Kantian principles. Her third approach to security studies is based on Grotian principles. For an application of the Haftendorn approach in a security studies curriculum, see Richard Shultz, "Introduction to International Security?" in *Security Studies for the 1990s,* ed. Richard Shultz, Roy Godson, and Ted Greenwood (Washington: Brassey's, 1993), 45-46.

12. Western Europe is not completely free of ethnic and religious dissension, as Basque separatists and IRA irredentists from time to time remind us.

13. See Azar and Moon, *National Security;* Ayoob, *Third World Security;* Norman A. Graham, ed., *Seeking Security and Development* (Boulder, Colo.: Lynne Rienner, 1994); Korany, Noble, and Brynan, *Many Faces;* see also Ali E. Hillal Dessouki, "Globalization and the Two Spheres of Security," *Washington Quarterly* 16, no. 4 (1993): 109-17 for a discussion of the implications of this distinction between security for the developed versus the developing nations.

14. Buzan, for example, selects five "sectors" corresponding to five types of threats: military, political, societal, economic, and ecological; *People, States, and Fear: An Agenda,* 116-34. Ayoob emphasizes the primacy in Third World countries of "political security" and acknowledges that when other sources of threats to state boundaries, political institutions, or governing regimes emanate from other variables "ranging from the economic to the ecological," they should also be taken into account; Ayoob, *Third World Security,* 8. Nye's focus in *Understanding International Conflicts* is on international economic and ecological issues. Azar and Moon focus on three major threats to national security: "physical" or military; economic; and ecological scarcity of resources that threatens organic survival; *National Security,* 286.

15. This chapter does not argue for maintenance of the status quo and does not intend to suggest that any particular regime is critical for national security or that stability of a regime is the goal of national security. There are tyrannical and totalitarian regimes that by their nature repress their populations and create threats to the national security of other states. It may still be a legitimate goal of policymakers of affected states in pursuing their own national interests to work to change such anathematized regimes.

16. See, for example, the classic approach to explaining war at three levels by Kenneth H. Waltz in *Man, the State, and War: A Theoretical Analysis* (New York: Columbia University Press,

1959); also, in *People, States, and Fear: An Agenda,* Buzan explores security at the three levels of individuals, states, and the international system.

17. Buzan uses a similar trichotomy: territory, society, and government; *People, States, and Fear: An Agenda,* 60. Ayoob sometimes uses the concept as more of a variable, i.e. "stateness" which requires "coercive capacity," "infrastructural power," and "unconditional legitimacy"; *Third World Security,* 4.

18. Durkheim noted this distinction in the use of the concept of the state to refer to either the government or the "political society as a whole," i.e., the people and its government. Anthony Giddens, *Durkheim on Politics and the State* (Cambridge: Polity Press, 1986), 38. For an exploration of the implications for the study of international relations if analysts adopted the sociological approach to defining state, see Fred Halliday, "State and Society in International Relations: A Second Agenda," *Millennium: Journal of International Studies* 16, no. 2 (1987): 215-29.

19. This definition of regime is akin to but not identical with the definition used by subscribers to the sociological tradition in defining state as the governing or coercive institution of society. Robert M. Fishman, for example, in "Rethinking State and Regime: Southern Europe's Transition to Democracy," *World Politics* 62, no. 3 (April 1990): 428, defines regime as "the formal and informal organization of the center of political power, and of its relations with the broader society."

20. Society has been defined in terms of societal institutions, groups, communities, and systems, including systems of actions and interrelations. Leon H. Mayhew, "Society," in *International Encyclopedia of the Social Sciences,* vol. 14, ed. David L. Sills, (New York: Macmillan and Free Press, 1968), 577-85.

21. Marion J. Levy, Jr., *Modernization and the Structure of Societies: A Setting for International Affairs* (Princeton: Princeton University Press, 1966), 707-8.

22. Durkheim, for example, defines the political society as "one formed by the coming together of a rather large number of secondary social groups, subject to the same one authority which is not itself subject to any other superior authority duly constituted"; Giddens, *Durkheim,* 34-35.

23. In 1994 Saudi Arabia spent approximately $14 billion (out of a gross domestic product of $128 billion) on defense, over five times as much as Iraq and Iran. Iraq spent $2.7 billion (out of a gross domestic product of $18.5 billion) and Iran $2.3 billion (out of a gross domestic product of almost $60 billion). The Kingdom has 295 combat aircraft compared to 316 in Iraq and 295 in Iran; International Institute for Strategic Studies, *The Military Balance, 1995-1996* (London: Oxford University Press, 1995), 133-34 (Iran), 134-35 (Iraq), and 145-46 (Saudi Arabia).

24. The Saudi airforce also serves as creditable support for a strategy of securing airspace so as to protect Saudi ports and infrastructure needed for the importation of United States ground forces. Thomas L. McNaugher, "Arms Sales and Arms Embargoes in the Persian Gulf: The Real Dilemmas of Dual Containment," in *The Powder Keg in the Middle East: The Struggle for Gulf Security,* ed. Geoffrey Kemp and Janice Gross Stein (Lanham, Md.: Rowman and Littlefield, 1995), 350-51.

25. Max Weber, "Politics as a Vocation," in *From Max Weber: Essays in Sociology,* trans. and ed. H. H. Gerth and C. Wright Mills (New York: Oxford University Press, 1958), 78-79. Weber's definition of political legitimacy identified three ideal types of willingness to comply with the political order: traditional, charismatic, and legal. Modern social scientists have recharacterized political legitimacy in other terms, such as David Easton's "specific" and "diffuse" supports for the government. David Easton, *A Systems Analysis of Political Life* (New York: Wiley, 1965). As applied to Middle East politics, political legitimacy has been defined as "the extent to which the relevant portion of the population *perceives* that the regime is behaving according to, or

violating the . . . norms"; G. Hossein Razi, "Legitimacy, Religion, and Nationalism in the Middle East," American Political Science Review 84, no. 1 (March, 1990): 70. See also Michael C. Hudson, *Arab Politics: The Search For Legitimacy* (New Haven: Yale University Press, 1977), who states: "The governmental system and leadership that is genuinely national, that partakes of the nation's history, that acts in accordance with the society's values, and that protects its broadest concerns is likely to be regarded as legitimate, even though particular decisions and leaders may be unpopular or unwise" (p. 2); and, adopting Dankwart Rustow, he summarizes the three prerequisites of modern political legitimacy as authority, identity, and equality (p. 4).

26. Regimes may also confer religious or historical significance on the territory or particular locations within the state, for example the Israeli Likud reference to the West Bank as Judea and Samaria, or the multiple claims in the Middle East to the sanctity of Jerusalem.

27. Gerard Chaliand, "Introduction," in *A People without a Country: The Kurds and Kurdistan,* ed. Gerard Chaliand (New York: Olive Branch Press, 1993), 7; Edmund Ghareeb, *The Kurdish Question in Iraq* (Syracuse: Syracuse University Press, 1981), 176-77.

28. Ole R. Holsti, "Theories of International Relations and Foreign Policy: Realism and its Challengers," in Kegley, *Controversies,* 43.

29. Cf. Marc A. Levy, "Is the Environment a National Security Issue?" *International Security* 20, no. 2 (fall 1995): 35-62; and Myron Weiner, "A Security Perspective on International Migration," *The Fletcher Forum of World Affairs* 20, no. 2 (summer/fall 1996): 17-34.

30. Buzan and Ayoob refer to regions as "security complexes" which are somewhat loosely defined as groups of states with linked security concerns from common enmities and amities. Buzan, *People, States, and Fear: An Agenda,* 188-202; Ayoob, *Third World Security,* 56-58. See also the "subordinate international systems" approach to defining regions in Louis J. Cantori and Steven L. Spiegel, *The International Politics of Regions: A Comparative Approach* (Englewood Cliffs, N.J.: Prentice-Hall, 1970), 1-41.

31. See, for example, Korany, Noble, and Brynen, *Many Faces,* for a definition of the "Arab" Middle East. This obviously excludes Israel and Iran, and includes the Arab North African states. This is not merely an academic issue. The inability to define the Middle East region also has implications for statesmen who are attempting to negotiate region-wide treaties such as a regional ban on weapons of mass destruction. *Wall Street Journal,* 6 September 1996, p. A6.

32. *Financial Times* (London), 11 April 1996, p. 4, reports that Turkey and Israel have entered into a military cooperation agreement pursuant to which Turkey is allowing Israeli jets to use Turkish bases for training.

33. For an attempt to measure external military threats, see John Jacob Nutter, "Unpacking Threat: A Conceptual and Formal Analysis," in Graham, *Seeking Security and Development,* 29-51. See also Buzan, *People, States, and Fear: An Agenda,* 96-107 for a summary measure of "weak" and "strong" states.

34. In this subjective sense, threats to national security constitute part of what has been referred to as the subjective determinants of perceived national interests, and involve collective needs and fears of a society and its elite. Herbert C. Kelman, "Social-psychological Dimensions of International Conflict," in *Peacemaking in International Conflict: Methods and Techniques,* ed. I. W. Zartman and J. L. Rasmussen (Washington D.C.: U.S. Institute of Peace, 1996), 5-7.

35. For an example of analyzing foreign policy choices as intertwined with domestic policy choices see Robert D. Putnam, "Diplomacy and Domestic Politics: The Logic of Two-Level Games," *International Organization* 42, no. 3 (summer, 1988): 427- 60.

PART I:
POLITICAL LEGITIMACY

CHAPTER TWO

Political Legitimacy and the Production of History: The Case of Saudi Arabia

MADAWI AL-RASHEED

*T*he political legitimacy of the Saudi state has been approached within two frameworks. The first is a Weberian model emphasizing the role of coercion, bureaucratization, and the general expansion of the state apparatus, believed to have succeeded in penetrating the basic fabric of society.[1] The Saudi state extracts legitimacy from its populace using a combination of variables, the most dominant being tribalism, Islam, and the expanding state bureaucracy.[2] The second framework derives from the rentier state model which deals specifically with the oil-producing countries of the Arabian Peninsula. The state gains legitimacy in the eyes of the population through redistributing oil wealth, a welfare system, and various other subsidies, bribes, and handouts.[3] Both stability and legitimacy are maintained as long as the state can channel excessive wealth to an untaxed constituency. Stability is expected to last as long as redistribution is kept flowing from the center—that is the state—to its populace. The state can only be threatened as a result of a sudden decrease in oil revenues which would undermine its ability to act as the main distributor.[4]

The stabilizing effect of bribes can easily be measured in the immediate present, but the long-term success of the equation—bribe = political loyalty/legitimacy—has not yet been fully assessed. The rentier state approach, according to Eric Davis, has succeeded in "fetishizing" the state by considering it to be situated beyond societal constraints, and failing to place it within a historical perspective.[5] Davis has correctly pointed out that it was only when the state realized the need to use oil wealth to create a national ideology to which the bulk of the populace could feel some affinity was it able to institutionalize a degree of stable rule.[6]

Stability is, however, not always to be understood as a sign of strength. Nazih Ayubi forcibly argues that Arab states, including the oil-producing ones, are "over-stated," by which he refers, first, to the remarkable expansion of the state in quantitative terms, meaning state industrialization, social welfare, public personnel, public organization, and expenditures. He argues that the process of expanding both the size of the state machine and the role of the state in the economy and society is a form of *étatisme*. Secondly, and most importantly, over-stating implies that the real power, efficacy, and significance of this state might have been over-emphasized. This is so because the Arab state

> is a "fierce" state that has frequently to resort to raw coercion in order to preserve itself, but it is not a "strong" state because (a) it lacks—to varying degrees of course—the "infrastructural power" (Mann, 1986a) that enables states to penetrate society effectively through mechanisms such as taxation for example; and (b) it lacks ideological hegemony (in a Gramscian sense) that would enable it to forge the "historic" social bloc that accepts the legitimacy of the ruling stratum.[7]

Ayubi successfully proves that the Arab state is not strong. His political economy approach, inspired by Antonio Gramsci's concept of hegemony, channels him towards the conclusion that the Arab state is not a hegemonic state in which the populace is persuaded to accept the ruling class's system of belief and to share its social, cultural, and moral values. In the Arab world, there is no hegemonic ideology involving all classes and groups. Consequently, the state remains a *gendarme* or "corporate" type.

Although Ayubi uses Gramsci's concept of hegemony, which incorporates the area of culture and ideological consent, and emphasizes the role of the state as educator, he does not fully investigate those areas of state practice that may show that most Arab states have been striving to achieve Gramscian hegemony, a form of social and political control that combines physical force and coercion with intellectual, moral, and cultural persuasion or consent.[8] Arab states have tried to establish both *coercive control* achieved through the army, the police, and the penal code, and *consensual control*, achieved through the institutions of civil society, such as the education system, religion, and the family. Consensual control is a subtle area of state practice that does not lend itself to straightforward analysis. It is opaque and, as such, has not been fully investigated either by Weberian-oriented researchers or by rentier state protagonists.[9]

While agreeing with Ayubi that the Arab state remains over-stated, I reexamine his Gramscian hegemony hypothesis by investigating the mechanisms by which the Saudi state establishes consensual control over society through the production of historical narratives, embedded in school history textbooks. I do not start, as Ayubi does, with the question of whether the state is weak or strong—a question beyond the scope of this chapter—but, above all, with a question that cannot be answered before agreement is reached on the standards and criteria against which strengths or weaknesses are to be measured. But, like Ayubi, I use Gramsci's extended concept of hegemony to show that constructing historical narratives is part of enforcing political legitimacy and consent.[10]

The historical narratives of the Saudi state create uncontested emotional bonds between rulers and ruled. More importantly, they establish consent, an important dimension in the exercise of power.[11] Official control over the production of history perpetuates particular representations that bind rulers and ruled. These representations are often called civic myths.[12] As will be shown in the analysis of official Saudi history textbooks, this integration seems to be successful because, as Davis has correctly pointed out, reinterpreting the past requires a strong sense of the factors that resonate emotionally with subaltern groups. It also entails an ability to reconstruct, synthesize, and even invent symbols that will touch a psychological nerve in the population.[13]

While I am not in a position to measure the success of Saudi historical narratives on psychological grounds, I endeavor to investigate these narratives from a sociological and political perspective by highlighting what they achieve at the level of society. Official historical narratives contribute to the mystification of the world—that is, they project both the past, and actors in the past, as natural and inevitable.[14] Also, through a careful process of selection, official narratives invoke the past to legitimate present relations of domination, thus perpetuating consent among the polity. I also endeavor to show that only in the last decade have these official narratives begun to be questioned by many voices of opposition in the country who are currently engaged in the construction of alternative narratives to counter official representations. The publications of two opposition groups, those of the Sunni Islamists and the Shi'is of the Eastern Province, will be consulted to demonstrate how counter-historical narratives can undermine those of the state, thus weakening the ideological foundation of the Saudi state and its political legitimacy.

THE STATE AND THE MYSTIFICATION OF HISTORY

Before the establishment of the state and the expansion of formal education, the country had known various forms and methods for the transmission of knowledge, literacy, and religious instruction. This took place in the oases and towns and tended to be absent in the countryside among nomadic groups. The traditional mosque-based *madrasa,* common in other parts of the Arab world, was the medium for educating children. Known in the local dialect as *kuttab* (mosque schools), these informal and unstructured gatherings were led by the mosque *imam* or other *'ulama'* whose main role was to teach the recital of the Qur'an and simple *fiqh* (jurisprudence), in addition to socializing children in proper Islamic conduct. Literacy and some mathematical skills were also part of this traditional education system. While some children attended the kuttab in the mosques, wealthy and elite families often held classes for their children in their own houses. This was widely practiced in Najd in the absence of formal education comparable to that which existed in the Hijaz, especially in Mecca, Madina, and Jiddah. In the Hijaz, where Ottoman influence was more established, there were over 50 schools by 1915, the most famous of which were the Fallah schools, founded by one of Jiddah's merchant families, the Alireza.[15]

Male children were often over-represented in the *kuttab,* whereas females were confined to learning from their mothers and other female relatives. The education of girls was limited and in most cases was restricted to reciting enough Qur'anic verses to allow them to perform prayers. In some exceptional elite families, a shaykh, often blind, occasionally visited the female section of the household to teach women the fundamentals of Islam. These visits were intensified during the month of Ramadan when the shaykh was expected to lead women during the special Ramadan tarawih prayers, after which discussion with the shaykh regarding religious matters such as fasting and ablution were common. This tradition continued even after the expansion of the female education system in the 1960s.

While joining the *kuttab* resulted in the acquisition of some knowledge, in particular religious instruction, the teaching of history was a different matter. With the exception of the *'ulama', quda* (judges) and learned members of society, in general people acquired knowledge about the past through the medium of oral transmission from previous generations. The history that people became accustomed to was embedded in *sawalif* (oral narratives) and a number of famous *qasa'id* (oral poems). The past was, however, not the concern of ordinary people; it was the preoccupation of the tribal elite and oasis amirs, who had a vested interest in the past as a source for explaining power relations, intertribal conflicts and alliances. Their history was one of battles, chivalry, and conquest, in which famous lineages and prominent shaykhs demonstrated their hegemony, and humiliated and defeated their enemies and rivals.[16] This history was not a master narrative, but a fragmented and contested knowledge which was constantly being defined and constructed in response to present concerns. It created a flexible social memory ready to be altered and changed according to the prevalent social and political relations between groups. For instance, the oral poetry of the Shammar dealt with their relationship with another famous Arabian tribe, the Anizah, often described in historical sources as a relationship of constant rivalry and enmity. However, an examination of Shammar oral narratives demonstrates that they oscillate between a celebration of Shammar hegemony over the Anizah during one period, and a celebration of Shammar friendship with them at other times. Accounting for the past did not involve the construction of narratives that transfixed political relations between groups. This would not have been possible in an ever-changing political context and a permanent state of flux.[17] Tribal history was an exercise in establishing claims to the past. These claims changed as much as those who advocated them. This history had no permanent heroes or fixed myths. Accounts of actors in history and their deeds constantly varied with shifting political relations and tribal alliances.

This historical tradition was undermined with the establishment of the state, the formalization of the education system, and the growth of state monopoly over the production of historical narratives, facilitated by oil wealth. The ruling elite was keen to establish an uncontested past, and continuity with the past, to justify its present role in politics; the traditional historical genre was altered in favor of master narratives, pregnant with moralization, mystification, and enchantment. The primary objective of these narratives was the enforcement of the legitimacy of the state and the strengthening of its internal security by persuading the population of the natural and inevitable development that led to the creation of the state and the consolidation of its Saudi rulers.

The establishment of a modern education system in Saudi Arabia is a recent development, attributed in large part to the availability of oil revenues. The first Saudi male elementary school was opened in 1925.[18] Female education did not materialize until the 1950s, amidst fierce opposition from the religious establishment. The first female school, Dar al-Hanan, was opened in Jiddah in 1956 by Iffat, the wife of King Faisal. It was followed by the formation of a royal commission in 1960, the purpose of which was to facilitate the expansion of female education under strict supervision from the 'ulama'. However, although modern schools became widely available in the country by the end of the 1960s, some would argue that education in any modern sense of the word really only began to advance after 1978.[19]

The initial slow and hesitant progress of both male and female education gathered momentum and reached a remarkable level in the 1990s. Saudi sources estimate the number of male students in primary, intermediate, and secondary education to be 1,380,387, and that of females to be 1,168,224, a total of roughly 2.6 million during the 1991 academic year.[20] This represents a substantial portion of the total population, a figure over-estimated by Saudi sources at 17 million. The United States Embassy in Saudi Arabia gives an estimate of between 5 and 6 million.[21] As in other Third World countries, the Saudi population remains very young. It is estimated that between 50 and 60 percent of the Saudi population is under the age of 21.[22] As the majority of Saudi children are currently enrolled in schools and higher education institutions, the history transmitted to them is of great importance in shaping their perception not only of the past, but also the present and future. What follows is an analysis of the content of official history textbooks, a total of 12 volumes, which are studied at schools by 2.6 million pupils—that is, almost a third of the population, over a period of 12 years, covering primary, intermediate, and secondary education.

HISTORICAL NARRATIVES

Two themes dominate the teaching of history, to the exclusion of other topics, in Saudi schools: Islamic history and Saudi-Wahhabi history. From the time a child enters school, at around the age of six, the historical knowledge acquired relates to understanding the interconnection between early Islamic history and modern Saudi history.[23]

Islamic History

History instruction prepares a pupil to understand the rise of Islam, the Prophet's biography, the establishment of the early Muslim state, the life and deeds of the early Muslim Caliphs, the later periods of the Umayyad and Abbasid Caliphates, the period of the Crusades, and finally the Ottoman Empire. This excludes a discussion of the pre-Islamic period, better known as *jahiliyya*. The documentation of time begins with the Prophet's call, celebrates the achievements of the various Islamic states that followed the call, and highlights the deeds of Muslim rulers. Islamic history is projected as a succession of episodes, each leading to the strengthening of Islam and Muslims, and the flourishing of Islamic civilization in all its intellectual, artistic, scientific, and military manifestations.

The celebration of Islamic civilization is checked by a discussion of a number of factors which led to *da'f* (weakness) and *inhilal* (dissolution of the *umma*, the Islamic community). These factors include, above all, "political dissent, sectarian conflict, the immersion of Muslims in luxury and the pursuit of worldly pleasures, and the proliferation of excessive Sufism."[24] The same source explains how the issue of leadership was one of the most divisive events in Islamic history, thus weakening the consensus of the *umma*. It is argued that the problem of succession resulted in the growth of religious sectarianism, thus contributing to division and disintegration. The narrative highlights the negative influence of the so-called *firaq munharifa*, sects that deviated from true Islam, listing for instance the Saba'iyya, Khawarij, Batiniyya, and Isma'iliyya, some of which have sunk into historical oblivion (e.g., Saba'iyya and Batiniyya). The source remains silent on the division over the succession of the first Caliphs, concerning the Prophet's cousin and son-in-law Ali, which in later years led to the development of Shi'ism. The omission of the Shi'is from history is not without significance. No mention is made of their establishment as a sect nor of their religious beliefs and practices. While the text reminds pupils of minor sects that do not have strong representatives in modern times, it overlooks one that has living followers in both Saudi Arabia and elsewhere, especially in neighboring Gulf countries—Iraq, Yemen, and Iran. Saudi pupils remain ignorant of the origins and beliefs of some of their compatriots, such as the Shi'is of the Eastern Province and neighbors such as the Iranians who in recent years have challenged Saudi Arabia's role in the Muslim world.

The text affirms that other factors affecting the disintegration of the Muslim community are related to *'asabiyya qabaliyya* (tribal solidarity). In the narrative, there is an unequivocal rejection of tribal solidarity, supported by evidence from the Qur'an (Sura 13) and hadith (words and deeds of the Prophet). The negative consequences of tribalism include ta'asub (fanaticism on the basis of descent and kinship loyalty) which, it is argued, should be replaced by loyalty to faith and the *umma*. This is a crucial projection as it is in line with Saudi policy towards tribal groups in the present. The text highlights the destructive aspects of tribalism, tribal conflict, and competition in the past and provides a justification for its suppression in the present. As evidence is drawn from Islam, the theme becomes clear, that a good Muslim should replace tribal loyalty with loyalty to Islam. The consequences of this discourse are paramount given the fact that, historically, Saudi society has been organized along tribal lines with kinship solidarity being one of the most cherished axes along which alliances and conflicts have been formed. The underlying message advocates a shift from tribal consciousness to Islamic consciousness.

The rejection of tribalism in historical texts is in line with the early detribalization policies of the state. Since its formation in the 1930s, the Saudi state has endeavored to break up the tribes, first through the *ikhwan* movement, and later through various legal and bureaucratic measures such as the abolition of tribal territories and the introduction of the 1968 Land Redistribution Law.[25] While members of the ruling elite entered into matrimonial relations with tribal groups, thus creating kinship bonds and dependencies, state ideology condemned tribalism. At the same time, state practices continued to enforce this policy and erode the underlying principles and structures of tribalism. The Saudi condemnation of tribalism in history textbooks calls into question the conclusions of scholars who consider it to be one of the crucial pillars in the legitimation formula of Saudi Arabia and of other Gulf states.[26] In Saudi Arabia, in particular, the state encapsulated the tribes and at the same time launched an indoctrination program through historical narratives, supported by Islamic evidence, which undermined their ethos.

While emphasizing the devastating effects of both religious diversity, manifested in the rise of sects in Islam, and cultural and social organizing principles such as tribalism, the texts give equal attention to so-called secular movements and ideas, believed to have contributed to the demise of Islamic civilization and society. These include, above all, Arab nationalism. In their negative representations of this movement, the narratives reiterate the opinion of the most respected religious authority in the country, Shaykh Ibn Baz, who describes Arab nationalism as:

> an atheist *jahiliyya,* a movement of ignorance whose main purpose is to fight Islam and shake its teachings and rules. Many Arabs adopted it; they are the enemies of Islam. This is celebrated and encouraged by atheists. It is a wrong movement and a falsification.[27]

Outlining the origin and characteristics of nationalism, the text highlights that it is "European in origin, Jewish in motivation, leading to conflict, division, chauvinism, and above all contradicting the integrating spirit of Islam."[28] Nationalism is represented as a conspiracy theory, promoted by the West and Zionism to weaken the unity of Muslims. This representation of Arab nationalism undermines the ideological foundation of a number of neighboring Arab regimes (e.g., Syria and Iraq). Also, the use of the rhetoric of atheism, *ilhad,* and *jahiliyya* (ignorance) presents nationalism as Islamically illegitimate. These strong judgments shape public opinion and create an atmosphere of hostility towards the atheist "others," while the labels are bound to be taken seriously by Saudi citizens.

Other secular movements with similarly dangerous influences are dealt with in the text. For example, communism is condemned on Islamic grounds. Karl Marx's famous view on religion as "the opium of the people" is used to illustrate the atheism of the movement, which contradicts the spirit of Islam. The consequences of communism are listed as leading to the enslavement of the individual by materialism, and the abandonment of spiritual and moral qualities.

Similarly, *al-taghrib* (Westernization) leads to the loss of Islamic ideals and practices, and social upheaval and conflict. More importantly, at the political level,

> Westernization leads to the introduction of Western political systems, political parties, and parliaments, to the detriment of social cohesion and consensus. Westernization promotes misery and suffering among Muslims.[29]

Socially, Westernization is believed to undermine Islamic conduct as it leads to a number of undesirable consequences including

> mixing between the sexes, opening night clubs, abolishing the veil, promoting a banking system based on interest, adopting Western holidays (e.g., Christmas, Mother's Day, and Labor Day), speaking European languages to the detriment of native tongues, and the enrollment of native students in local missionary schools.[30]

Another movement, which calls for the institutionalization of colloquial Arabic, *al-'ammiyya,* as a means of instruction to replace classical Arabic, is seen as equally damaging to the Muslim community. This is "an internal force aiming at destroying the intellectual and linguistic heritage of the *umma.*" Its most damaging effect stems from the fact that "it undermines people's ability to understand and appreciate the messages of both the Qur'an and classical Arabic literature."[31]

In summary, Islamic history is taught in Saudi schools with a strong sense of mystification. First, this history is constructed in such a way as to highlight its inevitability. It marks the beginning of historical time; it is the starting point for any historical narrative. Secondly, through this process of mystification, history unfolds a story of a civilization marked by achievement and success, only to be undermined by the acts of those who did not remain faithful to the spirit of Islam. Both internal sectarian divisions and secular movements combined with external threats weakened the unity of Muslims and, more importantly, led to the adoption of alien styles and behavior, to the detriment of indigenous Islamic conduct. Stagnation became the fate of the *umma*, which abandoned its faith in favor of foreign concepts. Thirdly, official historical discourse aims to replace tribal loyalty in favor of total Islamic allegiance. Local tribal identities and regional Arab sentiments are projected as belonging to the era of *jahiliyya*.

The "logical" conclusion that the text alludes to is the urgent need for action to correct this historical diversion. It is at this juncture that the Wahhabi movement and the subsequent foundation of the Saudi state are introduced. These two become inevitable corrective mechanisms, a prelude to the restoration of order and unity among a Muslim community that had lost these virtues.

The Wahhabi Movement and Saudi History

In their final year at school, Saudi pupils are presented with a comprehensive volume that deals with the rise of the Wahhabi movement, the three Saudi states, and ends with a summary of the economic, social, political, and educational achievements of the present regime.

The starting point for Wahhabi and Saudi history is "the state of chaos that loomed large among the Muslims of the Arabian Peninsula" in the eighteenth century. The country is divided into four regions: the Hijaz, the Southwest, the East, and Najd. It is argued that a general state of moral, intellectual, religious and political decay was prevalent. Only Najd and the Hijaz are referred to by their traditional names. The names al-Hasa (the Eastern Province) and Asir (the Southwest), which were common appellations for these two regions, are not used. This is not without significance. While Najd and the Hijaz are not reduced to merely "the Central Province" and "the Western Province" respectively, Asir and al-Hasa become geographical areas, deprived of their traditional regional identity.

After a brief introduction to local leaders of the four regions, the text describes the political conditions as being characterized by competition, rivalry, and *tafakuk* (disintegration). According to the narrative, peaceful coexistence among various local groups was absent. The economy was diversified but in general rested on a combination of pastoral nomadism, limited agriculture, trade and *hajj* (pilgrimage) revenues, benefiting beduins, merchants, local rulers, and city dwellers. The economic prosperity of the country was constantly undermined as a result of the predominance of strife, political instability, and rivalry. Education was limited except in the towns of the Hijaz and other oases in central Arabia where some quda and 'ulama' instructed the population in the most important matters of religious worship.

However, the most emphasized attribute in the pre-Saudi-Wahhabi era is the general spread of *bida'* (innovations) and *khurafat* (myths) both of which contradicted "proper Islamic principles." The text points, in passing, to the presence of the Shi'is in the Eastern Province, coexisting with the Sunnis, which led to the promotion of an "intellectual atmosphere," but it refrains from exploring how this had happened or what its manifestations had been. Immediately, the text reverts to asserting that this region had witnessed the same religious innovations that plagued the rest of the Arabian Peninsula and diverted its population from following the true path of Islam.[32]

The discussion of the pre-Saudi-Wahhabi era leads to an important conclusion stated in the text as:

> all regions which later became part of Saudi Arabia were in need of religious reform *(islah dini),* to abolish elements which were against Islam, and political reform *(islah siyasi)* to unite the regions and the tribes for peace and stability.[33]

According to the text, the region that was the most predisposed to promote both religious and political reform was Najd because of its geographical position away from the Ottoman centers and because it had escaped direct Ottoman control. Therefore, the rise of the Wahhabi movement in Najd was the most "natural" event in a region believed to be predestined to play a leading role in the course of religious reform and political unification. Najd is not only the geographical center of the Arabian Peninsula but also its political and religious heart. Both the Wahhabi movement and the Saudis originated in Najd. As such, the region's significance is paramount not only in the past but also in the present and the future.[34]

Saudi historical narratives create a memory of a population riven by warfare, instability, and rivalry as a prelude to the paramount role of the call to Wahhabism, to be adopted by al-Saud in the Najdi town of Dayr'iyya. More importantly, the narrative asserts the leading role of the Najdi population, who were the first to accept the Wahhabi call and fight under the banner of al-Saud to deliver the rest of the country from "ignorance and chaos."

The superficiality of the historical narratives of the pre-Saudi-Wahhabi period, preoccupied as they are with the representation of political divisions, fragmentation, and moral degeneration, creates consensual control over the imagination. *Islah* (the reform of the Saudi-Wahhabi movement) is portrayed as a historical necessity, thus contributing to its legitimacy in the eyes of the populace. Moreover, the movement becomes hegemonic as an ideology at the heart of establishing peace and stability. It is projected as an inevitable response to urgent political, social, and economic crises.[35] This discourse generalizes the interests of the Najdi Saudi-Wahhabi leadership over other regions which, according to the text, should appreciate their delivery from the state of *jahiliyya* into which they had sunk, thanks to the movement and its adoption by al-Saud.

Having established the inevitability of the Saudi-Wahhabi reform movement, the text introduces the first attempt, in the mid-eighteenth century, to unify the country under the banner of the Saudis. This is followed by a discussion of the disintegration of this first attempt in the early decades of the nineteenth century as a result of the Ottoman Egyptian campaigns of Muhammad Ali. The importance of *bay'a* (confirmation of ruler in office) between Muhammad Ibn Saud and Muhammad Ibn Abd al-Wahhab in 1744 is projected as a crucial pact according to which the foundation of the first state was consolidated. Underlying the pact is a division of labor whereby the Saudis assumed political and military roles, and the Wahhabis acted in a moral and religious capacity. This pact is cherished as a unique historical event.

The division of labor between politics and religion laid the foundation for not only the first Saudi state (1744-1818), but also the second realm (1824-91) and, more importantly, the present third state (1932-). The text insists that this division guaranteed that those who played political roles acted under the guidance of the religious authority. While the boundaries between religion and politics were initially blurred—for example Saudi rulers of the first and second states were called *imams* and even Abd al-Aziz Ibn Saud was referred to as *imam* until he adopted first the title of sultan and later king—the gap between them has widened with the development of the state apparatus and bureaucracy. The expansion of government bureaucracy allows religious functions to operate under a separate agency, but within state control.

The narrative describes the formation of the modern state in the twentieth century. The key word in this process is the "unification" of the regions referred to earlier. This unification is projected as reclaiming the historical right of al-Saud to rule over these territories. The text emphasizes the process of unification rather than conquest. It fails to explore fully the resistance of the various tribes and regions to the loss of their autonomy and their eventual encapsulation by the Saudis. Furthermore, the text remains silent regarding the atrocities inflicted by Ibn Saud's army, the ikhwan, on the various regions during the so-called unification process. For example, the pillaging of Ta'if, which was committed by the *ikhwan* as they entered this Hijazi town, is given little attention. It is attributed to the actions of local *badiya,* beduins, who joined the *ikhwan* army with the hope of capturing booty. The beduins were responsible for atrocities committed in Taif. These were stopped only after the intervention of the *ikhwan* commanders.[36]

This narrative obviously takes the responsibility for this incident away from the Najdi *ikhwan* and their leadership. The event is represented as the work of greedy Hijazi nomads, a representation that reiterates official discourse on the negative aspects of both nomadism and tribalism.

This is followed by a celebration of the achievements of the Saudi realm since 1932, including the development of the educational, communication, and institutional infrastructures of the state. The texts also celebrate the roles of the kingdom in the regional Arab context, such as participation in the Arab League and support for the Palestinian cause. At the international level, the narrative reasserts the leading role of Saudi Arabia in supporting Muslim issues as a result of its participation in and financial support of Islamic international organizations.

THE OPPOSITION AND STATE RHETORIC

It is worth noting that the messages embedded in Saudi historical narratives remained unchallenged for a long time. Official representations of the past, both of Islam and recent Saudi history, were hegemonic in the sense that they did establish consensual control over the imagination of the populace. As such, these narratives allowed the state to enforce its political legitimacy and extract from the polity acceptance of its historical right to rule. Since 1932 the Saudi state has enjoyed remarkable stability in a volatile region characterized by political change, coups d'état, and civil unrest. While oil wealth guaranteed both economic and political security, historical narratives were ideological weapons enforcing the legitimacy of the state and its ruling group, whereas other states sought for legitimation formulae including Arab nationalism, Ba'thism, and Nasserism. Official narratives conditioned the population to accept the status quo as inevitable and natural. More importantly, these narratives altered consciousness from one that celebrated regional diversity, tribal loyalty, and political autonomy, to one that unquestionably accepted both Saudi-Wahhabi hegemony and the political predominance of one region, Najd, over the rest of the country.

Until the early 1980s, serious political upheavals only occurred when the 'ulama' resented their confinement and marginalization, a process that accompanied the consolidation of the state. For example, the early *ikhwan* revolt of 1927-30 undermined the legitimacy of the division between politics and religion. The *ikhwan* revolt was an attempt to reassert their political authority, which had gradually been eroded by Ibn Saud. The consolidation of the state meant that the *ikhwan* were denied any political function. They were confined to playing social, religious, and military roles. Similarly, Juhaiman's seizure of the Great Mosque in Mecca in 1979 was indicative of the malaise among members of the religious circles over their increasing subordination to the state. These incidents represented an infringement by the religious establishment of the political sphere, so far monopolized by al-Saud and represented by historical narratives as natural.

The Islamists of the 1990s have gone a step further in voicing their discontent and opposition to the regime. They have exposed its official rhetoric and scrutinized its most cherished legitimation formula. They are using official Saudi narratives and drawing on the very same Islamic tradition to undermine both the regime and the right of al-Saud to rule. With this opposition, the country is witnessing for the first time a systematic criticism of official historical discourse through regular publications that draw on the same official sources, but offer a reinterpretation of history.

The situation in Saudi Arabia in the 1990s demonstrates that Islam can be both a legitimizing and a regime-subverting ideology. While the regime enhances its legitimacy by invoking its Islamic Wahhabi foundation as its historical narratives demonstrate, the Islamists of the 1990s have been undermining the plausibility of this legitimation formula using the same rhetoric. For instance, one *risala* (message), entitled *Kashf al-ghamma 'an 'ulama' al-umma* (The unveiling of the distress of the umma's 'ulama'), by Shaykh Safar al-Hawali, Dean of Islamic Studies at Umm al-Qura University in Mecca, shows how Islam has become the medium of protest in a state that historically has relied on it for its raison d'être.[37] It is this text addressed to Shaykh Ibn Baz, the official head of the *'ulama'*, together with a number of Friday sermons criticizing the regime, that led to al-Hawali's imprisonment after the Gulf War.

Al-Hawali represents what the Islamists call *'ulama' al-sahwa* (the *'ulama'* of the reawakening), in contrast with *al-'ulama' al-rasmiyyun* (official *'ulama'*), who supported the regime. Al-Hawali's criticism of the regime was adopted by the well-known Islamist opposition groups: the Committee for the Defense of Legitimate Rights in Saudi Arabia (CDLR), led by al-Mas'ari and the Committee for Reform (CAR), led by al-Faqih (hence the importance of the latter's rhetoric, which has so far been one of the strongest inspirations for the Islamic opposition).[38]

Al-Hawali's *risala* was instigated by the official acceptance by the *'ulama'* of the invitation of foreign troops to defend the Kingdom during the Gulf crisis, which took the form of a fatwa issued by Shaykh Ibn Baz. Al-Hawali argues that his message is an exposure of facts that have escaped those who issued the *fatwa* legitimating the invitation of Western troops. This exposure involves both a reading of history and a reinterpretation of Islamic concepts such as that of *isti'ana* (assistance by foreign military forces). Al-Hawali's vision of history is one that centers on the conflict between the West and Islam, giving the Crusades as an example—a line of argument echoing official state narratives.[39] Given this interpretation, the Gulf crisis and the subsequent invitation of the troops were seen as a step towards perpetuating Western hegemony over the Islamic world in general and Saudi Arabia in particular.

As far as his interpretation of the Islamic concept of isti'ana is concerned, al-Hawali argues that a distinction must be made between the position of fiqh regarding the use of infidel troops for the defense of the umma, and the context in which such use is to take place. Isti'ana is justified only if "Muslims can guarantee that they will not be treated treacherously by the infidels, and that Muslims can resist them if they side with their enemy."[40] According to al-Hawali, these conditions were not met during the Gulf crisis; therefore the invitation, in his opinion, did not fulfill the legal criteria of isti'ana. As such, it was illegal. This genre of argument, which above all relates to a political issue—the decision of the Saudi government to use foreign assistance—is reinterpreted and represented within the same Islamic framework that the government has relied on in both its general quest for legitimacy and its security concerns during the Gulf War. Using the rhetoric of Islam, al-Hawali challenges the Islamic fatwa on which the Saudi state based its decision. More importantly, he questions whether the regime is genuinely Islamic as projected in its official rhetoric and historical narratives.

In his conclusion, al-Hawali distinguishes between two categories of states: dawlat al-'aqida, the state of creed "where jihad and the prevention of vice and propagation of virtue are supreme, and dawlat al-rafahiyya, the state of luxury where worldly desires and al-taghrib (Westernization) are its ultimate goals."[41] Here there is an implicit recognition that the Saudi state initially fell within the first category. But more recently, both modernization and corruption have led to a swing in the direction of the second, where there remain "slogans of piety and skeletons of traditional institutions which claim to be Islamic."[42]

It is worth noting that in al-Hawali's risala, there are points of congruence with official historical narratives. This is apparent in his unequivocal rejection of Arab nationalism, Ba'thism, and Westernization. Al-Hawali agrees with state rhetoric that "Arab nationalism is a misguided ideology, a diversion from Islam, and an illusion," a description that echoes the official rhetoric referred to earlier. The Ba'thist version of this ideology is, in his opinion, the ultimate jahiliyya. Similarly, Westernization is, in his opinion, more likely to enforce itself in the land of Islam, especially after the invitation of foreign troops during the Gulf crisis. Here al-Hawali accepts official representations of these movements.

Another example of the congruence between state and Islamist rhetoric is al-Hawali's unquestioning acceptance of the historical value of Wahhabism. This reformist movement remains the framework within which both the state and the Islamists operate. The present Islamic opposition may undermine and question Saudi legitimacy in the political field, but so far it has not cast any doubt on the validity of Wahhabism as a religious movement capable of providing the ideological foundation of the state.

However, the congruence between Islamist and state rhetoric gives way to a rejection of the role of al-Saud in perpetuating the movement and applying the rules of the *shari'a* (Islamic law). Islamists question the degree to which al-Saud, including the founder of the state, Abd al-Aziz Ibn Saud, have remained faithful to the tenets of Wahhabism and whether the movement is best guarded by them at the present. *Al-shar'iyya,* the CDLR monthly magazine, continues to attack the Saudi leadership. The title of one article, "Psychological Reading in al-Saud's Personality," captures the group's understanding of the relationship between religion and al-Saud. The article claims:

> The gap is wide between the slogan of applying the *shari'a,* which al-Saud claim to respect, and the reality of the situation which contradicts not only the *shari'a,* but also religion in general.[43]

This gap, according to the magazine article, is reflected in the way Saudi official rhetoric continues to

> deceive the umma by excessively using religious rhetoric and formulae. Words such as *al-'aqida, rabb al-'izza wa-al-jalal, rida' al-allah* are overused in the King's speeches and those of other members of the royal family.[44]

The magazine claims that King Fahd repeated the word *al-'aqida* (creed) 30 times in one of his speeches, and reports an amusing anecdote concerning his son Faisal who, when asked about the reasons for the construction of the Riyadh stadium, replied: "To please God."[45] As the Islamists subject official narratives to scrutiny and ridicule, these narratives become trivialized and less convincing. More importantly, they lose both their potential to establish consensual control and their sacrosanct quality.

In addition to citing the "deception" resulting from excessive use of religious jargon, the CDLR gives other reasons to support the claim that Saudi rule has departed from the true path of Islam. One such reason relates to how the *'ulama'* are treated in the country. This is described as the

> *drama of respect,* in which even the most loyal *'ulama'* are greeted in the king's *majlis* according to rituals whose ultimate purpose is to humiliate them and ensure their subordination. Those *'ulama'* who disagree with the regime continue to face imprisonment and torture.[46]

Furthermore, the state tradition of distributing land and real estate among the *'ulama'* confirms, according to the magazine article, that al-Saud gain the loyalty of the *'ulama'*, not by strictly following their advice, but by bribing them.

While the reinterpretation of official historical discourse continues to be a priority for the Islamists, the project seems to be equally high on the agenda of the Shi'i minority. The Shi'is cannot compete with the rhetoric of Wahhabism, which describes them as *rafida* (a sect outside the true path of Islam), as long as Wahhabism and its specific interpretations remain dominant. They can only hope that the government will intervene to limit the circulation of Wahhabi theological discourse, which so far has condemned their beliefs and practices.

However, the Shi'is have been active in rejecting official historical representations of themselves. This has crystallized in a rewriting of their regional history, especially that of al-Hasa, where the majority of the Shi'i community live. As official narratives deny the Shi'is a position in history, as shown by their total omission from history textbooks, the community—through its intellectuals and leadership—constructs counter-historical narratives whereby the Shi'is are reintroduced into history as active agents with a separate, but not totally alien, regional identity. The writings of Hamza al-Hassan, Shi'i opposition spokesman for *Al-harakat al-islahiyya,* the Reform Movement, previously known as *Munathamat al-thawrat al-islamiyya,* the Organization of Islamic Revolution, represent one of the systematic attempts to achieve this goal.[47] Al-Hassan's objectives in writing this seminal historical work are twofold: to introduce the authentic history, culture, and identity of the Saudi Shi'i community, which in his opinion are omitted from Saudi narratives as if "they do not exist," and to highlight the discrimination to which the Shi'is are subjected under Saudi rule, described as promoting sectarian divisions among people.[48]

Al-Hassan's work presents the origins of the Shi'i community as dating back to the times of the Prophet Muhammad. He lists the major Shi'i tribal groups in al-Hasa and Qatif, in the eastern provinces, and the Hijaz in the western parts of the country. He acknowledges the fact that Shi'i tribal origins cannot be easily traced because the community had been settled in towns, oases, and cities longer than the rest of the population of Saudi Arabia. Sedentarization was accompanied by the weakening of tribal allegiances and marked genealogies. This combined with the fact that Shi'sm constituted the main bond uniting these sedentary communities led to the dissolution of tribal identities, which were replaced by allegiance to Shi'ism. Furthermore, al-Hassan dismisses the claim that, because its dialect has a resemblance to the Iraqi dialect, Shi'ism originated in Iraq. This resemblance is interpreted as a function of the theological and religious links that the Saudi Shi'is maintained with the Iraqi centers of religious learning. From this exploration of the question of origin, dialect, and identity, al-Hassan concludes that the Shi'is are an indigenous group well rooted in Saudi Arabia, a claim that counters that of the state, which has continued to spread the idea that the Shi'is have their origins in neighboring countries, mainly Iraq and Iran. The rest of the volume, a summary of the history of the community in the nineteenth century, highlights the various Saudi attempts to subjugate the Shi'is and the discrimination that resulted from their incorporation in the first and second Saudi dynasties. Al-Hassan also celebrates the intellectual developments, mainly in literature and theology, which flourished among the Shi'is at that time, an elaboration of the theme that is alluded to in Saudi history textbooks, but without any clarification.

The most interesting account in al-Hassan's work is his reinterpretation of the incorporation of the al-Hasa region in the Saudi realm. While official narratives describe this as a function of the "unification" process, al-Hassan's counter-narrative labels it as the "occupation" of 1913. Al-Hassan dismisses the Saudi justification, described in Ibn Saud's words as "a restoration of my ancestor's historical rights over this territory," by showing that in the nineteenth century, Saudi hegemony over al-Hasa lasted for only 31 years and was disrupted by various local revolts. According to al-Hassan, this does not represent a sound argument. Similarly, Saudi claims that they entered al-Hasa on the basis of local complaints inviting them to rescue the population from Turkish rule, echo the well-established official story which depicts Saudi unification as rescuing local communities from the pervasive state of moral, social and political degeneration. This argument is used in relation not only to al-Hasa, but also to all regions that in subsequent years became part of Saudi Arabia.

Al-Hassan's study is one attempt to rewrite regional and community history inspired by a political agenda. His themes are reiterated in other Shi'i publications, including the magazine *Al-jazirat al-'arabiyya,* whose publication was suspended after the reconciliation with the regime in 1992-93.[49] This magazine provided a forum for highlighting the theme of regional identity, not only that of the Shi'is, but also of other groups such as that of the Hijazis, which are believed to have been undermined by *siyasat al-tanjid* ("Najdization"), a reference to the supremacy of Najd and its ruling group over other communities in Saudi Arabia. In a leading article, one author questions official representations of this supremacy, describing it as delivering the rest of the Arabian Peninsula from political and moral degeneration.[50] Instead, his interpretation deconstructs this official myth by emphasizing that the present unity of the regions is based on two pillars, so far endorsed by al-Saud: *'asabiyya najdiyya* (Najdi solidarity) and *'asabiyya madhhabiyya* (sectarian solidarity). This resulted in a forced unity and dependency, to the detriment of local autonomy and regional character. Above all, the so-called unification process replaced the traditional economic and social interdependence by utter dependency on Najd and its population, which began to occupy a superior position vis-à-vis other areas and local communities. The rhetoric of this argument centers on the concepts of *taba'iyya* (subordination), *saytara* (authority), and *ilhaq* (attachment), all pointing to the political and social inequality between Najd and the rest of the country. The text concludes by highlighting the potential threat of division, *al-taqsim*, stemming from this inequality. The solution, in the author's opinion, lies in a genuine attempt by the ruling group to introduce wider political participation, taking into account regional interests, cultural and religious specificity, and local political and economic aspirations. Moreover, this would involve the revival of *mujtama'at al-madaniyya*, urban civilization as described by Ibn Khaldun, which is most conducive to the development of urban culture and intellectual pursuits. According to the same source, Najdization has undermined the urbanity of the Hijaz and al-Hasa in favor of the Najdi beduin solidarity.

The starting point of this intellectual activity is the deconstruction of the well-established official vision of polity, society, and history. It demonstrates that the official narratives of the regime are beginning to be challenged by those groups who have been underrepresented or misrepresented, such as the Shi'is. It remains to be seen whether other regions, especially the Hijaz, will in the future produce similar attempts to rewrite their own version of their past and their vision of its future within a larger entity, that of Saudi Arabia, both state and society.

CONCLUSION

Official historical narratives constitute one of those areas so far neglected as a window through which to examine both the state's political legitimacy and its security. Saudi historical narratives are an important part of what Barry Buzan calls "the idea of the state," which provides the major bindings holding the territorial-polity-society package together.[51] Historical narratives created a sociopolitical cohesion that guaranteed the security of the state by providing a coherent ideology propagated by the state through its controlled educational institutions. These narratives were widely endorsed by many Saudis.

Since its creation in 1932, the Saudi state has been playing the role of an educator which has at its disposal enormous oil wealth. Through education, official history is disseminated to a large section of society. This history creates a world view that celebrates Islam, Wahhabism, and the leading role of al-Saud. Moreover, this history replaces traditional regional and tribal consciousness with one that centers on loyalty to a larger entity, Saudi Arabia, under the supremacy of the Najdi ruling group and religious elite. The origins of the state are projected as a product of a unification process, facilitated by the Saudi-Wahhabi alliance, which delivered the various regions from their initial state of moral, economic, and political disintegration. The Saudi state becomes an inevitable historical event. Its legitimacy lies in its historically justified idea. These narratives establish consensual control over the population; above all they generalize the interests of those who control the state to the rest of the constituency.

The content of these narratives remained unchallenged until recently when counter-narratives were produced by opposition groups. This has only taken place as a result of events that were not products of internal mechanisms. The preeminence of the Islamists' trend is to a large extent attributed to the events of the Gulf War and the political debate that it generated. Similarly, the Shi'i counter-narratives were stimulated by events outside Saudi Arabia, mainly the success of the Iranian revolution. Both the Islamists and the Shi'i opposition have been active in producing counter-visions of society and politics.

The legitimacy of the Saudi state has not been entirely dependent on the predominance of its official historical narratives. However, these narratives remain important in maintaining the security and legitimacy of the state. Their importance equals other well-documented means available to the state including institutions, external support, economic largesse, and coercion. What distinguishes the efficacy of these narratives is their ability to create long-lasting consciousness in support of the idea of the state; the complete dismantling of this idea may take the present opposition into the twenty-first century.

NOTES

1. Ghassan Salamé, for instance, writes that it is remarkable in a tribal society that one tribe has been able to gain the degree of hegemony attained by the al-Sauds. He explains this historical anomaly by referring to the "crucial Wahhabi connection which gave the Sauds a supra-tribal ideology to manipulate in their drive to establish a permanent principality, rather than one of those numerous volatile and short lived tribal confederations." See Ghassan Salamé, "Political Power and the Saudi State," in *Power and Stability in the Middle East,* ed. Berch Berborglu (London: Zed Books, 1989), 70.

2. Gregory Gause, in his analysis of the legitimation formula deployed by many Gulf states, including Saudi Arabia, accepts Islam and tribalism as crucial pillars upon which the hegemony of rulers had been resting. However, he expands these factors further and shows how they affect politics now, a position that enables him to analyze a wide range of phenomena such as dress, the manipulation of the media, the revival of *turath* (heritage) and other interrelated issues. He forcibly argues that regimes in these countries have been largely successful in taming and using Islam and tribalism as institutional and ideological supports. However, they have not monopolized these concepts, and other political forces have emerged that contest the regimes' interpretations. This describes the situation in Saudi Arabia in which both the state and the Islamists are drawing on the same tradition and historical narratives. See F. Gregory Gause III, *Oil Monarchies: Domestic and Security Challenges in the Arab Gulf States* (New York: Council on Foreign Relations, 1994), 41.

3. Hazem Beblawi and Giacomo Luciani, eds., *The Rentier State* (London: Croom Helm, 1987) and Giacomo Luiciani, ed., *The Arab State* (London: Routledge, 1990).

4. This view is sustained in Gause's work on the Gulf states referred to earlier, in which he emphasizes the role of oil wealth in the successful transformation by rulers of ideologies such as Islam and tribalism. However, Jill Crystal remains skeptical about this assertion, arguing that the state has no monopoly on ideas. She adds that "although they invoke religious and other symbols, such as *turath*, or heritage, from time to time, they have not developed an elaborate ideological justification of their rule, a set of antidemocratic ideas. Certainly, they have not been successful in selling such a justification to the populace." See Jill Crystal, "Civil Society in the Arabian Gulf," in *Civil Society in the Middle East,* vol. 2, ed. Augustus Richard Norton (New York: E. J. Brill, 1996), 273.

5. Eric Davis, "Theorizing Statecraft and Social Change in Arab Oil-Producing Countries," in *Statecraft in the Middle East: Oil, Historical Memory and Popular Culture,* ed. Eric Davis and Nicolas Gavrielides (Miami: Florida International University Press, 1991), 9.

6. Ibid., 10.

7. Nazih Ayubi, *Over-Stating the Arab State: Politics and Society in the Middle East* (London: I. B. Tauris, 1995), 3.

8. Antonio Gramsci, *Selections from the Prison Notebooks of Antonio Gramsci,* ed. and trans. Quentin Hoare and Geoffrey Nowell Smith (New York: International Publishers, 1971) and Paul Ransome, *Antonio Gramsci: A New Introduction* (London: Harvester Wheatsheaf, 1992).

9. Writing about the formation of the Saudi state, Ayubi highlights the crucial role of Wahhabism and tribal support, which Ibn Khaldun had emphasized and projected as the basis of central authority in the Islamic world. According to Ayubi, the modern Saudi state gained legitimacy by deploying three strategies: tribal alliances and marriage, bureaucratization, and patronage. See Ayubi, Over-Stating the Arab State.

10. This has been explored by Davis and Gavrielides who investigate the cultural and ideological foundations of legitimacy and power. This is coined *statecraft,* the processes or mecha-

nisms whereby a state enhances its power and authority. It entails the effort of those who control the state to generalize their interests to the populace at large. While oil revenues and their distribution by the state may create patronage networks, economic dependency, and consequently loyalty, statecraft creates bondage of a social and ideological nature. See *Statecraft in the Middle East,* 12. In another publication, Davis pays special attention to the role of historical narratives in maintaining the hegemony of one particular group in society over others. He argues that subaltern groups must internalize the ideology of the ruling class if that class is to exercise hegemony. For further details, see Eric Davis, "History of the Many or History for the Few? The Historiography of the Iraqi Working Class," in *Workers and Working Classes in the Middle East: Struggles, Histories, Historiographies,* ed. Zachary Lockman (New York: State University of New York Press, 1994), 301. Freitag discusses the importance of the project of rewriting history from the perspective of Arab nationalism; see Ulrike Freitag, "Writing Arab History: The Search for the Nation," *British Journal of Middle Eastern Studies* 21, no. 1 (1994): 19-37.

11. Godelier has rightly pointed out that while the power to dominate always combines violence and consent, for this consent to exist, in some way dominators and dominated, exploiters and exploited must share the same representations. See Maurice Godelier, "Mirror, Mirror on the Wall . . . The Once and Future Role of Anthropology: A Tentative Assessment," in *Assessing Cultural Anthropology,* ed. Robert Borofsky (New York: McGraw Hill, 1994), 97-112.

12. Jill Crystal argues that in Qatar the ruling elites' myths and the symbolism they invoke remain unclear and contested as they fail to integrate the past and the present in a coherent ideology. See Jill Crystal, *Oil and Politics in the Gulf: Rulers and Merchants in Kuwait and Qatar* (Cambridge: Cambridge University Press 1990; reprint, 1995), 161.

13. Davis, "Theorizing Statecraft."

14. David Kertzer argues that one is struck not by rebellions of the oppressed who rise up to destroy the political system that exploits them. Rather it is the overwhelming conformity of the people living in such societies that is most impressive. Both ritual and ideology make the social order appear natural and inevitable through a process of "mystification." See David Kertzer, *Ritual, Politics, and Power* (New Haven: Yale University Press, 1988), 39. This statement seems to explain why some regimes enjoy stability as a result of the dominance of their official representations of history.

15. Michael Field, *The Merchants: The Big Business Families of Saudi Arabia and the Gulf States* (New York: Overlook Press, 1985) and Jerine Bird, "Revolution for Children in Saudi Arabia," in *Children in the Muslim Middle East,* ed. Elizabeth Fernea (Austin: University of Texas Press, 1995), 276-94.

16. I have dealt with these issues elsewhere in the context of Shammar tribal history. Suffice it here to say that the outstanding feature of this history was that it was oral. For further details, see Madawi Al-Rasheed, *Politics in an Arabian Oasis: The Rashidi Tribal Dynasty* (London: I. B. Tauris, 1991), 159-83.

17. This genre of historical tradition is common in other parts of the Arab world. John Davis documented how Libyan tribes are concerned with the construction of history, in this case a product of a specialized group who tell stories about past events which they witnessed themselves or heard about from their ancestors. See John Davis, *Libyan Politics: Tribe and Revolution* (London: I. B. Tauris, 1987), 207. Similar work has been done on Yemen where there is a tradition of competing historiographies. See Paul Dresch, *Tribes, Government, and History in Yemen* (Oxford: Clarendon Press, 1989).

18. Bird, "Revolution for Children," 280.

19. Delwin Roy, "Saudi Arabian Education: Development Policy," *Middle Eastern Studies* 28, no. 3 (July 1992): 477-508.

20. Saudi Arabia Monetary Agency, *Annual Report* (Saudi Arabia, 1994), 114.
21. Peter Wilson and Douglas Graham, *Saudi Arabia: The Coming Storm* (New York: M. E. Sharpe, 1994), 12.
22. Ibid., 13.
23. In theory Saudi children can enter school at the age of six but not many children are sent to school at that age. It is not uncommon for some children to enter school for the first time at the age of 14 or 15.
24. *Al-sira al-nabawiyya wa-tarikh al-dawlat al-islamiyya,* for secondary schools, vol. 1 (Saudi Arabia: Wizarat al-ma'arif, 1993), 71-72.
25. Ugo Fabietti, "Control and Alienation of Territory among the Bedouin of Saudi Arabia," *Nomadic Peoples* (1986): 39.
26. Scholars who advocate this view include among others Salamé, Gause, and Ayubi.
27. *Al-sira,* 89
28. Ibid.
29. Ibid., 93.
30. Ibid.
31. Ibid., 91.
32. *Tarikh al-mamlaka al-'arabiyya al-sa'udiyya,* for secondary schools, vol. 3 (Saudi Arabia: Wizarat al-ma'arif, 1993), 11.
33. Ibid., 12.
34. This is accepted even by the Islamists who continue to be drawn from Najd. For details on the composition and regional background of the Islamist opposition, see Hrair Dekmejian, "The Rise of Political Islamism in Saudi Arabia," *Middle East Journal* 48, no. 4 (autumn 1994).
35. Again Wahhabism is central in the discourse of the present Islamist opposition to the Saudi regime. For further details, see Madawi Al-Rasheed, "Saudi Arabia's Islamic Opposition," *Current History* 95, no. 597 (January 1996): 16-22.
36. The encapsulation of tribal groups by the Saudis is the subject of Madawi Al-Rasheed and Loulouwa Al-Rasheed, "The Politics of Encapsulation: Saudi Policy towards Tribal and Religious Opposition," *Middle Eastern Studies* 32, no. 1 (January 1996): 96-119.
37. Safar al-Hawali, *Kashf al-ghamma 'an 'ulama' al-umma* (n.p.: Dar al-hikma, 1991).
38. Dekmejian, "The Rise of Political Islamism" and Al-Rasheed, "Saudi Arabia's Islamic Opposition."
39. Hawali, *Kashf al-ghamma,* 138.
40. Ibid.
41. Ibid., 43.
42. Ibid.
43. *Al-shar'iyya* 1, no. 8 (February/March 1996): 15.
44. Ibid.
45. Ibid.
46. Ibid.
47. Hamza al-Hassan, *Al-shi'a fi al-mamlaka al-'arabiyya al-sa'udiyya,* vols. 1 and 2 (Beirut: Mu'assasat al-baqi li ihya' al-turath, 1993).
48. Ibid., 8-9.
49. For further details on the Shi'i opposition, see Al-Rasheed and Al-Rasheed, "Politics of Encapsulation."
50. *Al-Jazira al-'arabiyya* 18 (July 1992): 24-30.
51. Barry Buzan, *People, States and Fear: An Agenda for International Security Studies in the Post-Cold War Era* (London: Harvester Wheatsheaf, 1991), 82.

CHAPTER THREE

Legitimacy and Security in Arab Countries
1989-1996

MUSTAPHA KAMEL AL-SAYYID

*T*he four major tasks of this chapter are to clarify how security and legitimacy are to be understood in a Middle Eastern context, to suggest ways of providing a quantitative basis for the two concepts, to strive to measure them in a representative group of countries in the Arab world, and, finally, to explore how legitimacy affects societal and state security in these countries in the 1990s.

DEFINING SECURITY AND LEGITIMACY

Security

For the concept of security to be useful, it should be disaggregated into its several components: societal security, state security and regime security, and the security of the ruler. A modified version of the classical definition of national security offered by Walter Lippmann in 1943 could serve as a common yardstick for all these dimensions of security. Lippmann defined national security in the following way:

> A nation is secure to the extent to which it is not in danger of having to sacrifice core values, if it wishes to avoid war, and is able, if challenged, to maintain them by such victory in such a war.[1]

Thus, the security of a society, a state, a regime, or a ruler can be seen, according to this definition, as the capability of any of them to maintain its core values, even in situations of conflict. A fundamental feature of security dilemmas in countries of the South is that these dimensions of security do not often go together. If the core values of society are different from those of the state, as seemed to be the case in Algeria in January 1992, then the attainment of societal security necessitates a radical transformation of the nature of the secularist national state. Societal security ran against state security. Likewise, the security of a particular regime might run counter to the security of the state. For instance, it could be claimed that the security of the post-Gulf War regime in Iraq is diametrically opposed to the security of the state of Iraq. A less authoritarian regime in Iraq or Libya might be better capable of defending state security in the face of domestic, regional, and international threats to the core values of these states. In the particular case of Libya, it is conceivable that the removal of Colonel Mu'ammar Qadhafi could contribute positively to the security of the Libyan regime, in the sense that the basic structures of the regime could be safely maintained in the absence of a particular leader whose probable involvement in specific decisions is the cause of the international sanctions imposed on the Libyan state since 1992 by the United Nations Security Council.

This incompatibility of the different dimensions of security in the postcolonial states is perhaps due to two important features of their political systems. One is the uneven incorporation of the different ethnic groups into them,[2] when members of these groups do not enjoy effective equal rights of citizenship on account of their ethnic origins. The other feature is their authoritarian nature and the lack of popular accountability of their rulers who are able to pursue personal interests at the expense of the majority of their peoples. Although the first feature is encountered in several countries of the North as well, the case of United States blacks and Hispanic citizens being the most notorious, the liberal nature of their political systems provides ways for reconciling the interests of society with those of the state and of ensuring that security of their political regimes is consistent with security of their states and societies, at least in the short run.

In the study of countries of the South, the concept of national security is applied as though these societies have become nation-states, in which the nation and the state are identical, and as though states enjoy legitimacy vis-à-vis their societies. As this is not generally the case, it would be better to substitute for the concept of national security the concepts of state, regime, and societal security.

State security can be defined as maintenance and promotion of a state's core values, including in particular its territory and natural wealth within the bounds authorized by the international system. Regime security is maintenance of the core values of the regime, especially maintenance of its basic rules and institutions. Societal security is protection of the core values of that society, namely, protecting the right to life of its citizens, safeguarding its national values, and ensuring its welfare, or at least satisfaction of the basic needs of its inhabitants.[3]

This conceptualization of these terms makes it possible to relate discussions of security to the reality of countries of the South, and to be able to distinguish the various types of threats to the security of these countries. For example, civil strife in Algeria mainly affected two Algerian regimes, while the Algerian state remained intact. In the case of Iraq in the aftermath of the second Gulf War, the Ba'thist regime has survived, despite much damage to the security of state and society. The demise of a particular ruler, as in the case of Sadat in Egypt, did much to enhance the security of the regime he established, although it had been temporarily weakened by his policies.

Legitimacy

The concept of legitimacy is less controversial than the concept of national security, but it is also quite problematic when linked to other political issues. It has been discussed very often in the context of comparing different types of political systems, each characterized by a specific foundation of political authority, or by a specific rationale in appealing to citizens to voluntarily accept it. Thus, following the famous trilogy of foundations of domination suggested by Max Weber, social scientists used to distinguish its rational, traditional, and charismatic bases. Raymond Aron explains this in the following way:

> That domination is rational which is based on a belief in the legality of domination and the legality of titles of those who exercise domination. That domination is traditional which is based on a belief in the sacred quality of long-standing traditions and in the legitimacy of those who have been called upon to exercise authority. That domination is charismatic which is based on an extraordinary devotion to the sacred quality of the heroic strength or exemplary character of a person and of the order revealed or created by him.[4]

Arab political systems have often been analyzed in terms of the Weberian typology.[5] A fourth type of foundation of domination, particularly relevant to countries of the South, including the Arab countries, is revolutionary legitimacy. Revolutionary regimes claim legitimacy by advocating the interests of the majority and striving to satisfy their most elementary needs for food, housing, education, health care, and some dignity. A majority of their citizens could forego for a while such regimes' disregard of civil and political rights so long as they offer them food and shelter. The stability of radical authoritarian regimes in the Arab world, like those of Libya, Iraq, and Egypt under Nasir, can be explained by this type of social contract where the government offers citizens a minimum of welfare services in return for their acquiescence to its denial of their right to political participation. When any of these governments failed to provide its citizens with this minimum of personal security, its own security was jeopardized, as was experienced particularly by Sadat in 1977.[6]

However, the question of legitimacy should also be raised in the context of comparing different types of political communities, as the definition of the political community itself, and not just the basis of political authority, is also questioned in many countries at present, not only in the South. This dimension of the legitimacy issue is particularly relevant in security studies, when the object of dispute is the appropriateness of maintaining specific groups within the boundaries of the same state. In this sense, the questions of legitimacy and national identity become closely interrelated, or become one and the same issue. If the boundaries of the political community itself do not enjoy the loyalty of a certain segment of its own people, it is highly unlikely that they view the political authority which presides over them as legitimate, regardless of the foundations it claims for its exercise of power. Persistent nationalist agitation by the Basque separatist movement ETA in northern Spain or by the IRA (Irish Republican Army) in Ireland are vivid demonstrations of this point.

The legitimacy crisis affects not only perception of the threat to national security by opposition groups in the country in question, but also its security performance. Its capacity to mobilize resources for purposes other than self-maintenance is limited by the fact that it devotes most of its resources, or a large part of them, to security purposes. Even the capacity to mobilize resources for internal security and defense purposes is curtailed by this lack of legitimacy which drives citizens away from any show of support for such regimes, complying with its commands in terms of the provision of material, financial, or human support only when forced to do so. They are likely to find ways to avoid fulfillment even of the most basic civic duties, such as payment of taxes or obligatory military service. Acts of non-cooperation shown by Lithuanian citizens towards Soviet authorities during the last months of the life of the Soviet Union are illustrative of this.[7] Finally, the task of security management is further complicated by the link between domestic opposition and foreign foes of the regime in question. The former seeks allies abroad and the latter are more than willing to offer their support to the domestic opposition.

Quantifying Levels of Legitimacy and State-Society Security

This section outlines an attempt to translate these concepts into indicators that can be measured for the five representative countries chosen for this study from 1989 to 1996. A translation of any concept into indicators cannot, in the best of circumstances, render justice to its full meaning. The list of indicators mentioned in this section is by no means exhaustive. A more detailed list might make it possible to refine measurement of both legitimacy and security, but it would be unlikely to lead to vastly different conclusions. In other words, the more exhaustive list could increase or decrease the combined score of certain regimes on some of these indicators, but would probably not change the final verdict on that regime from being legitimate to being illegitimate, or from being one that offers its citizens little societal security to one offering them maximum security.

Legitimacy, interpreted as people's voluntary acceptance of their political community and its structures of power, can be manifested through absence of politically-motivated murders; absence, or a small number, of prisoners of conscience; resort to ordinary courts in settlement of political disputes; absence of restrictions on certain freedoms such as those of expression, political activities, associations; absence of involuntary disappearances, political exiles, and economic migrants; and orderly change of government.

Broadening the concept of security to allow us to make the distinction between the security of the regime and that of the state and the society can be justified on the grounds that threats to one do not necessarily pose a threat to the other two. Successful management of external and internal threats to core values constitutes a solid foundation for their security. In the case of the state, its security would require that it successfully manages foreign and domestic military threats relying either on its own resources or on involvement in symmetric alliance relationships. Security is also ensured if the state does the same with respect to external economic threats. Other indicators of state security include movement towards more interdependent relationships with other countries in the world market; more government expenditure on welfare than on security and defense; and low military/total manpower and defense/government expenditure ratios. Societal security is manifested in lower crime rates, regardless of the type of crime; low levels of unemployment and poverty; and many of the human development indicators used in the report published annually by the United Nations Development Program.[8] This chapter will focus on those indicators related directly to physical survival of citizens.

How is legitimacy related to national security? Lack of legitimacy influences each dimension of security. Regarding regime security, citizens, or groups of citizens who do not accept a certain regime as legitimate, and who do not find adequate channels for the expression of their discontent or to effect a change of system, might resort to armed methods in their opposition to the regime. Depending on the magnitude and effectiveness of this armed opposition, this might endanger the security or even the survival of the regime. They might also penalize other citizens for their cooperation with or acquiescence to the regime, or simply to demonstrate the incapacity of the regime to maintain law and order. The collapse of law and order as a result of a protracted armed struggle might encourage more people to defy the law by engaging in acts of vandalism, theft, attacks on property, and the like. Societal security would thus be endangered. Even when the lack of legitimacy is not manifested in open challenge to the incumbent regime, large numbers of citizens might cease to co-operate voluntarily with the regime in carrying out its policies or implementing its programs and projects in different areas. This withdrawal of support might tax the regime a lot in terms of loss of financial and human resources which would make it more difficult for it to attain its own goals, thus contributing further to the erosion of its legitimacy.

The lack of legitimacy might not necessarily impact state security as such. A state, as opposed to a regime, can survive a crisis of legitimacy if those who challenge an incumbent regime aspire to take hold of the state itself. This is the case in countries who do not have a separatist movement within their population, and where even minority groups are committed to maintenance of the existing state. This is not the case, however, where the legitimacy crisis is rooted in minority groups who perceive their emancipation to be through establishment of their own states. In such cases, the lack of legitimacy, combined with an intercommunal conflict, could indeed become a threat to state security.

Failure of the incumbent regime to deal effectively with threats to state, societal, or even regime security could impair its legitimacy. The first function of the state is to defend its territory and to ensure security and some justice in the settlement of disputes to its citizens. If an incumbent regime fails in carrying out these basic functions, its legitimacy might be weakened or undermined and its citizens might seek an alternative regime. A perceived weakness of the regime might encourage opposition groups to escalate the scope and methods of their opposition, to stiffen their demands and to seek domestic and foreign allies in their opposition to the regime. An initial failure to provide regime, societal or, state security would therefore widen the crisis of legitimacy of the regime and aggravate its security dilemma.

However, the link between legitimacy and security in all its dimensions is never a direct one. It is mediated by a host of other variables, including the position of the counter-elite as to whether or not its members are willing to cooperate with the incumbent regime in alleviating causes of the crisis; the position of foreign powers and their willingness to offer support to those opposed to the regime; and the capacity of the incumbent regime to embark upon policies that strike at the roots of the legitimacy crisis by changing policies, personnel, or even the structures that provoked the legitimacy crisis in the first place.

MEASURING LEGITIMACY AND STATE-SOCIETAL SECURITY IN FIVE ARAB COUNTRIES

This section aims to measure levels of legitimacy and state-societal security in five Arab countries held to be representative of the various types of political regimes in the Arab world. Arab countries exhibit at present four types of such regimes: liberalized regimes (represented here by Egypt and Algeria), single party (Iraq), military or no party regimes (Libya) and neo-traditional monarchies (Saudi Arabia). Admittedly, these countries might not be perfect representatives of their categories. For example, is Algeria at present a liberalized or a military regime? The election of Lamin Zerual as head of state in the autumn of 1995 in a fairly competitive election qualifies it for membership of this group, while it was a full-fledged military regime prior to that election. Did the election fundamentally change the character of the Algerian regime?

The five countries are compared along different dimensions of legitimacy and state-societal security. The scores on these indicators have values varying usually from 1 to 5. If a country's score on any of these indicators is close to 1, this signals a positive rank along this specific indicator. If the score is close to 5, this signals a negative ordering, meaning low levels of legitimacy or deteriorating level of state-societal security.

This method of ranking countries helps overcome a problem related to measurement, namely, the lack of quantified data on some indicators such as levels of freedom of expression and association, orderly change of government, and the state's management of external military and economic threats. For such indicators, qualitative data, for example reports of human rights organizations or other reliable surveys of foreign relations, can be used in order to rank them in the same way as if quantitative data were available. Complete freedom of expression translates into rank 1. Few restrictions is a middle rank or one close to the top. Frequent restrictions accompanied by harassment of people who express views hostile to the government or complete lack of freedom rank at 4 or 5. The same kind of reasoning is used with respect to all indicators which are not based on readily available quantified data. An explanation of the logic of rankings is to be found for each of these indicators under the relevant tables.

MEASURING LEGITIMACY

Number of Political Prisoners or Detainees

Figures for political prisoners or detainees published by human rights organizations or even official sources in the Arab world indicate an increase in their numbers in the sample countries in the 1990s due to the impact of the second Gulf War in Saudi Arabia and Iraq, suspension of the second round of the legislative elections in Algeria, and the flare-up of armed opposition by Islamist groups in Egypt. In terms of the total number of political prisoners, Saudi Arabia has the lowest number, followed by Libya, with Egypt third, and Iraq and Algeria occupying the highest ranks (table 3.1).

TABLE 3.1
Number of Political Prisoners or Detainees[a]

YEAR	EGYPT	ALGERIA	IRAQ	LIBYA	SAUDI ARABIA
1989	18,027 (812)[b]	202	hundreds	162	60
1990					
1991	2,014 (640)	8,000 (2,976)	15,105[c]	467	842
1992	2,454 (1,780)	30,000	13,594	550	700
1993	(2,000)	(4,000-8,000)	10,320	800[c]	1,000
1994	3,000 (2,000)	(5,000-7,000)	5,638[c]	613	600 (150)
1995	16,708	thousands	4,045	6,000	200

[a]3,045 people disappeared between 1976 and 1988, an annual average of 254 throughout the five countries. For 1992, 1993, and 1994, the figures are 7,000, 10,570, and 15,781, respectively, in Iraq and for 1993, 52 in Libya, according to UN sources.

[b]Figures in parentheses are official figures; other figures come from Munazzama al-'arabiyya li-huquq al-insan (Arab Organization for Human Rights), *Huquq al-insan fi al-watan al-'arabi* (Human rights in the Arab world) (Cairo, 1989-1996).

[c]Including those who were temporarily detained and released.

The ranking might be slightly different when numbers of political prisoners are seen in relation to the population of each country and, more particularly, if an average annual number of prisoners is shown in relation to the median population of each country, as in table 3.2. Non-official figures are relied on here. They might not be very accurate but are probably more credible than official figures, which tend to under-report such numbers.

TABLE 3.2
Countries Ranked According to the Average Annual Number of Political Prisoners[a]

COUNTRY	POPULATION IN MEDIAN YEAR (1992) MILLIONS	AVERAGE ANNUAL NUMBER OF POLITICAL PRISONERS	AVERAGE ANNUAL NUMBER OF POLITICAL PRISONERS/ MILLION POPULATION	RANK
Egypt	53,807	3,785	70	2
Algeria	26,720	7,168	1,024	5
Iraq	19,010	6,465	923	4
Libya	4,510	370	82	3
Saudi Arabia	16,929	457	27	1

[a]Based on table 3.1

Weighted averages show Algeria and Iraq in the lowest position, the average numbers of political prisoners reaching hundreds per million of population while not exceeding a few tens per million in the case of the three other countries.

People Killed in Political Conflict

A second indicator of the legitimacy of a political system or a community is the number of people killed in political conflict. If both the political system and community enjoy legitimacy, it is not likely that citizens would risk losing their lives in political conflict. A political conflict is one involving political actors, who could be the government and opposition groups, or ordinary citizens dissatisfied with actions on the part of the government or a political organization. There are cases in which citizens are willing to risk their lives to express their discontent with the ruling regime, or with their presence in a certain political community, or when that regime finds no other way to get citizens to comply with its commands except through the frequent use of force outside the legal channels. There are even cases in which some citizens lose their lives accidentally as a result of fighting between a particular regime and its opponents. In all these cases, the legitimacy of the regime or the political community is impaired since a fundamental basis for the legitimacy of any state is its capacity to secure lives of its citizens from violent, illegal assaults. It is difficult to get data related to violent encounters, such as the number of people injured or merely involved in such incidents.

Data in table 3.3A show an increase in the number of victims of political conflicts in all five countries during the 1990s. The largest number was recorded in Iraq due to the second Gulf War in 1991, and in later years because of attempts by Iraqi authorities to suppress revolts in the north and south of the country. Some of the reported killings were due to infighting between rival guerrilla factions as well as the Turkish military expeditions in Kurdish areas. Suppression of the revolt in the south and limitations imposed by the United States and its allies on the use of Iraqi airspace contributed to the drop in the number of such reported deaths, and Algeria replaced Iraq at the top of the list from 1993. The total number of victims of the Algerian civil war was estimated to have reached more than 50,000 by 1996, exceeding estimated numbers of Iraqi deaths throughout the 1990s. Political murders in Algeria and in Egypt, which is third on the list, were caused by the armed confrontation between Islamist groups on the one hand, and security forces and some civilians and foreigners on the other. Murder cases reported in Saudi Arabia were due mostly to fighting among Iraqi refugees but tended to increase after 1995 as a result of armed attacks which targeted Saudis, other Muslims, and American soldiers. The most serious of these armed actions was the huge explosion which targeted the American military base in El-Khober in the summer of 1996 which cost the lives of 19 Americans and injured to about 400. Libya also started to experience violent confrontations between Islamist militants and security forces and clashes between rival factions of armed forces involving those opposed to Colonel Qadhafi and his supporters. If the method used in table 3.2 is applied, the five countries are ranked according to the average annual level of deaths caused by acts of political violence and reflecting their varied population sizes as shown in table 3.3B

TABLE 3.3A
Number of Deaths Caused by Political Conflicts

YEAR	EGYPT	ALGERIA	IRAQ	LIBYA	SAUDI ARABIA
1989	35	4	750	2	17
1990	52				
1991	14	300	$(55)^a$	$70-105^b$	$7,000^c$
1992	85	870	21,000	$(1,429)b(5,000)^c$	7
1993	212 (179)	1,250-1,600	462^d	12	13^e
1994	279	$8,000 (6,388)^f$	209	16	
1995	366	20,000	727, plus thousands in the Kurdish areas	circa 100	19

[a]Figures in parentheses are official figures.
[b]Military casualities.
[c]Civilian casualities.
[d]Figure does not include 97,000 more deaths caused by economic blockade.
[e]Including nine Iraqi refugees.
[f]The Algerian News Agency estimated the number of deaths caused by confrontation between Islamist groups and the government since September 1995 to be 30,000 Algerians and 90 foreigners; Munazzama al-'arabiyya li-huquq al-insan, *Huquq al-insan fi al-watan al-'arabi* (1995), 93.

TABLE 3.3B
Countries Ranked According to Average Annual Levels of Political Violence

COUNTRY	POPULATION IN MEDIAN YEAR (1992) MILLIONS	AVERAGE ANNUAL NUMBER OF POLITICALLY -MOTIVATED DEATHS	AVERAGE ANNUAL NUMBER OF DEATHS PER ONE MILLION OF POPULATION	RANK
Egypt	53,807	142	2	2
Algeria	26,720	4,308	161	4
Iraq	19,010	14,200	746	5
Libya	4,510	16	4	3
Saudi Arabia	16,929	7	0.44	1

Table 3.3B demonstrates once more the differences between Iraq and Algeria and the other three countries. Politically-motivated murders shed doubts on the legitimacy of any regime, even when the murders are very few, but when their numbers reach tens and hundreds for every million of population, the legitimacy of regimes is undermined.

Politically-motivated killings that do not target representatives of the incumbent regime but are caused by armed conflict among certain factions of the opposition, foreign aggression, or even attacks on foreign military personnel, are also considered to be indicators of lack of state or regime security, since security means maintaining the core values of a community, including defense of the right to life of its citizens. The legitimacy of both the state and the regime is at stake in all these situations, since all bases of legitimacy are accepted by citizens because of the perceived capacity of the regime to impose law and order on a rational legal basis, have charismatic leadership, or uphold the sacred tradition. If the regime fails to control certain parts of its territory, discipline factions of the armed forces, or halt a foreign aggression, then the belief in its perceived capacity to do any of these things would be shattered.

Freedom of Expression

If freedom of expression is measured through the degree of freedom of the press, according to the data of table 3.6 restrictions on freedom of the press increased in two of these countries, namely, Egypt and Algeria in the 1990s, but the same level of heavy restrictions on freedom of the press continued in the other three countries. Algeria was distinguished by the fact that it moved from being a country with complete freedom of the press in the late 1980s and early 1990s to a country with both tough official censorship measures and the highest number of killings of journalists and writers at the hands of armed Islamist groups. An informal interview conducted by the author with a group of young Egyptian political scientists suggests that the state is considered more legitimate in countries where a measure of freedom of expression exists, even if people who use this right pay a price for it in terms of political or societal expression. There is less legitimacy where there is no freedom of expression at all, with people exercising self-censorship, thus leading to a lower number of cases of persecution of writers and journalists. Thus, if absence of freedom of expression is weighted, countries would be ranked as shown in table 3.4.

This ranking is based on two sub-indicators, namely, the presence of an opposition press and physical assaults on media people. A country with free opposition press, where media people are not punished for their independence of mind, would deserve rank 1, few restrictions on freedom of expression would put the country in rank 2, more restrictions accompanied by assaults on media-people correspond to rank 4, while massive restrictions and assaults on all people who might express dissenting views unacceptable either to the government or to particular societal groups would put a country at rank 5.

TABLE 3.4
Countries Ranked According to Freedom of Expression

COUNTRY	RANK
Egypt	1
Algeria	5
Saudi Arabia	3
Iraq	4
Libya	2

Freedom of Association

Absence of restrictions on freedom of association is a good indicator of the legitimacy of a political order. Data in table 3.7 exhibit the same trend manifested in the preceding three tables, namely, increasing restrictions on freedom of association in all five countries in the 1990s, with Egypt and Algeria allowing the presence of some autonomous associations while such associations were virtually unknown in Libya and Iraq. Freedom of association is not recognized for most citizens in Saudi Arabia. The five countries would rank as in table 3.5.

TABLE 3.5
Countries Ranked According to Freedom of Association

COUNTRY	RANK
Algeria	1
Egypt	2
Saudi Arabia	3
Iraq	4
Libya	5

TABLE 3.6
Freedom of Expression as Measured by Freedom of the Press[a]

YEAR	EGYPT	ALGERIA	IRAQ	LIBYA	SAUDI ARABIA
1989	3	2	3	3	3
1990					
1991	2	1	4	3	3
1992	2	5	4	3	4

YEAR	EGYPT	ALGERIA	IRAQ	LIBYA	SAUDI ARABIA
1993	2	5	4	3	4
1994	3	5	4	3	4
1995	4	5	4	3	4

1=complete freedom
2=opposition press with a degree of governmental control
3=no opposition press
4=journalists pay the price for exercise of freedom of the press
5=massive violations of freedom of expression by both the government and opposition groups

TABLE 3.7
Freedom of Association

YEAR	EGYPT	ALGERIA	IRAQ	LIBYA	SAUDI ARABIA
1989	3	1	4	4	5
1990	3	1	4	4	5
1991	3	1	4	4	5
1992	3	3	4	4	5
1993	3	3	4	4	5
1994	3	3	4	4	5
1995	4	3	4	4	5

1=no restrictions on freedom of association
2=minor restrictions
3=serious restrictions
4=monopoly of the right to association by the state
5=no freedom of association

Absence of Restrictions on Citizens' Political Involvement

A legitimate political order does not impose any, or many, restrictions on citizens' political activities, whether these take place through peaceful assembly or political parties. The five countries under study did all strive to constrain these activities, although the type of restrictions varied from one country to the other, and even sometimes varied within the same country. Most restrictions were lifted in Algeria between 1989 and 1992, but were renewed after the ban of the activities of the Islamic Salvation Front in January 1992. The Egyptian government continued to ban the establishment of either Islamist or communist organizations. All opposition parties were prohibited in both Libya and Iraq and all party activities are banned in Saudi Arabia. The countries are ranked according to data in table 3.8.

TABLE 3.8
Countries Ranked According to Restrictions on Political Involvement

COUNTRY	RANK
Algeria	3
Egypt	3
Libya	4
Iraq	4
Saudi Arabia	5

1=complete freedom of political participation
2=few restrictions on political participation
3=more restrictions on political participation by specific groups
4=political participation is accepted only in government-controlled organizations
5=no political activities are authorized

TABLE 3.9
Absence of Restrictions on Involvement in Public Affairs

YEAR	EGYPT	ALGERIA	IRAQ	LIBYA	SAUDI ARABIA
1989	3	1	4	4	5
1990	3	1	4	4	5
1991	3	1	4	4	5
1992	3	4	4	4	5
1993	3	4	4	4	5
1994	3	4	4	4	5
1995	3	4	4	4	5

1=no restrictions, complete transparency
2=no restrictions, incomplete transparency
3=some restrictions, incomplete transparency
4=massive restrictions, no transparency
5=no chance for involvement in public affairs

Orderly Change of Government

An important test of the legitimacy of the political order over a long period of time is the organization of succession at the highest levels of the government. If that succession takes place in a peaceful, orderly manner and according to well-defined rules, this is considered evidence of elite and possibly also mass consent to the basic rules of the political game. If such succession is often marred by violent resistance, on a massive scale, this could point to the opposite, namely, partial or total lack of legitimacy of the ruling regime, depending of course on the frequency and scope of this violent resistance. The lack of legitimacy affects security in different ways. Violent resistance to succession of one head of state could signal opposition to a particular ruler, but not necessarily lack of legitimacy of the regime itself. When one particular head of state or government is associated with certain policies that provoke mass protest, his replacement by another leader who adopts different policies without changing the basis of the political system might enhance legitimacy of the regime if this succession is accepted by the majority of citizens. Thus it seemed for some time in the early 1980s in Egypt that the coming to power of Husni Mubarak, following the assassination of Sadat, had reinforced the legitimacy of the political system of his predecessor. Both regimes were characterized by a small number of parties, liberal economic policies, a peace treaty with Israel, and close relations with the United States. Sadat's political system, however, was threatened by his harsh treatment of all opposition groups. This policy was abandoned by his successor.

The most influential official in the five countries is usually the head of state. Four of the five countries did not witness any change of the head of state during the period under study. Few would expect their heads of state to disappear voluntarily from the political scene in the near future. Two heads of state, Egypt's and Iraq's, went unopposed through a presidential referendum, in 1993 and 1996 respectively, which they won, not unexpectedly, by more than a 96 percent majority. No such referendum took place in Libya. In Saudi Arabia, the head of state inherits the throne. In Algeria, one head of state was removed through a palace coup in 1992, his successor was assassinated six months later, and the third head of state was replaced by the defense minister who won a fair competitive election two years later. In neither Egypt nor Algeria did the violent succession of the head of state signal a change of regime. But assassination of the head of state means rejection, by at least some parts of the elite or the masses, of the official formula for his succession, which sheds doubts on the legitimacy of this element of the political system.

The posts of head of state and head of the government are separated in the four republican regimes included in this sample, but the fate of the prime minister always depends on the head of state. In tables 3.10 and 3.11, the five countries are ranked according to the frequency and orderliness of recent changes of government.

TABLE 3.10

Countries Ranked According to Frequency of Orderly Change of Government or Regime

COUNTRY	RANK
Saudi Arabia	1
Egypt	2

(continues)

(continued)

COUNTRY	RANK
Libya	3
Iraq	4
Algeria	5

TABLE 3.11
Orderly Change of Government or Regime

YEAR	EGYPT	ALGERIA	IRAQ	LIBYA	SAUDI ARABIA
1989					
1990					
1991			2		
1992		5			
1993	1	3			
1994		2			
1995		2			
1996	2				

1=orderly, peaceful change of government
2=peaceful change of government
3=violent change of head of state
4=violent change of cabinet
5=violent change of regime

Presence of Exiles and Economic Migrants

Two other indicators of the legitimacy of a political order are political exiles and economic migrants. A large number of political exiles signals large-scale rejection of the political order, on the assumption that more citizens would have left the country had they been able to. A highly repressive regime might physically eliminate all its opponents leaving no chance for any of them to seek political asylum abroad. Presence of economic migrants also suggests dissatisfaction with economic conditions in the home country. The implication is that citizens have withdrawn support for the political regime which drove them away from their families to go through the risk of attempting to earn a living in a foreign country where they do not enjoy the rights of full citizens.

Although it is not easy to obtain figures, political exiles from four of these countries are known to form large communities abroad. This is the case for Iraqi, Algerian, Egyptian, and Libyan opposition figures who live mostly in European countries, while some Egyptian and Algerian Islamist militants are known to be living in Arab and Muslim countries and even in the United States. Saudis have also sought political asylum in Europe in recent years, as a result of the clampdown by Saudi authorities on activities of the Society for the Defense of Shari'a Rights.[9] The United Nations High Commissioner for Refugees (UNHCR) has published data on countries of origin of major refugee communities. Figures are available for political refugees from three Arab countries—Iraq, Sudan, and Somalia—up to July 1996. Iraqi refugees were estimated at 630,000, living in Iran, Saudi Arabia, other Middle Eastern countries, and Pakistan. No figures are available on other Arab countries included in this study. A good number of Algerian, Saudi, and Egyptian exiles are to be found in European countries, particularly France, Great Britain, and Germany. Some also sought asylum in the United States, as was the case of the Egyptian Islamist leader, Shaykh Omar Abdel Rahman. UNHCR sources point to the difficulty of determining national origins of refugees, particularly in advanced countries. This difficulty is compounded by the fact that some political exiles do not like to declare themselves as political refugees, either because of administrative obstacles in getting this status, or because they do not like to attract the attention of authorities in the host countries to their political affiliations.[10]

As for economic migrants, Egypt and Algeria are known to be countries of out-migration, with millions of Egyptians and Algerians seeking a better living in other Arab countries, Europe, and the United States. Numbers of economic migrants were estimated in the range of 2.9 million Egyptians and 400,000 Algerians in 1990, just before the second Gulf War.[11] Economic migration can be considered an indicator of dissatisfaction with economic conditions; acceptance of all the hardships involved in the migrant worker's life, in Western Europe as well as in the Gulf countries, must have been motivated by extreme dissatisfaction with living conditions at home. On the basis of whatever data are available, the five countries could be reasonably ranked in terms of numbers of political exiles and economic migrants, as in table 3.12.

TABLE 3.12

**Countries Ranked According to Size of Communities
of Political Exiles and Economic Refugees**

COUNTRY	POLITICAL EXILES	ECONOMIC MIGRANTS/ MILLION OF POPULATION	RANK
Saudi Arabia	2	none	1
Libya	2	few	2
Egypt	3	56,700	5
Algeria	4	1,600	4
Iraq	5	few thousand after 2d Gulf War	3

TABLE 3.13
Number of Political Exiles

YEAR	EGYPT	ALGERIA	IRAQ	LIBYA	SAUDI ARABIA
1989	2	1	4	3	2
1990	2	1	4	3	2
1991	2	1	4	3	3
1992	3	3	5	4	3
1993	3	4	5	4	3
1994	3	4	5	4	3
1995	3	3	5	4	3

1=none; 2=few; 3=some; 4=large numbers; 5=massive numbers

TABLE 3.14
Economic Migrants

YEAR	EGYPT	ALGERIA	IRAQ	LIBYA	SAUDI ARABIA
1989	5	5	1	1	1
1990	4	5	1	1	1
1991	4	5	1	1	1
1992	5	5	1	1	1
1993	5	5	1	1	1
1994	5	5	1	1	1
1995	5	5	1	1	1

1=none; 2=few; 3=some; 4=large numbers; 5=massive numbers

Summarizing Measures of Legitimacy

Table 3.15 offers a summary of indicators of legitimacy measured for each of the five countries.

TABLE 3.15
Indicators of Legitimacy: A Summary

INDICATOR	SAUDI ARABIA	LIBYA	EGYPT	IRAQ	ALGERIA
Political prisoners	1	3	2	4	5
Political murders	1	3	2	5	4
Freedom of expression	3	3	1	3	2
Freedom of association	3	4	2	5	1
Restrictions on political involvement	5	4	3	4	3

INDICATOR	SAUDI ARABIA	LIBYA	EGYPT	IRAQ	ALGERIA
Orderly change government/regime	1	3	2	4	5
Political exiles	2	2	3	4	5
Economic migrants	1	2	4	5	3

Since not all these indicators hold the same weight for political legitimacy, they should not be treated as statistically similar. Political prisoners, politically-motivated murders, restrictions on political activities, and the seeking of political asylum are strong indicators of the lack of political legitimacy. If the first two of these strong indicators are weighted, with their scores multiplied by three, and the last two with their scores multiplied by two, the overall scale is constructed as in table 3.16.

TABLE 3.16

Weighted Scale of Political Legitimacy for Selected Arab Countries, 1989-1995

INDICATOR	SAUDI ARABIA	LIBYA	EGYPT	IRAQ	ALGERIA
Political prisoners	3	9	6	12	15
Political murders	3	9	6	15	12
Freedom of expression	3	3	1	3	2
Freedom of association	3	4	2	5	1
Restrictions on political involvement	10	8	6	8	6
Orderly change of government/regime	1	3	2	4	5
Political exiles	4	4	6	8	10
Economic migrants	1	4	10	6	8
Total	28	44	39	61	59
Average	2.10	3.40	3	4.70	4.50

Most legitimate=1; least legitimate=5.

What is striking about this index is the position occupied by Saudi Arabia, whose government is the least liberal of the five. It emerges as having relatively the most legitimate, or the least illegitimate, political order. This is due to the impact of vast oil wealth in a country less populated than the other four countries, which are heavily populated or have squandered their oil wealth in military adventures, or which cannot benefit from this oil wealth because of international economic sanctions. Egypt and Libya come in close second and third positions despite important differences in their respective types of formal political structures. Algeria with its civil war and Iraq with the grave consequences of the second Gulf War are close in fourth and fifth ranking.

There is a lack of legitimacy in the five countries. In Saudi Arabia it is moderately lacking, but tends to increase in Libya and Egypt, and reaches serious proportions in Algeria and Iraq. The individual indicators pointed to a deteriorating situation from the early 1990s in all five countries.

MEASURING STATE AND SOCIETAL SECURITY

Successful Management of External Military Threats

Countries can be ranked according to their capacity to deal on their own with foreign threats to their stability or territorial integrity. Few countries are completely immune from foreign threats which, if they materialized, could lead either to the loss of parts of state territory or extreme disruption of the functioning of its institutions. The capacity to counter such threats depends on the economic and military power of the state and on the skill and wisdom of its foreign policymakers who may either reduce the number of hostile countries or placate them by engaging in different kinds of cooperative behavior.

A country facing no foreign military threats is more secure than one facing such threats. But a country that can deal with such threats is more secure than a country that needs an alliance with a foreign power in order to be able to do so. A symmetric rather than an asymmetric type of alliance is preferable as the latter poses more threats to the independence of its weaker partner and might be resented by domestic opposition groups who find it an offense to national dignity. Failure by a country to deter a foreign threat casts doubts on the capacity of its regime to defend its state security as was the case in both Kuwait and Saudi Arabia in 1990 and Iraq in 1991. In terms of the capacity of the five countries to successfully manage external military threats, detailed data appear in table 3.17. They can be ranked as in table 3.18 .

TABLE 3.17
Successful Management of External Military Threats

YEAR	EGYPT	ALGERIA	IRAQ	LIBYA	SAUDI ARABIA
1989	1	1	1	1	1
1990	3	1	5	2	4
1991	3	1	5	2	4
1992	1	1	5	1	1
1993	1	1	5	1	1
1994	1	1	5	1	1
1995	1	1	5	1	1
1996	1				

1=no external military threat
2=successful management on its own
3=successful management in alliance with Third World countries
4=successful management with a foreign power
5=failure

TABLE 3.18

Countries Ranked According to Success in the
Management of External Military Threats

COUNTRY	RANK
Algeria	1
Libya	2
Egypt	3
Saudi Arabia	4
Iraq	5

Most legitimate=1; least legitimate=5.

Successful Management of External Economic Threats

The global nature of the world economy renders all countries vulnerable to negative economic implications of events taking place outside their borders. Rates of growth in Japan and Western Europe were seriously affected by the October war of 1973 in the Middle East, but these economies were capable of a fast adjustment to the crisis in the oil markets; they became less dependent on petroleum as a source of energy and were thus less vulnerable to similar threats in the future. Countries of the South are more vulnerable to economic threats, being more dependent on foreign trade than countries of the North. Foreign trade is crucial to their economies since many of them are still exporters of one or very few products, mostly raw materials and energy, whose prices have tended either to decline in recent years or to witness sharp fluctuations. Although state and societal security can be positively affected by these movements of international trade, it can also be hard hit by decisions of other countries or international economic actors, through deprivation of vital goods or services that seriously disrupt the functioning of an economy or standards of living.

Two of the countries under study were subject to such situations in recent years. Iraq was punished for its short-lived annexation of Kuwait in July 1990 through the UN Security Council Resolution which imposed serious economic sanctions, cutting Iraq completely off from international trade until the winter of 1997. The dispute between Libya and the United States, the United Kingdom, and France over the explosions aboard an American and a French airliner led to the imposition by the UN of sanctions, which severed Libyan international maritime and air links with other countries. These measures have seriously affected the economy, welfare, and health of the populations of the two countries, taking Iraq back to the pre-industrial age, according to a UN report.

A detailed table on the evolution of successful management of external economic threats is included in table 3.19. Based on this table, the five countries are ranked as in table 3.20.

TABLE 3.19
Successful Management of External Economic Threats

YEAR	EGYPT	ALGERIA	IRAQ	LIBYA	SAUDI ARABIA
1989	2	2	3	1	1
1990	2	2	3	1	2
1991	3[a]	2	5	1	2
1992	1	2	5	4	1
1993	1	2	5	4	1
1994	1	2	5	4	1
1995	1	2	5	4	1
1996	3				

[a]Although the West forgave Egypt a large part of its debt in 1991, the aid was approved only in May. A large number of Egyptian migrant workers came back empty-handed from Kuwait and Iraq and Egyptian exporters lost out temporarily as a result of troubles in these countries.

TABLE 3.20
Countries Ranked According to Successful Management of External Economic Threats

COUNTRY	RANK
Saudi Arabia	1
Egypt	2
Algeria	3
Libya	4
Iraq	5

1= most successful; 5=least successful.

Lower Military-to-Welfare Expenditure by the Government

It is evident that a government not facing a serious threat to state or regime security will not have to devote a large proportion of its public expenditure to security. Security expenditure includes spending on police and the army, together with their affiliated services, particularly the various types of intelligence activities. There may also be other causes of increased expenditure on some branches of the military apparatus, for example the capacity to intervene in armed conflicts abroad or to provide employment and income to certain regions of a country.

TABLE 3.21
Military Expenditure as % of Gross Domestic Product and of Total Spending on Education and Health[a]

COUNTRY	MILITARY EXPENDITURE AS % OF GDP			MILITARY EXPENDITURE AS % TOTAL SPENDING EDUCATION/HEALTH 1990[b]
	1990	*1992*	*1995*	
Egypt	4.6	6.0	8.5	57
Algeria	1.5	2.7	1.7	18
Iraq	20.0	21.1	25.9	511
Libya	8.6	6.3	6.2	56
Saudi Arabia	17.7	11.8	19.6	177

[a]United Nations Development Program, Human Development Report (New York and Oxford: Oxford University Press, 1990-1996). See 1993,1995,1996, tables 21 and 14 respectively.
[b]Figures were not available for 1992 and 1995.

Table 3.21 suggests two tendencies that coexist: countries that spend too much on their military and countries that spend very little. Iraq and Saudi Arabia belong to the first group and Algeria is the perfect example of the second. Egypt and Libya occupy middle positions. This ranking has no obvious link to the internal security situation in these countries. High military expenditure in Iraq and Saudi Arabia preceded the second Gulf War and is due most probably to a heightened sense of external military threat to security. Internal troubles in Egypt, Algeria and, to a certain extent, in Libya did not entail increased spending on their armed forces. Available data do not distinguish between internal security forces and the regular army. Confrontation with Islamist groups in Egypt and Algeria does not seem to require intervention of the regular army and is left to special branches of the security forces. Unfortunately, it was not possible to obtain data on welfare expenditure in three of the five countries for the period following the second Gulf War. The year 1990 was a year of high tension all over the Arab world. This was particularly true of the second half of that year due to the outbreak of the second Gulf War which led to military confrontations in January and February 1991 between the international alliance forces led by the United States, and the Iraqi forces which were occupying Kuwait. Three of the countries in the sample—Iraq, Saudi Arabia, and Egypt—

were involved in this confrontation. Thus 1990 was an exceptional year in terms of military expenditure. However, the level of military expenditure relative to expenditure on welfare continued to rise in the three countries in the following years. In terms of data in table 3.21, the five countries can be ranked as in table 3.22.

TABLE 3.22
Countries Ranked According to Levels of Military Expenditure

COUNTRY	RANK
Algeria	1
Libya	2
Egypt	3
Saudi Arabia	4
Iraq	5

Crime Rate

Security implies safety of citizens; a culture of peace is prevalent, with no resort to violence and confidence in security forces. Interpol provides figures on crime rates, not related to political violence, in different countries. Using the 1990s data in these annual yearbooks, it is possible to rank the countries under study as in table 3.23.[12]

TABLE 3.23
Countries Ranked According to Crime Rate

COUNTRY	RANK
Saudi Arabia	1
Iraq	2
Algeria	3
Libya	4
Egypt	5

Unfortunately, not all the relevant Interpol yearbooks were available, and data for all countries for the same years could not be found. In the case of Iraq, data were not available for the post-Gulf War period. Comparison of the five countries is therefore based on figures for 1991, with the exception of Iraq, for which the 1990 data are used, although this might not be the best year for comparison. It is meaningless to consider such limited data as representative of the societal security in the five countries in the 1990s; the impact of the second Gulf War in Iraq, the civil war in Algeria, and the UN Security Council sanctions against Iraq and Libya would only be apparent in later years in statistics that were not available.

TABLE 3.24

Levels of Crime in Selected Arab Countries, 1990-1991[a]

INDICATOR	SAUDI ARABIA	LIBYA	EGYPT	ALGERIA	IRAQ
Military threats	12	6	9	3	15
Economic threats	2	8	4	6	10
Welfare expenditure	4	2	3	1	5
Crime rate 1990-91	3	12	15	9	6
Total	21	28	31	19	36

[a]International Criminal Police Organization (Interpol), Statistiques criminelles internationales. International Crime Statistics (Saint-Cloud, France: Secretariat générale de l'O.I.P.C, 1991-1992).

The ranking of the five countries according to crime rate, the most relevant indicator for measuring societal security, is considerably different from the ranking according to other indicators. Saudi Arabia comes first, not unexpectedly, as societal security is related as much to economic conditions as to local culture. Iraq, however, jumps to second place. If the figures are correct, this probably reflects fear on the part of citizens and foreign workers alike of the severe penalties and the strength of security agencies in the suppression of crimes. The situation has deteriorated in the wake of the second Gulf War, a deterioration reflected in stiffer penalties for ordinary crimes. Table 3.24 suggests a qualitative difference between Saudi Arabia and Iraq and the other three countries; the average level of offenses increases by more than 200 percent between Iraq and the third ranked, Algeria. Algeria and Libya occupy a middle position. But the limited data available for these two countries for 1992 point to a big increase in the number of all crimes, with thefts mounting by one-fourth in Libya and more than doubling in Algeria. Murders increased by one-third in Libya and by 42 percent in Algeria.[13] Figures provided by the Egyptian Ministry of Interior do not show a rise in the level of crime for the same period.

State-Societal Security: Concluding Remarks

Assessing the relative importance of the four indicators of state and societal security, two would seem particularly crucial, namely, successful management of external military threat and lower crime rates. If the state fails in effectively resisting foreign military threats to its independence or territorial integrity, or in ensuring a safe life for its citizens, there can be neither state security nor societal security. External economic threats may be connected with the international economy, over which no country has complete control, or with perceived unfairness in decisions of international organizations. They may impair state and societal security when they affect the capacity of the state to ensure supplies for the maintenance of its armed forces or satisfaction of the basic needs of its population. A lower ratio of welfare expenditure compared to expenditure on the military and security forces does not always mean that welfare levels of citizens are going to deteriorate: citizens may seek to attain reasonable standards of health and education through private institutions if their levels of income so permit. Thus, in a combined score of state-societal security, successful management of external military threat and lower crime rates are more important. However, as data on crime cover only 1990, the combined indicator should be understood to refer only to that year. The score of the five countries is shown in Table 3.25.

TABLE 3.25
Scores of State-Societal Security in Selected Arab Countries, 1989-1995

INDICATOR	SAUDI ARABIA	LIBYA	EGYPT	ALGERIA	IRAQ
Military threats	12	6	9	3	15
Economic threats	2	8	4	6	10
Welfare expenditure	4	2	3	1	5
Crime rate 1990-91	3	12	15	9	6
Total	21	28	31	19	36
Av. score	2.62	3.50	3.87	2.37	4.50
Total excluding societal security	18	16	16	10	30
Av. excluding societal security	3	2.66	2.66	1.66	5

Table 3.25 shows quite clearly that security is lacking in varying degrees in all five countries. The best scores, whether societal security is included or not, are close to the median point, suggesting a medium level of security. Three countries facing different security threats—Egypt, Algeria, and Libya—gravitate towards the middle point. Libya is suffering the impact of sanctions imposed by the UN Security Council; Algeria is facing a serious armed opposition movement; and Egypt was involved in 1990-91 in an international conflict far from its borders. However, if the second Gulf War is excluded, Egypt's score improves, making it the country facing the fewest threats to its state security.[14]

It is apparent from table 3.25 that state security does not always coincide with societal security. The Algerian state did not have to face either external military or economic threats, but societal security was nearly undermined by a high rate of criminality. Saudi Arabia emerged as the country with the highest levels of state and societal security, but this was obtained with a high ratio of military expenditure compared to expenditure on welfare. As is to be expected, Iraq did badly on all indicators, while Egypt occupied a middle level with regard to crime rate and did well on the management of external military and economic threats. It should be noted that despite a relatively high crime rate in Algeria and Iraq, levels of crime in all these countries were far lower than was reported by Interpol for some of the highly developed countries, including the United States.

Table 3.25 casts strong doubts on the wisdom of including all security indicators in one score. Algeria faces a civil war situation, but survival of the state is not at stake. Libya is also suffering from international sanctions which, while influencing societal security, do not seem to be preventing the regime from perpetuating its hold over the people; nor does the Libyan state seem to be on the verge of collapse. Saudi Arabia, on the other hand, is experiencing major threats to its state security, but there are no indications that societal security is in any danger.

COMBINING LEGITIMACY AND STATE-SOCIETAL SECURITY

In an attempt to examine how state and societal security are related to indicators of legitimacy, the indicators of state and societal security are separated. The score of successful management of external military threats is taken as a proxy indicator of state security, and the rank on the criminality indicator is taken as a proxy indicator of societal security. The five countries appear as shown in table 3.26.

TABLE 3.26

Ranks for State Security, Societal Security, and Legitimacy

COUNTRY	RANK: STATE-SOCIETAL SECURITY	RANK: LEGITIMACY
Saudi Arabia	1	1
Egypt	2	2
Libya	3	3
Algeria	4	4
Iraq	5	5

For statistical correlation analysis to be valid, there should be a larger number of cases, and the study period should be longer. Given data limitations, this exercise should be considered an exploratory one, to test the relevance of this particular way of thinking about security problems in countries of the South. Table 3.26 is useful, however, as some countries occupy the same position on the three indicators. Iraq occupies the lowest rank in terms of legitimacy, state security, and societal security, whereas Egypt and Libya occupy middle positions on those indicators, suggesting moderate levels of security and legitimacy, although Egypt scores a little lower. On the other hand, Saudi Arabia and Algeria offer contrasting examples, with the former short on state security but low on both legitimacy and societal security, whereas Algeria is high on state security but low on both legitimacy and societal security.

In the countries under study, despite the increasing prominence of economic and environmental threats to national security at the end of the twentieth century, external military threats are the most serious. They do not seem to be directly related either to societal security or to the legitimacy of the regime. According to the data, the legitimacy of the Saudi regime is not very much in doubt, nor is the societal security of the Saudi population, even though it perceives external threats to its security. Neither the territorial integrity of the Algerian state nor its survival are in doubt, although daily clashes with militants of Islamist groups and a high level of criminality seem to threaten it security. Could such "disarticulation" of dimensions of security last long? The history of other countries suggests that, sooner or later, a society that lacks security finds ways to topple a regime incapable of offering it this security, or that a regime incapable of providing defense against external military threats encourages dormant opposition to remove it, benefiting from the resentment created by the regime's reliance on foreigners for its own security.

If an attempt is made to combine summary indexes of legitimacy and security for the five countries, the ordering is as shown in table 3.27.

TABLE 3.27
Combined Ranks for State-Societal Security and Legitimacy

COUNTRY	RANK: STATE-SOCIETAL SECURITY	RANK: LEGITIMACY
Saudi Arabia	1	1
Egypt	2	2
Libya	3	3
Algeria	4	4
Iraq	5	5

Table 3.27 suggests that there is a strong relationship between legitimacy and total security. Countries that did less badly than others in terms of legitimacy, e.g., Saudi Arabia, ranked higher in terms of state and societal security, and vice versa, and the country that is lowest in legitimacy, i.e., Iraq, is also the lowest in terms of state security. The Algerian regime, which lacks legitimacy, does not seem to face any serious threat to the survival of the state itself.

TENTATIVE CONCLUSIONS

How to explain an apparently strong link between legitimacy and state-societal security? Shortage of legitimacy influences perception of threats to state and societal security. In Algeria and Egypt the major threat to security is perceived to be lying within their borders, embodied in the Islamist movement. This perception of the threat was shared by the government of Saudi Arabia from the early 1980s, and particularly since the second Gulf War and the resort by Saudi Arabia to American military support. Iraq and Libya, on the other hand, see their major threats presently coming from outside, due to sanctions imposed by the UN Security Council and incursions of Turkish troops into Iraqi territory.

A country with a shortage of legitimacy seems vulnerable to foreign intervention. Repressive policies of the Iraqi and Libyan regimes encouraged Western governments to impose sanctions on them in the hope that with a little external pressure the two regimes would crumble. However, it does not seem that shortage of legitimacy alone poses, in the short term, much threat to the survival of either the incumbent regime or the state. Repression of the opposition enables an authoritarian regime to withstand the dissatisfaction of the population. It can also buy off their loyalty through its welfare policies.

The case of Iraq, while showing the capacity of a regime to maintain itself despite failure to provide either state or societal security, also demonstrates the potential danger to the security of the regime when it ceases to be able to buy the loyalty of the population through its welfare policies. Risky foreign adventures might be a price that has to be paid in order to keep the unity of a shaky domestic front. Consequences of such adventures are not always what such regimes like: failure might be disastrous for both the regime and the state, opening the way for foreign intervention on the part of those who oppose the regime. Survival of the regime and the state, under these conditions, would be possible only at the cost of ever-increasing repression, which would further weaken the regime's legitimacy and increase its vulnerability either to coups d'état or popular revolutions, or both.

On the other hand, regimes which initially enjoy a considerable degree of legitimacy might squander their stock of legitimacy and possibly regime security when they seek to ensure their security through military alliances with foreign powers. Security of the Saudi regime was effectively challenged in 1995 and 1996 and opposition to its policies escalated following the stationing of large numbers of American troops on its territory in 1991. The huge explosions that wrecked American military installations twice in 1995 and 1996 were carried out most probably by militant Islamist Saudis who hated to see their country relying on a foreign power to maintain its territorial integrity. Participation of Egyptian troops in a military alliance led by a foreign power contributed also in the eyes of Egyptian opposition to a further shrinking of the legitimacy of the Egyptian regime.

Shortage of legitimacy also influences the performance of political regimes. It becomes difficult for them to mobilize resources for any purpose, particularly for national defense. The Iraqi regime, for instance, had to impose severe penalties on citizens who escaped the military service, since many young Iraqis did not show much enthusiasm to defend a regime that led their country to a series of disastrous adventures.

Shortage of legitimacy not only influences the effectiveness of incumbent regimes, but also impairs its efficiency. Regimes incur a heavier cost in terms of time, effort, and resources in order to implement their policies. It becomes difficult for them to coordinate their domestic and foreign policies. There are examples of disagreements on major policies in both Algeria and Egypt. Disagreements among Algerian leaders on how to deal with the Islamist movement led to frequent changes of government, some of which were not exactly peaceful, e.g., the cases of former presidents Ben Jadid and Bou Diaf. Disagreements among Egyptian officials on the same question enabled the radical Islamist groups to increase their strength and to expand their ranks in Upper Egypt in the late 1980s and early 1990s.

As the question of legitimacy is one of the most intricate and complex issues in political science, it is risky to believe that it can be accurately measured by any index or to foresee the consequences of its shortage for the survival of incumbent regimes or maintenance of the territorial integrity of their states. Who could have predicted the fall of socialist regimes in Eastern Europe and the disintegration of the Soviet Union and Czechoslovakia? When early signs of weakness of regimes that lack legitimacy but are apparently stable appear, their domestic opponents, who have avoided showing their resentment for fear of regime reprisals, are encouraged and mount resistance strong enough to topple these regimes. Signs of legitimacy shortage should be looked at over time. A mounting trend of such signs could point to the increased strains suffered by a regime attempting to maintain itself despite resentment of important sections of its population. Collapse of such regimes is likely if they do not introduce the necessary adjustments to an ever daring opposition. Otherwise, the cost of repression would continue to escalate.

Finally, it does not seem that precarious societal security, measured by the level of crime, poses much threat to the survival of incumbent regimes or states. Regimes with variable amounts of legitimacy can endure while their population experiences lack of personal safety. How can states endure when they fail to fulfill what Hobbes argued was their most elementary function, i.e., ensuring personal security of their citizens? The answer is simple: such states survive because they perform this function very well for the fortunate elite that rules them. As for the ordinary masses, they do not count for much, until they show signs that they might threaten the survival of such states and regimes.

NOTES

1. Walter Lippmann, quoted in *The Many Faces of National Security in the Arab World,* ed. Bahgat Korany, Paul Noble, and Rex Brynen (New York: St. Martin's Press, 1993), 2.
2. Walter Connor, "Ethno-nationalism," in *Understanding Political Development,* ed. Myron Weiner and Samuel Huntington (Boston: Little, Brown, 1987), 196-220.
3. For a similar discussion, see Barry Buzan, "People, States, and Fear: The National Security Dilemma in the Third World," in *National Security in the Third World: The Management of Internal and External Threats,* ed. Edward E. Azar and Chung-in Moon (Aldershot, U.K.: Edward Elgar, 1988), 14-43.
4. Raymond Aron, *Main Currents in Sociological Thought,* vol. 2 (Harmondsworth, U.K.: Penguin, 1982), 240.
5. Michael C. Hudson, *Arab Politics: The Search for Legitimacy* (New Haven: Yale University Press, 1977), 1-30; Sa'd al-Din Ibrahim, "Masadir al-shar'iyya fi al-anzima al-'arabiyya" (Sources of legitimacy in Arab political systems), in Sa'd al-Din Ibrahim et al., *Azmat al-dimuqratiyya fi al-watan al-'arabi* (Crisis of democracy in the Arab motherland) (Beirut: Markaz dirasat al-wahda al-'arabiyya, 1984), 403-30.
6. Husayn 'Abd al-Raziq, *Misr fi 18 wa-19 yanayir: dirasa siyasiyya watha'iqiyya* (Beirut: Dar al-kalim, 1979).
7. Bernard Gwertzman and Michael T. Kaufman, eds., *The Collapse of Communism* (New York: Times Books, 1990), 21-22, 313-14.
8. United Nations Development Program, *Human Development Report* (Oxford: Oxford University Press, 1990-96).
9. Munazzama al-'arabiyya li-huquq al-insan (Arab Organization for Human Rights), *Huquq al-insan fi al-watan al-'arabi* (Human rights in the Arab world) (Cairo, 1996), 129.
10. United Nations High Commissioner for Refugees. *Facts and Figures* (UNHCR, 1996).
11. Aaron Segal, comp. and ed., *An Atlas of International Migration* (London: Hans Zell, 1993), 44.
12. This ranking is based on data contained in International Criminal Police Organization (Interpol), *Statistiques criminelles internationales. International Crime Statistics* (Saint-Cloud, France: Secretariat générale de l'O.I.P.C, 1950/52-).
13. Ibid., 1992, 4.
14. The second Gulf War of 1990-91 lowered Egypt's score on state-societal indicators because it was a highly divisive issue in Egypt. Some opposition parties and sections of public opinion did not accept that Egypt would fight another Arab country under a foreign flag.

CHAPTER FOUR

Political Challenges to Middle East Governments in the Twenty-First Century

FARHAD KAZEMI AND AUGUSTUS RICHARD NORTON

*I*n the 1980s and 1990s there has been much debate on the possibility of applying democracy in the Middle East, and especially in the Arab world. This has been an interesting debate, although sometimes more revealing of observers' biases than of the shape of contemporary politics in the region. Of course, it is important to understand the impediments to democracy, but in this chapter we argue that the focus on the question of democracy is a diversion from the really interesting question, viz., how—short of democracy—will the existing regimes address burgeoning demands for accountable, efficacious, honest, and fair government? Across the region, from Morocco to the Gulf, governments claim to be trying to meet calls for change. To date, these efforts have enjoyed only limited success, often because rulers have been prone to announce rather than implement political reforms. The demands for reform will grow more urgent in the years ahead. Although none of the region's governments is in imminent danger of revolution, each faces rising pressure for change as the region's fast-growing population bursts the seams of the major cities while government revenues fail to keep pace with growing needs.

When the rhetoric of democracy is adopted by those who rule, as well as those who seek to rule, there is room for considerable doubt about intentions and goals.[1] Meanwhile, in the popular discourse, democracy in its Western manifestation is frequently perceived to embody corruption, injustice, and hostility to Muslims. In contrast, the quest for fair treatment at the hand of government gives rise to a less equivocal discourse. The arbitrary abuse of power by the government—whether by interfering in successful informal associations, capriciously imposing taxes, fees, or service charges, or harshly quelling dissent—is a common source of complaint. Among Middle East intellectuals, one can find a lively debate challenging the universality of human rights as understood expansively in the West, but there is little disagreement that egregious violations of the dignity of the individual through torture and arbitrary imprisonment are as unjustifiable as they are widespread in the region. Thus, while democracy is broadly touted as the solution to the region's ills by some Western policymakers and a small but articulate minority of activists within the Middle East, the more relevant critique engages more basic issues of reform.[2]

The objective challenges facing many governments in the Middle East are formidable. Although generalizations must be applied carefully, rich and poor states share problems. If the richest governments in the region are less threatened by economic disaster, they are, like the poorer governments, viewed with suspicion and disapproval by large segments of the population. Governmental inefficiency, ineptitude, and corruption are omnipresent complaints across the boundaries of rich and poor states. The physical abuses inflicted upon citizens by their governments are widely known, even if people are often reluctant to speak publicly about them. High population growth rates are common in the region, and in less wealthy states—notably Algeria, Egypt, Jordan, Morocco, and Syria—the provision of public services is often stretched to the point of disappearance. Meanwhile increasing demands for jobs in economic systems with already saturated labor pools create the potential for wide-scale unrest and oppositional mobilization in the near future.

The sheer immensity of these socio-economic factors will not in itself cause political change. Only when the absence of housing, the paucity of jobs, and the general inadequacy of public services is perceived as a failure of politics do these factors acquire political meaning. In this sense, economic inequity, unemployment, poor housing, and public services have become politicized. The success of the Islamist opposition movements in mobilizing political support largely stems from their constructive response to these complaints.

We anticipate that the twenty-first century in the Middle East will be characterized by broadening patterns of politicization and, therefore, increasing opportunities for oppositional movements to gather followings. As a result, governments will continue to seek economic and political reforms that target material need, but also divert political energies into regime support. In order to appreciate the context for these efforts, it is germane to begin with a consideration of the political economy of the regimes.

THE POLITICAL ECONOMY OF THE STATE

The Middle Eastern state extends well beyond the seraglios of the rulers. Outside of agriculture, the state is the leading employer. Thus, many citizens have a stake in the state, and their interests lie not in destroying it but in improving its performance. Government dominates the formal economy, in some instances through a phalanx of public sector companies, in others through the flow of oil and other rents directly into the state coffers. As a result, government expenditures in the Middle East often make up a larger share of the GNP than in countries outside of the region of comparable income level. In some cases, the government spending amounts to nearly half of the GNP (e.g., Egypt), compared to less than 25 percent in middle-income countries generally.[3]

While the state's grip on the economy is important, considerable economic activity and resources lie outside of its control. A significant amount of largely undocumented economic activity occurs in the realm of the informal sector, which encompasses an array of craftspeople, doctors, lawyers, petty traders in licit and illicit goods, atelier operators, piece-workers, criminals, and many others whose income is undocumented by the state. In post-revolutionary Iran, the informal economy has mushroomed dramatically and is pointedly visible in the urban areas in a variety of crucial money-lending institutions.[4] In Egypt, the informal economy is commonly estimated to be comparable in size to the formal economy.[5] In effect, the steady growth of the informal sector has been a natural by-product of failures in the formal sector. The informal economy is an important site for undermining and quietly contesting the state's authority.

Yet, the state is resistant to change. A serious impediment to reform in the Middle East has been the place and role of rentier states in the system. The emergence of the rentier state in the Middle East has had a detrimental effect on both economic development and political liberalization. Its economic impact can be seen in the state's dependency on rents, extracted primarily from oil, as its essential source of revenue. This has in turn discouraged the emergence of an independent bourgeoisie that can engage the state in economic give and take or contest the state in delineation of rights, responsibilities, and obligations. The state has in effect attempted to satisfy the population at large through provision of a host of services and economic activities paid through income received from rents. As long as rents from the outside world are available, the state will respond only to those concerns of the population that it finds necessary for maintaining its power and position. Moreover, the rentier state's often extensive economic programs tend to engage the bourgeoisie fully and reward it economically in projects conceived and funded by the state. Hence the bourgeoisie's fortunes come to center on the state and its defined economic goals.

The rentier state tends to become increasingly autonomous. The state can use the income from rent to enlist compliance and to pursue goals not necessarily in the best interests of society. Since most of the state's revenues are not extracted from the population, the corollary sense of obligation and responsiveness to the society does not necessarily develop. Rentier states find themselves increasingly reluctant to liberalize their political systems. As Giacomo Luciani indicates, the oil rent becomes "a factor perpetuating authoritarian government."[6] This stands in sharp contrast to what Luciani calls "production states" where income is based primarily "through taxation of domestic economic activity."[7] In Luciani's view, taxation and the widening of the state's fiscal base are essential inducements for democratization. He further posits that a state facing fiscal crisis and forced to resort to increased taxation will generate demands from within the society for accountability and democratic institutions. Recent programs of political reform in Jordan and Morocco bear out Luciani's argument, in that each state sought through political reform to salve the pains of extensive economic belt-tightening and tax increases.

But taxation alone will not create the sense of obligation, responsibility, and accountability among the rentier regimes. Aside from the differential impact of taxation by type—direct versus indirect—in prompting political demands, any of a number of intermediary variables may affect demands for accountability.[8] The fiscal crisis of the state may serve as one intermediary variable. The leadership role of top political operators may serve as another. In addition, where direct taxes are imposed, tax collection has often proven incredibly inefficient. Rather than prompting demands for participation, direct taxation often has the effect of promoting shifts to the informal economy, where income is characteristically undocumented and untaxed. Thus, it is difficult to see any direct relationship between rentierism and accountability when the essential features of rentierism remain intact. Political liberalization and reform is not the natural tendency of rentier states. Only when the rentier states are forced to rethink the fundamental form of the state's relationship with society does reform appear as an option.

The link between fiscal crisis, reduction of rentier dependency, and political liberalization receives some support in the case of Jordan. From the earliest days of its inception, the Jordanian state was dependent on foreign subsidy (external rent) for its income and revenue. The extent, form, and continuity of this subsidy made rentierism the prime feature of the Jordanian state. Rentierism peaked in 1981 with important increases in "the two primary features of Jordan's rentier economy—workers' remittances and petro-dollar foreign aid."[9] Both of these sources of revenues declined as the price of oil dropped and many of the expatriate workers from the Gulf returned unemployed, seeking jobs at home. The resultant budgetary deficits were not rectified with increased taxation but through domestic borrowing.

As the economic crisis continued unabated, austerity measures were introduced which elicited widespread protest and public outcry against corruption and inequalities. As Rex Brynen explains, "these calls for economic reform were soon taken up in anonymous pamphlets, in appeals by East Bank community leaders in Karak, Salt, and elsewhere, and by the Amman-based (predominantly Palestinian) professional organizations, who added to them calls for greater political freedom and participation."[10] The Jordanian government began a process of incremental political liberalization in 1989, although there is no mistaking the state's capacity to suspend or even roll back its concessions. Jordan's transition from rentierism, fostered by an incipient fiscal crisis, ushered in a form of political liberalization that has allowed for a relatively free press, contested parliamentary elections, and reduced restrictions on freedom of association. The role of individuals at the helm of power is a key factor in the decision to liberalize or repress. The decisive role of Jordan's King Hussein in promotion of political liberalization and inclusionary politics was quite significant since many states facing a similar situation have resorted to repression instead.

It is quite possible that some of the rentier Gulf states, given the degree of citizen complicity with the state, may also choose a path similar to that of Jordan. In F. Gregory Gause's words,

> as the role of the state in these countries has grown, it has begun to call forth new demands for representative institutions and responsible government from society. These demands spring from the very processes of state growth and expansion occasioned by the oil boom. The recent upsurge in political activity in the Gulf monarchies is not only consistent with the realities of the rentier state and its relationship to society, but is in fact generated by those realities.[11]

Ghassan Salamé argues that in small Arab states such as Kuwait and Lebanon, a different combination of factors, which include a hostile regional environment, absence of regional ambition, and the "fragility of the state entity," may help nation-building and sustain incipient impulses for political liberalization.[12] Although this seems accurate for Kuwait and Lebanon, where parliamentary life is reasonably vibrant and the rulers' powers are sometimes held in check. In contrast, in most Gulf monarchies the impulses for political liberalization are weak. In the other Gulf rentier states, other than Kuwait, citizen expectations of the government in the Gulf states are not predicated on the principle of "taxation therefore representation" but rather on the continued operation of efficient rentierism. As Gause says, "much as taxpayers want responsible governments to spend their money, the beneficiaries of rentier states want responsible governments to sign their checks."[13]

Where credible opposition forces do exist, some scholars have suggested the promulgation of pacts between government and opposition that would specify the terms of reference for the opposition in return for political concessions by the state.[14] In principle, the pact permits the rulers to maintain control while ceding some political authority to their opponents. In Algeria, arguably, the negotiation of a pact between the government and the opposition, viz., the Islamic Salvation Front (FIS), would have mitigated some of the factors that were used to justify the army's seizure of power in January 1992. In practice, however, pacts have been only a limited success. In Jordan, King Hussein oversaw the drafting of the National Pact of 1991, which opened the way for the legalization of political parties, widened space for civil society, increased freedom of the press, and formally ended martial law.[15] In Tunisia, Ben Ali, realizing that the (Islamist) al-Nahda enjoyed a base of popular support, shelved the pact negotiated in 1988.[16] The Emir of Kuwait, seeking sanctuary in Saudi Arabia during Iraqi occupation of his country, did agree to the renewal of the Kuwaiti parliament and free elections, but (unsuccessfully) attempted to welsh on his promises once he was restored to his throne in 1992. Yemen's experiment with pact-making was overwhelmed by the civil war that erupted in 1994. In Lebanon, where the Ta'if accord of 1989 spelled out the terms for an end to the civil war that wracked Lebanon from 1975, the pact has often been observed in the breach especially with respect to the provisions requiring Syrian cooperation.

The case of Syria gives another twist to the argument that economic crisis followed by a relatively steady economic liberalization leads necessarily to political reform. As is the case in some other authoritarian states, Syria has controlled the bargaining process in its economic liberalization program by confining it "to within a narrowly delimited arena that typically includes only a small set of privileged institutional or individual participants."[17] Although there is an important political dimension to Syria's economic restructuring, the concern has been "to insulate the regime from the political consequences of its economic mismanagement, to prevent the economic crisis from provoking genuine democratization."[18] The partially liberalized economy has kept the affected part of the private sector dependent on the state. Consequently demands for a "democratic pact" and a mutual sense of dependency have not so far emerged on the Syrian political scene.

In a related vein, the examples of Iran and Turkey also shed some light on this issue. In Iran, rentierism came to define the state in the 1970s. Its systematic growth was conclusively evident after the oil boom following the 1973 Arab-Israeli war. Supremely confident of its economic and political positions in domestic, regional, and international arenas, the state's economic policies resulted in two simultaneous developments. The state created a heavily dependent commercial and industrial modern bourgeoisie that benefited enormously from the state's policies but remained subservient to it. The private sector's influence "was limited to implementation. Being totally dependent on the state, Iran's rentier bourgeoisie had neither the incentive nor the means to capture the state."[19]

Growth of rentierism also made the state essentially oblivious to the concerns and priorities of civil society. The pre-revolutionary Iranian state decided what was good for society and acted accordingly. The gap between the two increased as none of the normal checks and balances emerged or were allowed to operate. When the state was eventually challenged during the revolutionary years, it was the traditional bourgeoisie from the bazaar, which had preserved some of its autonomy from the state, that took the lead and in reality bankrolled the revolution. Using the well-established bazaar-mosque alliance networks, the opposition legitimized its attack on the Pahlavi state utilizing powerful Islamic ideology. The sharp lines of cleavage were defined in cultural and moral terms, much more so than economic ones, in order to mobilize support and attack the state where it was most obviously vulnerable.[20] The bazaar provided the funds, and the clerics the organizational structure and networks of mobilization. Their expression of opposition surfaced under a strong Shi'i Islamic code with deep resonance in the society at large. This was once again an example of pragmatic use of Islam to gain advantages in the political arena. The Iranian rentier state, alienated from significant segments of civil society, and confronted with a major political challenge that was expressed in moral and cultural terms, proved incapable of sustaining itself. Political liberalization, granted under intense revolutionary pressures, came too late in the game to help preserve the state.

The Turkish case advances a sharply different model. Although certain features of rentierism, such as remittances from workers abroad, are also present in Turkey, the state's income is based primarily on domestic sources, not external rent. Hence rentierism has not dominated the Turkish economy. To increase revenues in the 1970s, the state had to increase taxation and domestic production. A number of policies, including import substitution industrialization, were adopted to increase domestic production and reduce external dependence. Although these attempts did not help Turkey's negative trade balance and foreign exchange crisis, they did prompt the state to engage in a serious give and take with the business community through chambers of commerce and industry.[21] The ensuing cleavages within the private sector led to the creation of several organizations devoted to management of commerce and industry. The National Salvation Party can be seen as an Islamist group that was established to protect the interests of the petite bourgeoisie against some of the more prominent organizations that were tied to the interests of larger industrial and commercial capitalists.[22] Economic issues defined much of the political agenda of this Islamist party as well as of the industrialists in their interactions with the Turkish state. Organized in a set of autonomous organizations, the private sector was a serious force in the society at large and in its relationship with the state. The private sector's concerns and demands could not be ignored by the state, as discussed by Hootan Shambayati:

In Turkey, the state adopted a corporatist structure to control and respond to the demands. In Turkey, however, corporatism was inclusionary. Associations were not merely instruments of government control; they also served as the channel through which civil society made claims upon the state. Furthermore, by the 1970s some sectors of society were financially and organizationally strong enough to make demands upon the state outside the corporatist structure. Since the Turkish state was financially dependent upon these groups, it could not afford to ignore their demands. In particular, the state had to be responsive to the demands of entrepreneurial classes. At the same time, since the state controlled scarce resources such as foreign exchange, the entrepreneurial classes had an incentive to institutionalize their ties with the state.[23]

The end result of the private sector's interactions with the state, through a set of autonomous and semi-autonomous economic and political organizations, was the growing pressures for political liberalization. In short, in the absence of fully developed rentierism, increasing domestic taxation and extraction, a foreign exchange crisis, and the willingness to engage opposition from within the society in an inclusionary way, combined to increase prospects for democracy in Turkey. This pattern stands in sharp contrast to the Iranian case in the pre-revolutionary decade where rentierism and exclusionary politics were the dominant norms.

THE POLITICS OF ELECTIONS

The bugbear for great power strategists is instability, and in the corridors of Western governments the introduction of freely-contested elections is often viewed as a recipe for chaos. So, in many corners of academe and government, not to mention among the incumbent Middle Eastern political class, the implications of democracy in the Middle East are viewed with alarm. The image of the present rulers in the region—in the face of full-fledged democracy—scurrying for safe havens or leaving on permanent vacations (as the Shah did in January 1979), powerfully dampens democratic advocacy, especially when hostile Islamist movements are perceived as the most likely beneficiary. This imagery benefits the ruling autocrats, of course, who tirelessly enliven such fears. The aborted Algerian parliamentary election of 1991, in which the FIS captured 48 percent of the popular vote and, potentially, three-quarters of the parliamentary seats, was a signal event. The Algerian debacle has become a constant presence in political discourse in the region. A closer examination of the electoral results yields a somewhat different picture. Only 25 percent of eligible voters actually cast their ballots for the FIS, and half of the eligible voters did not even cast a ballot. Moreover, the winner-take-all system magnified the FIS victory. Free and fair elections need not follow the Algerian model, and proportional schemes have tended to dissipate Islamist votes.

Unfortunately, not only are elections relatively unimportant as measures of political freedom in the Middle East, and other locales as well, but several elections in recent years have actually had corrosive effects upon political liberalization as well as on incipient processes of democratization. The cases of Algeria and Yemen are obvious examples. In Algeria, from 1989 until 1992, when a poorly designed electoral process was aborted by a coup d'état, an impressive array of autonomous associations emerged and one veteran analyst argues that the country was on the brink of real democracy.[24] In Yemen, one of the most traditional societies on the globe, the 1993 election destabilized a more or less successful power-sharing arrangement and curtailed a fascinating period of experimentation with liberalization. Elections that serve the cause of autocracy are problematic, but those elections that curtail projects of political reform are profoundly counter-productive.

Important exceptions to this general pattern can be seen not only in Israel but also in recent elections in Turkey and in the Palestinian entity where participation was remarkably high in the inaugural election of January 1996 (over 90 percent in Gaza). It is clear that in these cases, the electoral process has become a significant avenue for political expression and participation. There is no guarantee that these exceptions will ever become the norms for the rest of the region. Electoral reform, nonetheless, remains one of the most important arenas, in both real and symbolic terms, for the opening of the political system and the promotion of institutionalized inclusionary politics.

Elections and Political Reform

In principle, there is much to be said for elections as a means of defining a watershed or solidifying popular support, and the rhetoric of democracy gives pride of place to elections. Middle Eastern rulers frequently toot their own democratic horns, declaring their commitment to freedom and democracy. The cynical rhetoric of the rulers is abetted by external powers. Western governments and institutions persist in using elections as reference points, as bona fide testaments to democratization if not democracy. Few of these claims are taken very seriously by the masses, even less the political elites. With some exceptions, elections have served as a hollow ritual for acclaiming support. In fact, in Egypt, where nominally contested parliamentary elections have been a feature of political life since 1979, abstention from voting in the parliamentary elections is widespread, especially in the higher reaches of society. In 1990, for instance, participation rates in some districts of Cairo were well below 5 percent of eligible voters. Within the ideological constraints of the Islamic Republic of Iran, there is a considerable amount of competition for parliamentary *(majlis)* seats. In fact, turnover in parliamentary seats has been 50 percent. Nonetheless, voter apathy, if not hostility, was reflected in dramatic declines in participation from a high of 80 and 90 percent to only half of eligible voters in the 1996 parliamentary elections. Like voters elsewhere, Iranians are perfectly capable of withholding participation to demonstrate their disenchantment with politicians and their promises, especially in the miserable economic conditions that now afflict Iran.[25] In this vein, it is very pertinent to note that in the landmark May 1997 presidential election, won by the reformer Muhammad Khatami, electoral participation was over 89 percent.

Elaborate Western-organized election monitoring operations have been mounted in Morocco, Yemen, and Palestine to determine whether a stamp of clean balloting is justified. Not only were the 1993 elections in Yemen certified as clean, but Yemen was praised as the "most democratically developed and stable Arab state," a year before civil war erupted.[26] Truly free elections, where the results are literally unpredictable, remain a rarity. Admittedly, election monitoring has no doubt promoted cleaner, even fairer elections, but to what end?

Examining electoral laws across the region, there is a pattern of modest liberalization, and nominally competitive elections have occurred in Egypt (1979, 1984, 1987, 1990), Iran (1980, 1984, 1988, 1992, 1996), Kuwait (1992), Lebanon (1992 and 1996), Yemen (1993), Morocco (1993), and Jordan (1989, 1993 and 1997). Nonetheless, even if the norm of blatant manipulation has been softened somewhat, the rules are still skewed heavily in favor of the governments and to the disadvantage of the opposition.

In a few locales, elections have improved governmental accountability, if not performance, and balloting has sometimes allowed for the ventilation of public demands for better, more responsive government. Vocal and active oppositions won seats in Jordan in 1989 and 1993, Kuwait and Lebanon in 1992, and Palestine in 1996. Moreover, in each case, we find a state (or state-in-formation, in the case of Palestine) in which the accommodation of dissent is instrumental in decreasing the opportunity for neighboring states to exploit internal divisions.[27] These were instances in which portions of the electorate were able to air their demands, and even send rebukes to the ruling autocrats. These are not examples to be dismissed. Yet, in all of these cases, significant segments of the population were under-represented in the electoral process.

In general, elections continue to be carefully choreographed affairs in which the results never include upsets or surprises. In the Islamic Republic of Iran, the government has routinely used the appointed Guardians Council, and a host of extralegal methods, to prevent opposition candidates from standing for elections.[28] In the 1996 parliamentary elections, approximately 40 percent of the candidates were disqualified on discriminatory and arbitrary grounds based on their alleged lack of loyalty, lack of commitment to the system, and insufficient "practical adherence to Islam." Nonetheless, the present regime in Iran does offer more scope for participation than the ancien régime. The former Shah of Iran was reputed to use a relatively simple formula in the 1950s and 1960s: he allocated two-thirds of the votes to the designated pro-government party and one-third to the designated opposition.[29] Some rulers have not been so generous, as in Egypt in 1995 when the opposition victors won scarcely enough seats in the 458-seat parliament to fill a minivan. Ninety-five percent of the seats went to the ruling National Democratic Party, and only 13 seats were won between four of the opposition parties. Only one avowedly Islamist candidate—running as an independent—won a seat. The Labor Party, a ship of convenience for moderate Islamists, who are barred from creating a party of their own, did not win a single seat. This was in marked contrast to the 1984 and 1987 elections when over 50 Islamists won parliamentary seats. In December 1995, some of the government ballot box stuffers were so over-zealous that they completed more ballots than could fit in the boxes, and the extras were dumped as trash in alleys adjoining the polling stations.[30] To argue that these elections have a family resemblance to democracy is only to sugar-coat authoritarianism.

If democracy has not had many takers, the same may not be said of political liberalization. Since the early 1980s, there have been myriad attempts to loosen some of the controls on the press, concede space to associational activities, and marginally increase government accountability. Absence of genuine political liberalization in Bahrain prompted serious clashes between the government and the forces calling for the restoration of parliament from late 1994 into 1996. There are few, if any, card-carrying liberals in top positions in Middle Eastern governments and, as one close observer notes, liberalization has been activated as a crisis management technique.[31] Reforms have also been initiated as a response to popular pressure. Indeed, in one instance after another, there is firm evidence of the increasingly tenuous popular support for government. In Egypt, the bread riots of 1977 pointed to the precariousness of the government's grip on public order. Four years later, the sullen reaction of the Egyptian public to the assassination of Anwar Sadat, who in his last months as president threw thousands of suspected opponents into prison, was a chilling message to Husni Mubarak. In Jordan, during 1989, violent demonstrations erupted among some of the monarchy's supporters, following the painful implementation of structural adjustment. The year before, massive riots in Algeria signaled that without some amelioration of economic conditions, worse might be yet to come. Given the sequence of events in each case, it is obvious that the subsequent liberalization efforts were intended to deflate anger.

AUTHORITARIANISM AND POLITICAL LIBERALIZATION

If incipient democratization has been manifested in the Middle East, it is only as an unintended by-product of strategies of survival that have been implemented to keep authoritarian regimes in power. The prevalence of authoritarianism in the Middle East is often explained by reductionist arguments emphasizing the imprint of Islam or the formative role of social structure in shaping politics. In contrast, we argue that the weakness of democracy in the Middle East stems directly from the behavior of the regimes. Authoritarianism is the defining form of government in the region. The regimes' often arbitrary and monopolistic control of the states' resources has allowed authoritarianism to persist across the region.[32] While there are certainly important differences from one state to another, there are striking similarities in terms of the regimes' responses to dissent, and even to relatively innocuous forms of social organization. Thus, to understand politics in the region it is necessary to look at the fate of civil society to reveal how the regimes have acted to strictly regulate, co-opt, or suppress associational life.

Whether monarchies or republics, the regimes have been more or less consistently intolerant of independent forms of association. In Egypt, for instance, the Ministry of Social Affairs is charged with enforcing Law 32, which was promulgated in 1964. The law permits the government to refuse permission for an organization to be formed, to closely regulate funding, to dissolve an organization or merge it with another, and to appoint a temporary governing board.[33] One energetic professor, an Egyptian woman with good connections and access to the media, revealed that she spent one year registering an association for young business people.[34] Law 32 is not an isolated case, and in many states of the region such associational restrictions are routine. In Syria, the ruling Ba'th party does not tolerate independent groups. "As a general rule, no private organization can exist without an important, if not dominant, Ba'th presence. As a minimum, no group can hold elections for its governing board unless the Ba'th screens candidates or heavily influences their selection."[35] In Iran, political parties have not been allowed to function ever since the regime's decision in 1988 to close the Islamic Republican Party, an organization used primarily to establish the Islamic government. The regime's fear of organized political forces that are not fully sanctioned and controlled from the top is yet another testimony to the widespread attempts to dominate civil society.

Where successful formal associations do nonetheless emerge, the state often acts promptly to control, circumscribe, or co-opt them. For instance, the Women's Union in Jordan (WUJ) was created in 1974, and established an impressive collection of programs, including child-care centers, cultural activities, and a campaign to improve women's social, economic, and political status. With many Palestinian members, the WUJ often took political positions that antagonized the palace. Although its own periodical was shut down by the state, the WUJ exploited the media when it could. Finally, in 1981, the ministry of the interior ordered the union closed on grounds that it had violated the constitution by "taking positions antagonistic to the country." The state created a replacement organization, the General Confederation of Jordanian Women, but the WUJ fought the closure order, and won a High Court ruling to rescind the disbandment order. Given the power of the ministry of the interior, the favorable court order was unenforceable. The result is that Jordan has two women's unions, one with a state patron, one without.[36] In the climate of controlled liberalization that has emerged in recent years, the WUJ has continued to survive—a testimony to its membership's commitment—but the government has not relented in its efforts to stifle criticism, particularly of its peace treaty with Israel, and organizations like the WUJ sometimes must walk on eggshells to survive. Despite the monarchy's declared commitment to democracy, the government has not hesitated to rein in critical elements in civil society, including the professional associations.[37]

In some instances the state has tolerated, even encouraged, independent secular associations as a counter to Islamist opposition forces. This has sometimes been the strategy of Tunisia's President Zine Abdine Ben Ali, as illustrated in the following case discussed by Eva Bellin:

> The [Tunisian] regime originally refused to grant a visa [i.e., a permit] to the Union des Femmes Démocrates [UFD] in 1989, in large part because the union was perceived as too independent and too daunting a competitor for its own state-sponsored women's organization, the UNFT [Union Nationale des Femmes Tunisiennes]. Ultimately, the regime granted the union a visa, not out of respect for free contestation but rather because it realized the UFD could mobilize a significant force of feminists behind the regime's campaign to battle the Islamists.[38]

Of course, the Tunisian government's tolerance for independent forms of association has been selective. In contrast to its handling of the UFD, the government so circumscribed the activities of the Human Rights League that the league's members decided, in 1992, to dissolve the organization rather than contend with state restrictions. Among other things, the league's defense of the rights of political prisoners, including Islamists, was an irritant to the regime. Under domestic and international pressure, the Human Rights League was tenuously reestablished in 1993.[39] Banning human rights organizations can be risky, especially for the poorer Middle Eastern states that are dependent to one degree or another on international financial institutions such as the World Bank. Rather than proscribe such organizations, the state may simply charter its own human rights organization. Sheila Carapico notes that in Yemen the central government prompted the creation of the Yemeni Organization for Human Rights, in 1992, to counter the creation of the Yemeni Organization for the Defense of Democratic Rights and Liberties, which enjoyed a broad, middle-class base. The government-sponsored organization held its founding meeting in the Sana'a Police Academy; the irony was unintended.[40]

Given the corporatist bias of many Middle East governments, it is not surprising that professional associations have often proved durable structures for the representation of interests vis-à-vis the state. Thus, lawyers, doctors, teachers, agronomists, engineers, pharmacists, and other professionals have found it possible to maintain some autonomy from state control. In Egypt and the Sudan, some of the professional associations *(niqabat)* have well-earned reputations for resisting government intimidation and standing firm on important matters of principle. In both countries, unfortunately, the state has moved aggressively to assert its control over the professional syndicates. In the Sudan, following the coup d'état of General Bashir, backed by the National Islamic Front, the new government moved quickly to rig associational elections and bring the leading *niqabat* under state discipline.

The case of Egypt is noteworthy. Particularly in the 1980s the Muslim Brotherhood (Ikhwan al-Muslimin) began to build a base of support in Egypt's most respected professional associations: the syndicates of doctors, lawyers, and engineers. Although the Ikhwan often did not constitute a majority of the membership, by mobilizing their supporters they were able to win syndicate elections and gain effective control of the *niqabat.* Even in the pharmacists' association, with a majority of Coptic Christian members, they captured a majority. Alarmed by the Islamist successes in the associations, President Husni Mubarak began to backpedal in his already limited support for political reform in Egypt. By 1993, despite the opposition of 17 out of 23 registered syndicates, the government imposed new electoral rules on the associations requiring a quorum of 50 percent for the first round of elections, and subsequent electoral rounds, and, most importantly, providing for "temporary" state governance of the associations. The result is that formal associational life in Egypt has regressed to the extent that the limited gains of the past two decades are now forfeit. The irony is that government policies have tended to favor populist Islamist forces, sometimes by design, but often as a side-effect of the suppression of potential or imagined opponents amongst the secular opposition.

The press has not been immune to intimidation by the state, as any reader of the press in Saudi Arabia, Syria, Tunisia, or Iraq can readily attest. Often censorship is tacit, and journalists and their editors learn to stay well shy of the red lines. In other instances, such as in Iran, the regime controls the press in particular and publications in general through the ministry of Islamic guidance.[41] Despite the omnipresence of authoritarian government in the Middle East, journalists have sometimes managed to maintain an impressive degree of freedom. While self-censorship is pervasive, the press in Egypt, Algeria, Kuwait, Lebanon, the Sudan, and in the nascent Palestinian state, to cite the notable examples, have resisted the state's control and highlighted some abuses of power by the powerful. The state has retaliated, citing the ruse of national security or the charge of libel to quell reporting of corruption and similar topics that go right to the heart of the (dis)honesty and (in)competence of the rulers. In Egypt in 1995, for instance, Fathi Srour, the speaker of the parliament, railroaded through Law 93 which imposes heavy fines and jail sentences on those who impugn public officials. The passage of Law 93 coincided with widespread accusations of misbehavior on the part of President Mubarak, his family, and especially his son 'Ala'. Against considerable odds, the journalists' syndicate succeeded in overturning Law 93, after a year's struggle. The defeat of Law 93 is an important reminder that authoritarianism is not blithely accepted in the Middle East, especially not by the professional classes.[42]

Of course, focusing on middle-class civil society only represents a portion of the picture. As Diane Singerman notes, the government has been much less successful in controlling the informal networks and associations that are pervasive in Egypt and the Middle East as a whole. Given the controls on state-regulated associations, it is often the informal level that is the most important site for quiet but effective resistance to the state.

> In the politics of everyday life among Egypt's popular sector, men and women are deeply involved in forging collective institutions that serve public and private needs. Through the vehicle of informal political institutions women and men both create public space and invade what is conventionally considered the public arena as they connect individuals and communities to state bureaucracies, public institutions, and formal political institutions. They organize informal networks that weave in and out of the bureaucracy, the offices of politicians, religious institutions, private charitable and voluntary institutions, workplaces, households, markets, schools, health clinics, the extended family, and the neighborhood in order to fulfill individual and collective needs. Informal activities, whether economic or political, are those that escape licensing, regulation and even enumeration by the state, and thus have an illegal or quasi-legal status.[43]

These networks are based on interpersonal relationships of trust and, as Jenny B. White argues, they function on the basis of reciprocity. Arguably, the success of the Islamist opposition forces lies with their ability to utilize such preexisting networks.[44]

Sustained political reform implies the toleration of secular forms of association in civil society as a counter-balance to Islamist oppositionists which, if unchecked, manifest the totalitarian tendency inherent in all social movements whether secular or religious in orientation. This does not mean that civil society equals democracy: the project of civil society is liberalization not democracy.

In their studies of democratization, i.e., the transition from authoritarian rule to democracy, Guillermo O'Donnell and Philippe Schmitter and their colleagues emphasize that with the political opening to change, there is almost invariably a surge in civil society.[45] For that matter, whenever repression lessens, whether by design or otherwise, "the first reaction is an outburst of autonomous organization in the civil society."[46] A number of such examples emerge in the studies conducted by the Civil Society in the Middle East program. The cases examined varied widely in terms of the political economy of the state, but whether in Algeria or Yemen, the lifting of state controls on free association was the occasion for civil society to grow rapidly if tenuously.[47]

The growth of civil society evinces new demands upon the state. Freed from the petty controls of the state, articulate voices clamor for change. Thus, measures that were intended to release pent up dissent develop their own momentum for further change. Closing this Pandora's box is always an option, but a messy one as Husni Mubarak has discovered in Egypt. This implies that the azimuth of reform is likely to include many detours.

When the Middle Eastern regimes have opened up political space, they have done so under internal and external pressure. Generally, it would be silly to presume that any Middle Eastern ruler has experimented with reforms in order to reduce his prerogatives, or dissipate his power. Using the rhetoric of freedom and democracy, the regimes announce reforms that are intended to reconsolidate power, to ensure regime survival, albeit with a broader base of social support. But liberalization is inherently unstable and typically leads to one or two polar results: democratization or a return to dictatorship.[48] As Adam Przeworski notes, "Liberalizations are either reversed, leading to grim periods euphemistically termed normalization, or continue to democratization."[49] The chances for liberalization efforts to fail, rather than to succeed, are generally greater. "Since liberalization is always intended as a process controlled from above, the emergence of autonomous movements constitutes the proof that liberalization is not, or at least is no longer, a viable project."[50]

ISLAMISTS AND POLITICAL REFORM

The attitude of the Islamists to incremental reform and to participation in the political process is obviously crucial. The major oppositional forces in the region are the Islamist movements, but these movements vary widely in their strategies. The Ikhwan al-Muslimin in Egypt, work at the grassroots to Islamicize society. Others, like the Committee for the Defense of Legitimate Rights, based in London, seek to delegitimize and topple the regime in Saudi Arabia. Whatever their tactics, the Islamist movements challenge the state's monopoly on symbolic production and, in that way, pose a basic challenge to the authority of the rulers.[51] Nonetheless, there are wide differences between the movements, especially in their assessment of the prospects for successful political reform. Some reject reform out of hand and, following the line of argument of the late Sayyid Qutb, cast the present regimes as *jahiliyya* (morally corrupt, anti-Islamic, i.e., secular), and so egregiously flawed as to be unredeemable. Other movements, for instance in

Egypt, Kuwait, Jordan, Lebanon, and Yemen, are attempting to work within the system by contesting elections.

The lack of enthusiasm for free elections in the Middle East is habitually rationalized by reference to the Islamist opposition forces. The unresolved attitude of the Islamists vis-à-vis free elections is a key issue for analysis. A number of leading Islamist thinkers and ideologues have emphasized their abhorrence for a political system that usurps God's sovereignty by assigning it to the people. Notwithstanding this position, there is suggestive evidence to show that the presumed alienation of the Islamists from democracy does not persist in practice.

This assertion, which will be explained below, does not diminish the anxiety and fear that the Islamists evoke in many circles in the region. Since the debacle in Algiers, the ardor of the Arab middle classes has cooled seriously on the question of democracy. For many people, the choice is not between autocracy and Islamic democracy, but between two variants of authoritarianism. Analytically, it is not difficult to show the manifest irrelevance of the cases of Iran and the Sudan— where militant Islamist regimes came to power through a revolution and a coup d'état, respectively—to instances of political reform and incremental change, but this cannot erase the fact that these cases impinge constantly on the minds of individuals.

Exclusion and the Islamists

Islamists in the Middle East offer a set of purportedly universalistic Islamic norms and use aspects of these norms to draw the demarcation line between themselves and others. Contemporary Islamist norms frequently emphasize differences and work to exclude individuals and groups who do not adhere to them. These attempts to exclude, particularly when they are given divine sanction, are detrimental to political reform and threaten social peace. The essential thrust of political reform is inclusion of the other, not exclusion.

Traditionally, the revivalist movements in Islam have generally concerned themselves with two broad themes of reform *(islah)* and renewal *(tajdid)*.[52] Their interest has been to reform the existing social order, since it has strayed from the Straight Path, in order to renew Islam in public life once again. Although the form of relationship between reform and renewal has varied from one group of Islamists to another, all groups have dealt with this problem.

An inherent element in the concern with reform and renewal is the reintroduction of some form of traditionalism in the discourse of the Islamists.[53] Traditionalism requires adoption of certain basic Islamic views and practices borrowed from the past. These deal with key issues such as the definition of sovereignty and citizenship, gender relationships in public and private space, and place and role of religious minorities. Although the precise differences among the Islamists on these issues are not always clear, there remain important variations among them on the direct relevance and applicability of these views to the political system. Since the impact of the differential impact of these views is potentially profound, it behooves us to emphasize points of convergence and divergence.

All Islamist groups maintain that sovereignty belongs to God. It is heretical to hold a contrary opinion. The Rousseauian idea of social contract with its explicit acceptance of people's sovereignty has no place among the Islamists. It is, however, possible to move beyond the debate on God's sovereignty and allow for the human agency to have extensive, if not complete, control over the organization of political life, including the legislative domain.[54] Islamic history is a rich depository of precisely this practical form of freedom to legislate in a vast array of fields for the interest of the polity.

It is also possible to conceive of the time-honored concept of *bay'a* (allegiance to the ruler) as a way to legitimize on theological grounds a form of contract between the ruler and the ruled. In its essential meaning this is clearly not a social contract. In its implementation, however, it can codify and underscore the existence of certain rights and responsibilities for both the rulers and the polity. It can also give rise to a sense of entitlement that is critical for holding regimes responsible and accountable to the citizenry.[55] It is perhaps not too far-fetched to think that the more modern notion of pacts between regimes and their adversaries is not unrelated to this practice. Pacts are predicated on agreements, rights, obligations, and entitlement. As Charles Tilly has shown, rights of citizenship have historically developed in Europe as part of bargains in the course of long struggles with the invasive state.[56] Rights do not emerge on the scene overnight. They have to be acquired and then preserved against all odds.

Durability of basic rights is largely dependent on its collective enforcement by the state and its citizens. Hence, definition of citizenship becomes highly poignant—a murky and problematic area for many of the Islamists. Again as Tilly says, "citizenship rights belong in principle (if not always in practice) to everyone who qualifies as a full-fledged member of a given state; membership in the category suffices to qualify a person for enforceable claims."[57]

The Islamist view of citizenship, and who is entitled to it, has different gradations and important differences. There are those Islamists (e.g., Jihad, Takfir wa-al-Hijra) whose view of citizenship is highly exclusionary. Even monotheistic religious minorities are basically denied such rights except as they are granted to them by virtue of the benevolence of the Islamists in power. This form of exclusion also extends to the Muslims—rulers and otherwise—who do not fully share the Islamists' view on the organization of the polity.

The introduction of the concept of *jahiliyya* (ignorance), by Sayyid Qutb and some of his followers, to modern Egypt is in essence a rejection of the existing society and its particular conception of rights and obligations. *Jahiliyya* has traditionally been used to refer to the conditions in Arabia before the rise of Islam. The Prophet eliminated *jahiliyya* through the force of monotheistic Islam. The term itself was used exclusively for this era until the Pakistani Islamist Abu al-A'la Mawdudi applied it in his writings to the modern period. In Qutb's further application, places such as modern Egypt are reincarnations of pre-Islamic Arabia in their ignorance of divine design and religious norms. As Qutb states emphatically, the *jahiliyya* society is Godless, subject to its own rules and regulations, and rejects the central place of divinity in human affairs.[58] It must, therefore, be fought by Muslim vanguards until it is overthrown. This is a decisive call to action on behalf of a rigid and exclusionary Islamic state.

Other Islamist groups have also made explicit denunciations of broadly defined non-Islamic groups. In his analysis of some of the Egyptian Islamists and their rejection of Western culture and ideas, Gilles Kepel refers to a broad set of rejected categories, the Four Horseman of the Apocalypse. They are the Jewry, the Crusade, Communism, and Secularism.[59] Those who adhere to these groups or their ideas are, then, denied citizenship rights in this particular form of an Islamic state. These Islamists do not make a distinction between Judaism and Zionism, collapsing them into one rejected category. The crusade refers essentially to the Egyptian Copts whom they denounce for their attributed links with Western culture. Clearly neither communism nor secularism can have any place in this rigid Islamist conception of the universe. After all, communists are godless and secularists reject the paramount role of religion in Muslim political life. They must all be eliminated.

This extreme rejectionist stand is in contrast to that of many other Islamists who not only have a more liberal conception of citizenship but also extend it to at least some religious minorities. The example of the Islamic Republic of Iran is of interest here. In conformity to the traditional Islamic treatment of monotheistic religious minorities, certain citizenship rights are granted to the Christians, Jews, and Zoroastrians. These include freedom to enact religious ceremonies, religious education, and personal status matters such as marriage, divorce, and inheritance. Although it can be argued correctly that there is an element of second-class citizenship that defines these rights, it is nevertheless clear that some formal and institutional rights have been granted to these religious minorities. The problem is, however, most severe when another religious minority, the Baha'is, is concerned. The refusal to recognize this significant group as a religious minority, and their arbitrary designation as a political group, has resulted in the regime's systematic persecution of them. In other words, citizenship rights have been denied to the Baha'is because of certain aspects of their doctrinal belief which the theocratic state finds fundamentally unacceptable.

The case of the Coptic Christians of Egypt is also illustrative. Copts and Muslims have lived side by side in Egypt for centuries. Coptic and Muslim traditions have shaped Egypt's culture, and while each community has sustained its unique rites and institutions, there is little to distinguish an individual Christian from a Muslim. Comprising less than 10 percent of the country's population, the Copts have admittedly been circumspect in their practice of religion. A leading Coptic personality, Makram Obeid, once said we are all Muslims culturally. This was repeated to us by Adil Hussein, a leading pro-Islamist politician, who noted: "In Egypt, all the people are Muslims. Some pray in churches, others in mosques."[60] In recent years however, the Coptic and Christian institutions in Egypt have come under steady attack by Islamist militants. More disturbing, arguably, is the fact that recent Egyptian governments have not generally encouraged Coptic representation in state offices. For instance, none of Egypt's 26 governors are Christian.

The right to religious freedom is a serious issue with implications that extend beyond the Islamists. Many Islamic countries do not fully appreciate the meaning of this fundamental right. This problem is evident in the 1990 Cairo Declaration on Human Rights in Islam, issued by the Organization of Islamic Conference which includes all Muslim countries. Endorsed by Saudi Arabia, Iran, and other Islamic countries, the declaration falls short of international human rights standards in not designating freedom of religion as "a fundamental and nonderogable right."[61] This failure is potentially detrimental to all non-Muslim citizens. However, as Ann Mayer points out, the failure to provide for religious freedom also has serious practical implications for Muslims, given the number of Muslim dissenters from officially-imposed constructs of Islam and members of local minority sects who have been mistreated, charged with apostasy from Islam, or subjected to pressures or threats to compel them to abjure nonconforming belief.[62]

The important point here, for our purposes, is to put the Islamist view on freedom of religion and religious minorities in proper contextual perspective. Clearly many militant Islamist groups have a negative perception of both religious minorities and secularists. This perception is, however, nurtured in a larger environment where even the moderate pro-Western regimes do not fully appreciate the fundamental right of religious freedom. This does not, of course, excuse either the Islamists or the moderate regimes. It only underlines a significant problem that needs to be addressed on a larger scale. It is unlikely that the problem would be resolved without some commitment to the principle of separation of religion and state. Without such a vision, ideas and solutions that are advanced will be piecemeal, incremental, and ultimately unsatisfactory.

Another problem area with special application to the Islamists is the issue of equality of women and gender rights. The difficulty here stems from two related sources. First, there is the essentially discriminatory nature of Islamic personal status laws, and the criminal code, when applied to women, and secondly the prevalence of certain patriarchal attitudes and views, learned through the socialization experience, on women and gender roles. The combination of these two factors places women in a highly disadvantageous position in the Islamist universe.

All Islamists emphasize the role of family and its critical importance as the backbone of a moral and ethical society. Women are praised as the carriers of virtue and as the key agents of socialization for children. Family values, and women's essential role in their propagation, are recognized and given special praise in the discourse of all Islamists. Nevertheless, and in spite of the recognition given to women, Islamic personal status laws discriminate against women in the areas of inheritance, divorce, and marriage rights. A woman's inheritance from her parents is half that of a male sibling. Despite certain restrictions, a man can divorce a spouse rather freely while a woman's right to do so is substantially more restricted. Men can engage in polygamy, women can not. In Twelver Shi'ism, marriage based on a temporary contract *(muta'a)* for a specified time is allowed.[63] Although women also partake of temporary marriage, restrictions on *muta'a* by women are more stringent. The Islamic criminal code emphasizes the importance of testimony by witnesses, but the testimony of a woman is valued as only half that of a man. Additionally, the testimony of women alone, irrespective of number and validity, is not sufficient to convict a murderer.

Since the establishment of the Islamic Republic of Iran, the collective and detrimental impact of a rigid Islamist view of women in the above areas has been made amply clear. In effect, there has been a codification and legalization of women's status as second-class citizens, even though the situation is now improving.[64] Similar restrictions are also evident in other Islamic countries, such as Saudi Arabia and Pakistan, where versions of the Islamic legal code are operative in matters of gender. Even the Cairo Declaration, which posits equality of woman and man in "human dignity," does not find the sexes equal in "rights."[65] Discriminatory treatment of women, then, is not a monopoly of the Islamists, even though they may be more readily prone to discuss and enact it.

Closely tied in with legal restrictions is the Islamist attempt to segregate women in public space. The moral imperative that dictates such a view may be hard to fathom but it is advanced by the Islamists as a justification for enforced separateness. Public space in this case includes public transportation, all levels of education, even parts of the workplace. The separateness is further reinforced through application of female veiling and the imposition of penalties for its non-observance. While voluntary veiling is also practiced for economic reasons, and at times as an act of protest, the relevant issue to the Islamists is state-imposed veiling.[66]

It is important to underline that Islamists in the Middle East are not a monolithic group. Those Islamists who obey the rules of the game, and abide by the pact with government, must be allowed to participate in the political system. The litmus test is the Islamists' political behavior in the public sphere, not what may be in their hearts. By the same token, those governments that agree to Islamist participation in the political process need to be prepared to clamp down on them firmly and quickly should their behavior violate the rules of the game. The ultimate hope is that the Islamists' participation in the political system will reinforce the evolution of centrist and moderate positions on key issues of governance. The example of Italy, as reported by Robert Putnam, where formal participation by radical politicians in the political process led to a measurable moderation of their views, holds out potential hope for the Middle East.[67]

CONCLUSION

A generation of scholars dealing with the Middle East have accepted Michael Hudson's characterization of Arab politics as a quest for legitimacy.[68] The burden of his argument is that regimes founded on personal or ideological legitimacy are precarious and insecure. There is no reason to doubt the insecurity of those who govern: their behavior is often consistent with insecurity. There is reason to question the notion of precariousness. In contrast to other areas of the developing world, the regimes in the Middle East have proven to be remarkably durable. This durability is, we have argued, largely a function of the political economies of the Arab regimes.

Although many of the Arab states are twentieth-century innovations, outside of border disputes in the Gulf there are few fundamental challenges to the physical definition of the state. Even in Lebanon, which suffered 15 years of horrendous warfare, initiatives to redraw the boundaries of the state enjoyed only narrow support. The state in the Middle East is a fact. Scholars have not established a very impressive track record for predicting revolution or social upheaval, but it does seem to be clear that none of the Arab states, including Algeria, is in the early throes of radical transformation. The apparatus of power, though under challenge, is sufficiently formidable to quell radical challenges.

While Islamist discourse emphasizes the co-identity of Muslims throughout the *umma,* it is a striking fact that Islamist oppositionists couch their demands and their programs in the context of the existing state. The tragic imbroglio in Algeria has reinforced this tendency and some Islamist thinkers have concluded that only an incremental strategy of seeking power will succeed in the face of a militant, entrenched state. Other Islamist thinkers question seeking power at all, and argue that the purpose of the Islamist movements is the spiritual renewal of Muslims, not the quest for political power.

We argue that the power of the state, its ability to postpone demands for economic justice, and its controlling role in the definition of both economy and politics, represents an opportunity to give shape to reform. Given the trends that we have discussed, standing still is not an option. The rulers face a choice between stagnation or worse, on the one hand, and creative, inclusive reform on the other. Liberal political reforms, as we have shown, are reversible and are only conditionally connected to democratization. While there are some risks, the merit of liberal reform is that the broadening of political rights necessarily attenuates the bipolarity that defines the impasse between the state and the Islamist opposition. Most importantly, liberal reform may begin a process of habituation in which those who are skeptical of democracy may grow accustomed to the politics of compromise with those who are contemptuous of democracy. Democracy defines a realm of bounded uncertainty and the negotiation of the boundaries of that realm is a continuous process. As Dankwart Rustow noted some years ago, the initiation of that process requires the adoption of a set of rules, not a collection of democratic true believers.[69] Navigating the shoals of reform in a climate of intense political fervor, when power is roughly contested in the streets, is extremely problematic. Timing matters a great deal, and those governments that reject creative, inclusive reform in favor of the status quo, if not political paralysis, may eventually face even tougher choices as the twenty-first century proceeds.

Notes

1. Aziz al-Azmeh, "Populism contra Democracy: Recent Democratist Discourse in the Arab World," in *Democracy without Democrats? The Renewal of Politics in the Muslim World,* ed. Ghassan Salamé (New York: I. B. Tauris, 1994), 112-29.
2. Kevin Dwyer, *Arab Voices: The Human Rights Debate in the Middle East* (Los Angeles: University of California Press, 1991); and Susan E. Waltz, *Human Rights and Reform: Changing the Face of North African Politics* (Los Angeles: University of California Press, 1995).
3. Mustapha Kamel Al-Sayyid, "Slow Thaw in the Arab World," *World Policy Journal* (autumn 1991): 716.
4. Said Saffari, "The Islamic Financial Sector in Iran: Locating the Informal-Organized Qarz al-Hasseneh Institution," paper presented at the conference on "State and Informal Economies," Harvard University, 22-23 February 1996.
5. See Diane Singerman, *Avenues of Participation: Family, Politics, and Networks in Urban Quarters of Cairo* (Princeton: Princeton University Press, 1995), especially 173-243.
6. Giacomo Luciani, "The Oil Rent, the Fiscal Crisis of the State, and Democratization," in Salamé, *Democracy without Democrats?*
7. Ibid., 131; Giacomo Luciani, "Allocation vs. Production States: A Theoretical Framework," in *The Rentier State,* ed. Hazem Beblawi and Giacomo Luciani (London: Croom Helm, 1987), 63-82.
8. John Waterbury, "Democracy without Democrats?: The Potential for Political Liberalization in the Middle East," in Salamé, *Democracy without Democrats?,* 30.
9. Rex Brynen, "Economic Crisis and Post-Rentier Jordan," *Canadian Journal of Political Science* 15 (March 1992): 84.
10. Ibid., 90.
11. F. Gregory Gause III, *Oil Monarchies: Domestic and Security Challenges in the Arab Gulf States* (New York: Council on Foreign Relations, 1994), 81.
12. Ghassan Salamé, "Small is Pluralistic: Democracy as an Instrument of Civil Peace," in Salamé, *Democracy without Democrats?,* 85-111.
13. Gause, *Oil Monarchies,* 81.
14. See the contributions by John Waterbury and Jean Leca in Salamé, *Democracy without Democrats?*
15. Laurie Brand, "'In the Beginning Was the State . . .': The Quest for Civil Society in Jordan," in *Civil Society in the Middle East,* vol. 1, ed. Augustus Richard Norton (New York: E. J. Brill, 1995), 149.
16. Lisa Anderson, "The Tunisian National Pact of 1988," *Government and Opposition* 26, no. 2 (spring 1991): 244-60.
17. Steven Heydemann, "Taxation without Representation: Authoritarianism and Economic Liberalization in Syria," in *Rules and Rights in the Middle East: Democracy, Law, and Society,* ed. Ellis Goldberg, Resat Kesaba, and Joel Migdal (Seattle: University of Washington Press, 1993), 78.
18. Heydemann, "Taxation without Representation," 82.
19. Hootan Shambayati, "The Rentier State, Interest Groups, and the Paradox of Autonomy: State and Business in Turkey and Iran," *Comparative Politics* 26, no. 3 (April 1994): 321.
20. See Ahmad Ashraf, "Bazaar-Mosque Alliance: The Social Bases of Revolts and Revolutions," *Politics, Culture, and Society* 1 (summer 1988): 538-67; and Shambayati, "The Rentier State."
21. Shambayati, "The Rentier State," 314.
22. Ibid., 316.

23. Ibid., 327; see also Henri Barkey, *The State and the Industrialization Crisis in Turkey* (Boulder, Colo.: Westview, 1990).

24. John Entelis, "Civil Society and the Authoritarian Temptation in Algerian Politics: Islamic Democracy vs. the Centralized State," in *Civil Society in the Middle East,* vol. 2, ed. Augustus Richard Norton (New York: E. J. Brill, 1996), 45-86.

25. *New York Times,* 7 March 1996.

26. National Democratic Institute for International Affairs, *Promoting Participation in Yemen's 1993 Elections* (Washington, D.C.: National Democratic Institute for International Affairs, 1994), 5.

27. Salamé, "Small is Pluralistic," 85-111.

28. Farhad Kazemi, "Civil Society and Iranian Politics," in *Civil Society in the Middle East,* vol. 2, ed. Augustus Richard Norton (New York: E. J. Brill, 1996), 139-40.

29. Richard Cottam, *Nationalism in Iran* (Pittsburgh: University of Pittsburgh Press, 1964), 297.

30. *Mideast Mirror,* authors' field notes.

31. Al-Sayyid, "Slow Thaw," 717.

32. See Jill Crystal, "Authoritarianism and Its Adversaries in the Arab World," *World Politics* 46, no. 2 (January 1994): 262-89; and Farhad Kazemi and Augustus Richard Norton, "Civil Society, Political Reform, and Authoritarianism in the Middle East," *Contention: Debates in Society, Culture, and Science* 5, no. 2 (winter 1996): 107-19.

33. Denis J. Sullivan, *Private Voluntary Organizations in Egypt: Islamic Development, Private Initiative, and State Control* (Gainesville: University Press of Florida, 1994), 17.

34. Field research notes from the authors' visit to Egypt, June-July 1995.

35. James A. Paul, *Human Rights in Syria: A Middle East Watch Report* (Washington, D.C.: Human Rights Watch, 1990), 97-98.

36. Brand, "'In the Beginning' was the State," 173-75.

37. "Jordan: Associations Cry Foul," *Civil Society: Democratic Transformation in the Arab World* 4, no. 48 (December 1995): 21.

38. Eva Bellin, "Civil Society in Formation: Tunisia," in *Civil Society in the Middle East,* vol. 1, ed. Augustus Richard Norton (New York: E. J. Brill, 1995), 146, footnote 54.

39. Ibid., 138-9

40. Sheila Carapico, "Yemen between Civility and Civil War," in *Civil Society in the Middle East,* vol. 2, ed. Augustus Richard Norton (New York: E. J. Brill, 1996), 308.

41. Middle East Watch, *Guardians of Thought: Limits on Freedom of Expression in Iran* (New York: Middle East Watch, 1993).

42. The fall of Law 93 is the subject of a study in progress by Farhad Kazemi and Augustus Richard Norton.

43. Diane Singerman, "Civil Society in the Shadow of the Egyptian State: The Role of Informal Networks in the Constitution of Public Life," paper presented at the conference on "Civil Society Debate and Middle Eastern Studies," University of California, Los Angeles, 29 January 1996.

44. Jenny B. White, "Civic Culture and Islam in Urban Turkey," in *Civil Society: Challenging Western Models,* ed. Chris Hann and Elizabeth Dunn (London: Routledge, 1996), 143-54.

45. Guillermo O'Donnell and Philippe C. Schmitter, *Transitions from Authoritarian Rule: Tentative Conclusions about Uncertain Democracies* (Baltimore: Johns Hopkins University Press, 1986) 48-56.

46. Adam Przeworski, *Democracy and the Market* (Cambridge: Cambridge University Press, 1991), 58.

47. The Civil Society in the Middle East Program was based at New York University from 1992 to 19995 and sponsored dozens of studies by leading Middle East scholars. See Norton, *Civil Society in the Middle East,* 2 vols.

48. Przeworksi, *Democracy and the Market,* 48.
49. Ibid., 60.
50. Ibid.
51. Lisa Anderson, "Liberalism, Islam, and the Arab State," *Dissent* (fall 1994): 439-44.
52. John Voll, "Renewal and Reform in Islamic History: Tajdid and Islah," in *Voices of Resurgent Islam,* ed. John Esposito (New York: Oxford University Press, 1983), 32-47.
53. Ali Banuazizi, "Social Psychological Approaches to Political Development," in *Understanding Political Development,* ed. Myron Weiner and Samuel Huntington (Boston: Little, Brown, 1987), 287; and Said Amir Arjomand, "Traditionalism in Twentieth-Century Iran," in *From Nationalism to Revolutionary Islam,* ed. Said Amir Arjomand (London: Macmillan, 1984), 195-232.
54. Ahmad S. Moussalli, "Modern Islamic Fundamentalist Discourses on Civil Society, Pluralism, and Democracy," in *Civil Society in the Middle East,* vol. 1, ed. Augustus Richard Norton (New York: E. J. Brill, 1995), 70-119.
55. Amartya Sen, *Poverty and Famines: An Essay on Entitlement and Deprivation* (Oxford: Clarendon Press, 1981), cited in Charles Tilly, "Where Do Rights Come From,?" paper prepared for the Vilhelm Aubert Memorial Symposium, University of Oslo, August 1990, p. 1.
56. Tilly, "Where Do Rights Come From?," 2.
57. Ibid.
58. Sayyid Qutb, *Milestones* (Kuwait: Islamic International Unity, 1978).
59. Gilles Kepel, *The Prophet and the Pharaoh: Muslim Extremism in Egypt* (London: Al Saqi Books, 1985); see also Walid Abdelnasser, *The Islamic Movement in Egypt: Perceptions of International Relations, 1967-1981* (London: Kegan Paul, 1994), 188-237.
60. Interview with Adil Hussein, Cairo, 11 July 1995.
61. Ann Mayer, "Universal versus Islamic Human Rights: A Clash of Cultures or a Clash with a Construct?" *Michigan Journal of International Law* 15 (winter 1994): 334.
62. Ibid.
63. Shahla Haeri, *Law of Desire: Temporary Marriage in Shi'i Iran* (Syracuse, N.Y.: Syracuse University Press, 1989).
64. See Mahnaz Afkami and Erika Friedl, eds., *In the Eye of the Storm: Women in Post-Revolutionary Iran* (London: I. B. Tauris, 1994).
65. Mayer, "Universal versus Islamic Human Rights," 330.
66. Arlene Macleod, *Accommodating Protest: Working Women, the New Veiling and the Change in Cairo* (New York: Columbia University Press, 1991).
67. Robert Putnam, *Making Democracy Work: Civic Traditions in Modern Italy* (Princeton: Princeton University Press, 1993).
68. Michael C. Hudson, *Arab Politics: The Quest for Legitimacy* (New Haven: Yale University Press, 1977).
69. As Dankwart Rustow noted in a seminal article: "The basis of democracy is not maximum consensus. It is the tenuous middle ground between imposed uniformity (such as would lead to some sort of tyranny) and implacable hostility (of a kind that would disrupt the community in civil war or succession). In the process of genesis of democracy, an element of what might be termed consensus enters at three points at least. There must be a prior sense of community, preferably a sense of community quietly taken for granted that is above mere opinion and mere agreement. There must be a conscious adoption of democratic rules, but they must not be so much believed in as applied, first perhaps from necessity and gradually from habit. The very operation of these rules will enlarge the area of consensus step-by-step as democracy moves down its crowded agenda"; "Transitions to Democracy," *Comparative Politics* 2, no. 3 (1970): 337-63, quotation at p. 363.

PART II:
ETHNIC AND RELIGIOUS TOLERANCE

CHAPTER FIVE

Religious Communities, Secularism, and Security in Turkey

SENCER AYATA AND AYŞE GÜNEŞ-AYATA

*P*ost-Cold War studies emphasize the consideration and analysis of a wide set of factors in identifying threats to security and ways of dealing with them.[1] The main focus in security studies has moved to different aspects and spheres of society, the relationships among different collectivities, and their relations with the state.[2] This chapter examines a set of ideological and political cleavages in Turkey based on religious factors which led to open conflict between various groups, communities, and the state. The threats and the threatened collectivities are analyzed in terms of a complex interplay involving three major actors: the Islamist movement, secularist forces, and Alevi—a religious minority—revivalism. The policies of successive governments' discriminating in favor of the majority Sunni branch of Islam have been a major factor behind the growing social and political unrest in the country. On the other hand, the Islamist movement itself has found its momentum mainly from the support of deprived or excluded groups, whose social status and standing are threatened by rapid social change, or those struggling to achieve a better place for themselves in society. The security of the state is threatened both by increasing strife and tension within civil society and by the efforts of Islamist groups and parties to undermine the secular nature of the regime.

SECULARIZATION AND RELIGION IN HISTORICAL PERSPECTIVE

The secularization process in Turkey has taken place in two major phases characterized by two different patterns of relations between politics and religion. In the first period (1923-46), the single party in power, the Republican People's Party (RPP), implemented a vast secularization program to effect a decisive removal of religion from public life. The secularization reforms targeted the obliteration of those Ottoman institutions deeply imbued with religion such as the Caliphate, the legal and educational systems, and Sufi brotherhoods (tarikats). Legislation, justice, administration, and education—indeed, the totality of the public sphere—were taken from the religious authorities and placed in the hands of the secular. Reforms such as voting rights for women (1926), the replacement of the Arabic by the Latin alphabet (1928), the ban on the wearing of costumes indicating religious status, and the adoption of the metric system and the Georgian calendar, were all directed towards the expunging of Arabic and Persian influences from Turkish culture and the weakening of groups and institutions that derived their power and legitimacy from Islam.[3]

During the second major phase, which started during the multi-party era in 1950, successive governments, mainly of center-right persuasion, laid greater emphasis on Islamic identity, religious education, and state sponsorship for the provision of basic religious services. The center-right governments defended the legitimacy of moderate tarikats and Islamic communities, developing strategies to incorporate them in mainstream politics. Although these governments have remained essentially loyal to the principle of the separation of state and religion, their supportive attitudes towards organized religious groups have facilitated the widespread penetration of the public sphere by Islamic activities. Two institutions are of note in this respect and have played a significant role in the Sunnification of the state. The first, the Directorate of Religious Affairs (DRA), which claims between 1 percent and 2 percent of the government budget,[4] is responsible for employing nearly 100,000 religious functionaries and operating the country's 80,000 mosques. As salaried employees of the government, the DRA personnel, especially those occupying the top positions, are highly receptive to the demands of government and generally espouse the views and the priorities of those in power. Nevertheless, among lesser officials and a sizable proportion of the preachers in the mosques, both the tarikats and the Welfare Party (WP) seemed to exert considerable influence.

In Islamizing the society, the government-sponsored religious schools, namely the Schools for Training Chaplains and Preachers (SCP), with their 500,000-plus students, have played an even more crucial role. As only a mere 10 percent of their graduates actually take on purely religious duties, the SCP has functioned as a religious alternative to the secular education system, producing hundreds of thousands of devout Islamist individuals. Their graduates who continue on to higher education end up as prefects, judges, bureaucrats, teachers, professionals, and businessmen, often gaining useful access to important decision-making bodies and economic resources. The Islamic movement in Turkey has gained pace and intensity largely as the outcome of the emergence of this Islamist stratum.

A third pattern that has gradually established itself in Turkish politics with the rise of the WP tends to reject the separation of state and religion, with the ultimate aim of implementing the sway of Islam over both society and politics.

THE WELFARE PARTY: SOCIAL BASIS, EVOLUTION, IDEOLOGY, AND ORGANIZATION

In the 1990s, the WP overshadowed the influence of the *tarikats* and Islamic communities, thereby claiming a virtual monopoly over Islamic political activity. The National Salvation Party (NSP), the predecessor of the WP, was founded by Necmettin Erbakan and his friends in 1972. The party stood in the general elections of 1973 and 1977, claiming 11.8 percent and 8.6 percent of the votes respectively, and took part in three different coalition governments: once with the center-left RPP in 1974 and, between 1975 and 1980, with center-right and extreme right parties. At that time, the party leadership was composed of a group of young, university-educated politicians, many of whom had studied the sciences and engineering, and who generally came from humble, provincial, and conservative families. The NSP gained a reputation for its concentration on moral and spiritual issues, as well as economic matters such as the development of heavy industry.[5]

The WP was founded in 1983, three years after the NSP, along with all the other political parties, was closed by the military leadership in 1980. Since Erbakan and some of his close associates had been barred from political activity by the 1982 constitution, the party remained in the hands of a group of trusted caretakers until the former regained their full political rights as a result of a referendum held in 1987. Neither Erbakan nor the WP was able to enter parliament until 1991, when an alliance with the extreme right Nationalist Action Party (NAP) brought the partnership 16.8 percent of the vote and 62 seats in the national assembly. Only three years later, in the 1994 municipal elections, the party achieved a sweeping victory, winning the mayorships in many of Turkey's major urban centers, including both Istanbul and Ankara. In the 1995 general election, it was able to emerge as the biggest party, in the extremely fragmented political landscape, with 21.5 percent of the vote. The WP came to power in July 1996 in coalition with Tansu Çiller's True Path Party (TPP); Erbakan himself, after more than a quarter of a century of political struggle, became the prime minister of secular Turkey's 50th government.

The foregoing discussion is limited to various ideological, organizational, and popular characteristics of the party that led to its perception by the military and secularist social groups in Turkey as a major threat to the secular regime. In its political ideology, the WP emphasized the central role of religion in individual and social life, and the necessity of making religious rules and values reign supreme in the public sphere, including such areas as education, law, and government. The Islamic viewpoint lays a special stress on society's moral issues and problems: the weakening of community ties; social atomization; the spread of utilitarian and material motives in social relations—which it views as the growing supremacy of selfishness, greed, and the free-market condition over community values based on companionship, sacrifice, and care for others; and the decline of religious faith and observance. Such problems are invariably seen as the consequence of a Westernization process which involved the wholesale adoption of Western institutions and thus, as part of this package, secularism, which divorced all that is spiritual, divine, and religious from social and political life. Islam is introduced as the only force capable of restoring individual faith, pulling the family together, and curing society's moral problems. The practical implications of these ideas for everyday life are: an attempt to strengthen the authority of the father/husband in the home; the encouragement of an, at least partial, return of women to the home so that they might devote their time and energy essentially to the rearing and education of children; a greater emphasis on moral and religious instruction at school; and the promotion of religious observance in the community.

Islam is envisaged as the major source of identification and allegiance for the wider community, over and above those of the tribe, ethnic group, nation, or race. Thus Turkey, whose population is 99 percent Muslim, needs to have an Islamic constitution and an Islamic system of law. The political unit, however, is conceived not as the universal community of Islam but as the national community of Turkey, for which full independence is held to be the ultimate goal. Economic development and increased military power are regarded as the fundamental means of undermining Western political domination and economic imperialism. The underlying reason for the country's political weakness and economic backwardness is seen as the total subservience of Turkey's secular elite to Western interests. Challenging the hegemony of the Western world also requires close collaboration among Islamic countries and the creation of new international economic and political entities organized on the basis of Islamic principles. Although, when in power, the WP leadership frequently reiterated Turkey's commitment to the Customs Union with the European Union (EU) and international alliances such as the North Atlantic Treaty Organization (NATO), both the party propaganda and the Islamist media tended to espouse strongly anti-imperialist and Third World views.[6]

Political Islam in Turkey is essentially an opposition ideology defined in relation to Western culture and institutions, which are invariably associated with imperialism, capitalism, materialism, and Christianity. According to this view, Western culture disseminates materialistic values whilst the capitalist economy generates social and economic inequality, injustice, poverty, and unemployment. The Western system increasingly makes people more insecure, dependent, and desperate. Secularism, another important aspect of the Western tradition, has undermined all that was once sacred in life and society, and Western nationalism has aggravated tribal instincts, leading to ethnic violence and lethal conflicts over artificial boundaries all over the world, even among people of the same faith. These messages are primarily directed at people who suffer from isolation, severe economic hardship, the absence of law and order in society, and oppressive rule. Political Islam is, by and large, a radical world view and a form of political protest for the frustrated and marginalized masses.

As regards the WP's party organization, several important aspects can be underlined. First, the same leadership clique was able to maintain a firm grip over both the NSP and the WP. Erbakan—as the person who gave birth to a political movement and eventually brought it to power—and his old guard appointed virtually all the candidates for the parliament, mayorships, and party positions in almost every single election from 1973. For instance, despite an extremely vigorous women's movement in the party, no woman was elected to an official political position in the party or nominated as a parliamentary candidate.[7]

Secondly, the WP was highly successful in expanding its membership. The party had a large body of well disciplined, highly committed, and strongly motivated activists. Thirdly, despite extreme centralization in its decision making, the WP was always able to maintain a steady flow of information and ideas between the party headquarters and local branches, enabling the party leaders to develop a good insight into local problems and the everyday concerns of the working people. The party members were highly differentiated in terms of their educational and occupational backgrounds and included university graduates, workers, employers, old-age pensioners, shopkeepers, artisans, students, and retired army officers. The activities of the party organization were directed towards major social groups in the form of special branches for women, youth, workers, businessmen, small entrepreneurs, and farmers. The WP also developed a highly complex organizational web of institutions, foundations, and voluntary associations affiliated to the party. It set up occupational organizations for major groups such as professionals, workers, and businessmen, which competed with their secular counterparts. Finally, the WP promoted the formation of separate residential communities where a distinctively Islamic lifestyle could be practiced.[8]

In terms of discipline, the extent of its membership, the range of its activities, and the efficiency of its propaganda machine, the WP far outstripped its rivals. Its negative image in the media encouraged the party members to emphasize face to face interaction in their propaganda, involving both house visits and encounters with people at emotionally loaded religious gatherings. The party organization and its affiliates distributed material benefits to needy people and helped them in their dealings with the bureaucracy. The WP activists and politicians were closer to the people in that they had similar social and cultural backgrounds, enabling the WP to understand better than their rivals the people's difficulties, worries, and expectations.

The social basis of the WP was made up of four major constituencies. First, the party was electorally strongest in the relatively isolated small and medium-sized cities of central and eastern Anatolia. Both economically and culturally, these settlements are centered around the activities of the bazaar people such as shopkeepers, artisans, and merchants. These groups try to uphold religious morality and to keep traditional community networks and social control mechanisms intact in order to defend their traditional lifestyles against Westernizing influences.

Secondly, the WP extended its support rapidly among the lower middle and, especially, low income groups in the big cities and metropolitan areas as a result of its efforts to fill the void created by the absence of state welfare institutions. The party also addressed the moral problems resulting from the weakening of traditional communal ties and anomic tendencies among migrant groups; these problems include excessive use of alcohol, drug abuse among the youth, increasing violence, and disputes aggravated by the absence of an effective justice system.

The third and fourth groups were of relatively more recent origin and smaller in size but were more advantaged in terms of access to economic resources and political opportunities. The export-led industrialization of the 1990s has helped to swell the ranks of small-scale and large-scale industrialists and merchants, who are now well connected to the global markets and the world economy. In many Anatolian cities, as well as in metropolitan centers like Istanbul, a significant section of the emergent entrepreneurial classes has leaned towards political Islam in order to challenge the privileged positions of the established business groups. These Islamist entrepreneurs financed and sponsored the welfare-oriented activities of the party and promoted the mobility of their religious companions who entered business. With their support, the WP gained additional power and leverage vis-à-vis both the state and other influential groups in the society.

Finally, for many students sponsored by Islamic communities and foundations, higher education proves an important source of social mobility, carrying them to the professions, as well as to bureaucratic and technocratic positions in the world of business, local government, and the state. Although not all acknowledge the debt they owe, recipients of sponsorship through higher education constituted a fourth major area of support for the WP. Much of the organizational vigor of the Islamic movement in Turkey can be traced to the new Islamic elite; the majority of the Islamist politicians, as well as the bureaucrats and business executives affiliated to the party, were recruited from among the ranks of this particular stratum.[9]

The social basis of political Islam in Turkey has extended and diversified considerably as new and dynamic groups have been incorporated into the movement: small and medium sized entrepreneurs, new middle classes, and the recent migrants to cities. Modern channels of social mobility based on education and entrepreneurship have played a major role in this process. What many of these groups have in common is an experience or feeling of exclusion by the dominant groups and classes. The resentment of the power, wealth, and lifestyles of the established groups tends to unite those who feel excluded, irrespective of whether they are rich or poor.[10] On the other hand, these groups often have divergent economic interests and varying political priorities and agendas. Increasing social diversity now poses a major threat to the ideological consistency and political coherency of the Islamic movement. This trend is becoming more conspicuous as differences in income, education, lifestyle, and political influence grow wider.

THE WELFARE PARTY IN POWER: THE CONFRONTATION BETWEEN THE SECULARIST AND THE ISLAMIST BLOCS

The political conflict between the WP and its rivals reached a climax when the party was in power and has gradually evolved into a societal polarization between Islamist and secularist. The WP-TPP coalition government that ruled the country for nearly one year between June 1996 and July 1997 did not attempt to Islamize the state, nor did it declare any intentions of introducing an Islamic regime in Turkey. The WP leaders were well aware that their electoral support was meager and that in government they were surrounded by powerful secular forces whom they could not dare to challenge. In the first six months of power, the WP tried to consolidate an image of a moderate Islamic party by pursuing liberal economic policies, showing at least outward respect to basic republican symbols, and stressing its commitment to democratic values. This attitude, however, tended to alienate both the more radical elements in the party as well as those in its constituency who felt excluded from the benefits of government. Furthermore, the frequent disputes and squabbles between rival factions began to damage the WP's image as a strongly unified party. Having failed to reform the economy and introduce changes to please the masses, the party leadership began to appeal to religious symbols and sentiments even more intensively. To compensate for its inaction in government, in January 1997 the WP authorities announced plans to build a huge mosque in Taksim Square in Istanbul, for which they legally expropriated the area used as green space. They also proposed a law that would enable Islamist women to wear the turban—an Islamist style of head covering—in public places such as government offices, schools, and hospitals. What were later called the "Sincan events" also added fuel to the escalating conflict. The WP-controlled municipality had organized a public event in Ankara's

Sincan district, which took place on 1 February 1997, to condemn Israel and show solidarity with the Palestinian people. The event, however, turned into a condemnation of Turkey's secular regime, as the mayor of Sincan fiercely attacked republican institutions in his speech. Furthermore, a play staged by a WP youth group espoused armed struggle against tyrannical secular rulers in Turkey. What really infuriated secular public opinion, however, was the presence of the Iranian ambassador and his provocative speech calling for an Islamic revolution in Turkey. The next day the military retaliated by organizing an exercise near Sincan and sending its tanks through the streets for hours. The WP mayor was immediately arrested and the Iranian ambassador was sent back to his country. The Sincan events marked the beginning of a new process in which the WP leaders and the military authorities confronted each other publicly with criticism and attacks. From then onwards, the deepening political cleft in Turkey was perceived as a contest for power between the Islamist WP and the secularist army.

The underlying reason for the conflict, however, was the appointment of the WP's Islamist followers to administrative positions in the bureaucracy, and the concerted efforts of Islamist groups to infiltrate the army. First, 146 Islamist officers and cadets were dismissed by the National Security Council (NSC)—a powerful organ of the state in which the president, the government, and the military high command meet to discuss and develop policies on national security issues. Ironically, the decision was taken with the approval of Erbakan, in his capacity as prime minister. It was, however, bitterly resented by the frustrated Islamists who interpreted the action as a humiliating defeat for Muslims, in view of the fact that an Islamic party was in power; the WP was accused of betraying its own children in order to stay in office.

Even more shattering for the WP were the so-called 28 February Resolutions of the NSC in which Islamic fundamentalism was identified as the major threat to the state. The resolutions also outlined a comprehensive strategy for the immediate elimination of this threat. More specifically, the NSC proposed that the government extend the minimum period of compulsory elementary education from five to eight years (a proposal subsequently embodied in the Eight Years Law), a measure that, in practice, foresaw the closing down of the middle level of the religious schools, which for years had been the spark of life not only for the WP but for the whole Islamic movement in Turkey. From then on, the secularist-Islamist confrontation, and the ensuing political crisis, which eventually undermined the WP-TPP coalition government, revolved around the Eight Years Law. As a result of a succession of resignations from Tansu Çiller's TPP, the government lost its majority in the parliament. The first priority of the new secular government led by Mesut Yılmaz was to pass the Eight Years Law, in August 1997, even though this entailed postponing the official summer closure of the parliament for nearly two months. The protests initiated by the mosque crowds calling for the repeal of the Eight Years Law continued for a time, but in the 1997-98 academic year no new students were admitted to the middle level of the SCP.

The rise of the WP, its ascendance to power, and the unfolding of the political and ideological conflict in the country have had profound effects on the nature and composition of secular groups. Women, who defend Ataturk reforms on the grounds of their contribution to the advancement of equality among sexes and the increased participation of women in public life, were among the first to recognize that Islamic fundamentalism could unleash the traditional exercise of patriarchal authority, and that fundamentalist Islam in general has a powerful bent towards confining women to domestic and family responsibilities. Hence, the civilian struggle against political Islam was initiated by women, and womens' networks and voluntary associations have spearheaded the secular protest movement, providing new behavioral and associational models for other groups. Secondly, the Alevi minority have perceived a major threat to their communal existence and identity. The Islamists have either strongly discriminated against them or tended to assimilate the Alevi by imposing Sunni views and values upon them without taking into account the important differences in interpretation and observance between the two sects. The Alevi, too, have played a pivotal role in secularist political parties and civic associations struggling to confine the rise of political Islam. Third, a number of groups and associations that define themselves as Kemalists have had a profound ideological and organizational influence on the whole secularist movement; these have mobilized diverse sections of society around the cause of defending republican values and institutions against what they described as "the threat of reaction." The Kemalists have organized meetings, conferences, discussion groups, and philanthropic ventures in order to convey secularist viewpoints and values to a wider public, and to strengthen solidarity among secular groups. One leading Kemalist organization, the Association of Ataturkist Thought (AAT), has been able to increase its membership to 45,000 in a matter of a few years by opening 355 local branches in almost every Anatolian town and city. The AAT is now the largest voluntary association in Turkey. The Association for Promoting Contemporary Life (APCL) has nearly 15,000 members, who are overwhelmingly women, and is particularly active in providing scholarships for needy students in order to challenge the predominant Islamist influence in this area. Fourth, the secularist RPP, the most ardent rival to the WP and its powerful grassroots organization, has acted as a magnet and umbrella for all secular opposition groups, especially in the small towns and the provinces.

Another major development was the so-called Civilian Initiative, an attempt by representatives of the leading occupational organizations to found a platform for united action against the WP-TPP coalition government. These included the two major trade union confederations: the confederation of small traders and artisans organizations, which has by far the largest membership in the country, and the leaders of the major employers' associations. The vast combined membership of these groups, and their agreement on a common plan of action despite their differences on other major issues, provided a wide basis of legitimacy for the secularist movement.

The secularist backlash took one of its most important turns when the organizations representing big business interests also started to give active support to the secularist groups. This was partly a response to the expansion of Islamic capital—which is by and large the result of favorable treatment by the WP municipalities and government—at the expense of established business interests. On the other hand, the big-business circles also recognized that their being identified with an Islamist government was doing serious damage to Turkey's standing and reputation in the Western world. The growing opposition from the business groups had two important consequences. First, the two most powerful groups in Turkish society, that is, the military and big business, whose interests seemed to have diverged on many issues in the last two decades, had joined forces to constitute a formidable power block against political Islam. Secondly, the leading mass media organizations, with their highly monopolistic ownership structure and general subservience to big business interests, then launched a massive media campaign against the WP and the government. The powerful three-pronged attack, involving the military, big business, and the mass media, played a major role in its downfall.

For secular groups, an Islamist threat means essentially four different things. First, the secular state, the secular political parties, and the secular public have tended to see political Islam as a major threat to the secular and the democratic regime. Secondly, the Islamist emphasis on traditional values, patriarchal relations, and a uniform Islamic way of life, has disturbed the urban middle classes, who are the main defenders of republican values and Western lifestyles. Third, scientists, artists, intellectuals, and the like see in fundamentalist Islam an underlying intolerance towards manifestations of personal eccentricity, free inquiry, artistic expression, and cosmopolitan values, which they regard as important for promoting civic society, an open public culture, quality of life, and scientific and artistic creativity. Finally, it was particularly the perceived threat to national security that mobilized the power elite against Islamic fundamentalism. In this, political as well as economic concerns played a role. For instance, there was the growing suspicion that, in foreign policy, the WP was abandoning Turkey's commitment to the Western world by forging new alliances with Islamic countries such as Iran, the Sudan, and Libya. Hence, a fear of isolation from the Western world started to grow. Similarly, the image of Turkey under Islamic rule was seen as ruinous for the international competitiveness of the Turkish economy, as evidenced by a sharp decline in direct foreign investments in 1996 and 1997, despite the Customs Union Agreement with the EU that took effect on 1 January 1996.

The developments summarized above contradict the well-established image in the minds of many foreign and Turkish observers that secularism in Turkey is exclusively the concern of the state elite. The secularist movement has proved at least as authentic, popular, and organized as the Islamic movement in both its composition and scope. The secular regime was defended by civilian associations and institutions as much as by the main pillars of the state such as the judiciary and the military.

To sum up, the rise of the Islamist movement in Turkey has generated a powerful secularist backlash in the form not only of a political struggle but also of a massive social movement. Although it includes the country's highly educated and globally-oriented urban middle class, the active participation of popular groups in the movement has indicated that secularism and the republican reforms have penetrated deep into Turkish society after nearly 75 years of implementation. This sharply contradicts the prevalent argument that Islam is the true indigenous and authentic culture in Turkish society, as well as the primary source of identity, cohesion, and solidarity among the ordinary people, whereas secularism and democracy are extraneous forces limited in their appeal to the small Westernized elite which is largely alienated from society. The secularist groups, by introducing new and highly imaginative forms of solidarity and resistance, have demonstrated that they too have considerable capacity for spontaneous and voluntary organization.

In what evolved into a major political crisis, the WP met with strong opposition from the organized powers of the state, the secular political parties, and an extremely vibrant civic movement. Through its mobilization of a wide range of social groups and the employment of a wide variety of tactics and strategies, this secular bloc has become a major obstacle to political Islam.

CLOSURE OF THE WELFARE PARTY

On 21 May 1997, when the WP was still in power, the chief prosecutor of the supreme court of appeal brought a suit against the party to the constitutional court, claiming that the actions of some of its members, including its leader Necmettin Erbakan, involved major violations of the constitution of the country. The hearing of the case took nearly eight months and, in the end, on 22 February 1998, the party was closed. The memorandum of the decision of the constitutional court stated that the WP had committed actions aimed at undermining the secular regime in Turkey. The leaders of the WP, expecting such a decision, had already founded a substitute party, the Virtue Party (VP), which the vast majority of its politicians and mayors entered in the following weeks. One major exception was Necmettin Erbakan himself, whose political activities were restricted for a period of five years by the same decision of the constitutional court.

What are the likely effects on the Islamist movement of the closing down of the WP? First, the Algerian syndrome, deeply feared by many inside and outside the country, remains a very distant possibility in Turkey; the WP leaders met the decision calmly, immediately calling on their supporters to avoid sensational action. The VP has substituted the WP in almost every respect. Erbakan is not in the foreground but he continues to rule the new party just as in the past. The WP did indeed represent a multitude of social groups, political communities, and ideological orientations. To the extent that the new party can take its place in Turkish politics, it can sound the views and interests of the same groups that supported the WP. Now the important question is whether the new party will be able to develop new ways of compromising with democracy, secularism, and the other political parties.

The new party has to reconcile two opposing demands: to play the game according to the rules of the dominant secular political system, and to meet the expectations of its constituency that insists on the distinctiveness of Islam both as a way of life and as a framework for political action. Before it appeared as a major political force in the 1994 municipal elections, the WP was more easily able to confine its propaganda to isolated local settings, face to face small group interaction, and various texts produced for internal consumption. From the time the party appeared on the forefront of the political stage, it was vigilantly scrutinized by a hostile media. In addressing people on matters of everyday interest, most of which were of secular concern, the need to give clear and consistent messages and appeal to common sense, rather than the expectations of special groups, became more deeply felt. This made the party leaders see politics in a more professional way, that is, as an activity which is an end in itself. In the party's everyday discourse in the media, religion either tended to recede into the background or was only symbolically expressed. As the WP politicized religion, it came to be dominated by politics itself. The shift from sectarian religious to national secular politics introduced a rift between the establishment-oriented party leadership and its more religiously motivated grassroots.[11] In the new party, the trend towards professionalization seems likely to be consolidated.

In a rapidly changing, differentiating, and diversifying society, the Islamic movement has tended to become increasingly heterogeneous in nature, complex in structure, and varied in membership composition. This has significantly increased the potential for internal divisions, tensions, and conflicts. Differences in social class, for instance, have become more obvious as the representation of professional and entrepreneurial groups has increased. In their lifestyles and political behavior, the latter renounce ascetic, collectivist, and radical values and orientations. Instead, they advocate an Islam based on affluence, moderation, and compromise. Improving relations with the Western world, commitment to the market economy and privatization, and compromise with secular groups through showing outward respect for Ataturk are among the more concrete manifestations of this tendency. On the other hand, the vast majority of those who voted for the WP, and its erstwhile rank and file—who were largely excluded from the benefits of power—strongly resent the changing lifestyles and world views of upwardly mobile Islamist individuals and groups. For them, priorities include stronger dedication to the ideal of Islamizing society, further emphasis on social justice and equality in party policy, a commitment to the withdrawal of Turkey from the capitalist world economy, and a more determined struggle against secularist groups and the secular regime.

The internal strife generated by the move towards the political center and the emergence of a bourgeois stratum seemed to threaten both the ideological consistency and the organizational unity of the party, especially when it was in power. However, the rapid polarization of Turkish society into the antagonistic secular and Islamist blocs threatened all groups in the party, rich and poor alike, thus making them act in unison, especially against secularist measures such as the closing down of the middle levels of the SCPs. This made the different groups and factions in the party feel that their collective interests were at stake.

The regime in Turkey has always been Janus-like in its approach to organized religious groups and political parties: restrictive, exclusive, and rejectionist as well as tolerant, accommodating, and compromising. Not only the WP but also its two predecessors were closed; similarly, there now exists a strong predisposition among some secular parties both on the left and right to exclude the successors of the WP from power. On the other hand, the WP and its predecessors came to power four times, the last time with the WP leader as the prime minister of the country. The tendency among the establishment-oriented, liberal, professional, and entrepreneurial groups in the new party is to avoid further confrontation and to adapt to the economic system and the regime. Provided that these groups can firmly establish their leadership, the VP can evolve into a modern conservative party, fully appropriating democratic values. Its leaders, and especially the moderates among them, emphasize that the new party should not repeat the mistakes of the old; for them, this involves a genuine commitment to democracy and the avoidance of unnecessary conflict with the secularist groups. The archetype for the younger generation of politicians is the Democratic Party of Adnan Menderes, with its emphasis on civilian rather than state interests, freedom of religion, and free enterprise. They well know that radicalism carries with it the risk of closure.

Furthermore, whereas a moderate Islamic party can come to power by establishing coalition partnerships, a radical one can expect only to be excluded from power. The WP came first in the 1995 elections with only 21.5 percent of the vote while the gross support for the center-right and center-left parties was 39 percent and 25 percent respectively. Ideological differences are negligible within both the center-left and the center-right parties, and the general expectation is that similar parties will eventually unite. This will move the WP's successor to third place in the party hierarchy and certainly make Islamic fundamentalism less of a threat for the regime. A further possibility is a decision on the part of the mainstream secular parties to rule out coalition partnerships with the WP's successor unless it makes a clear commitment to the secular democratic regime. As a matter of fact, in the 1995 election campaign, all four secular parties presented their leading missions as being the exclusion of the WP from power. Tansu Çiller's decision to go into partnership with the WP almost ruined her party as more than one-third of TPP MPs resigned even though the TPP was in power, and almost all poll results indicate that support for the TPP was considerably reduced at the last general election. Although the threat of exclusion from government would generate a moderating influence on the new party, any commitment made to counter this requires the approval of the radicals. Such dilemmas clearly indicate the structural contradictions and the ideological ambivalences of the WP/VP and the Islamist movement in Turkey.

THE ALEVI

The members of the Alevi minority sect make up a sizable proportion, nearly 20 percent, of Turkey's population. Secularism, understood as the separation of state and religion, constitutes the very core of Alevi identity since this group sees its basic communal existence in Turkish society as dependent on a position of neutrality, maintaining an equal distance from all citizens, irrespective of their religious beliefs. In the last few decades, however, the Alevi have tended to become more skeptical about the secular nature of the regime in Turkey, and increasingly worried about developments through which Sunni Islam, the religion of the majority, has gained an establishment status. The Sunnification of the state has been most visible in areas such as expansion of religious education, introduction of a compulsory course on religion in the secular schools, the efforts of the DRA to present Sunni Islam as "true religion," and the growing importance of a Sunni discourse in politics, the mass media, and most aspects of public life. Furthermore, since the 1970s, there have been several incidents in which the Alevi have suffered violent attacks by extreme nationalist and Islamic fundamentalist groups in which many have lost their lives. The Alevi have begun to resent what they see as the rapid erosion of their distinctive identity and serious threats to their communal well-being. Their feeling of exclusion has increasingly alienated them from the state, politicized their identity, and activated political conflict that would otherwise have remained dormant.

The Turkish Alevi have their origins in the Turcomans who began to migrate from central Asia to Anatolia and the Balkans in the twelfth and thirteenth centuries. These nomadic warrior tribes had converted to Islam and played a significant role in the Turkish conquest of Anatolia. The rising Turkic princedoms, among them the Ottomans, based their military power essentially on these groups. The expanding Ottoman state, however, in order to reduce its dependence on the autonomous, undisciplined, and untrustworthy tribal leaders and confederations, attempted to consolidate its power by developing alternative sources of recruitment for its army. Parallel to their exclusion from the state, the Turcoman tribes were forced to settle as farmers as their traditional nomadic lifestyle and economy had become antithetical to the requirements of sedentary agriculture. Exclusion and repression led to the emergence of a resistant subculture which, throughout Ottoman history, was never successfully integrated into the main fabric of society. One major element of this culture was its peculiar blend of central Asian shamanistic beliefs and practices with Sufi teachings strongly influenced by Shi'i Islam. The religious heterodoxy of the Turcoman groups clashed with the orthodox Sunni Islam of the Ottoman state, occasionally taking the form of organized revolts manipulated by the Shi'i dynasties in Iran. Later known as the Alevi, the Turcomans were seen as a highly dangerous threat by the Ottoman state.[12]

The Alevi, however, fully supported Mustafa Kemal in his efforts towards establishing a modern secular republic, one that would not base governmental authority on religion and would not align itself with any one religious group. Hence, in the republican period, the Alevi always lent their support to the secularist-modernist tradition in Turkish politics: first, to the modernizing single party regime, and later to the secularist center-left in the multiparty era.

Before the 1960s, that is, before the beginning of mass migration to the cities, the majority of the Alevi lived in isolated rural settlements in central Anatolia, as well as in scattered villages and village clusters in other parts of the country. The rural Alevi population is now depleted as the vast majority live in metropolitan centers like Ankara and Istanbul. The early Alevi migrants were able to find work in factories and large-scale formal organizations: jobs were on the increase due to rapid industrialization and the growth of the public sector in the 1960s and 1970s. In the big cities, the Alevi formed homogeneous residential communities, and in the workplace they joined trade unions, taking part in the frequent strikes and urban protest movements. Those who worked for the government and the municipalities as unskilled low-ranking civil servants enjoyed the security of employment and social benefits that state institutions provided. Both in the factories and in government, the Alevi were employed in numbers significantly out of proportion to their share of the population. In the same period, leftist working-class politics had wide appeal among organized private employees as well as among civil servants, as evidenced by the strong support of these groups for the RPP, the party founded by Ataturk which adopted a social democratic ideology in the 1970s. In this period again, the working population benefited significantly from rises in real wages. The Alevi thus consolidated their position both in politics, as modern working-class people, and in the economy, as modern consumers. Their group expectations were raised as they began to send their children to secondary schools and universities, investing heavily in education in order to achieve social mobility. These years were also the heyday of the left, as evidenced by the RPP's greatest ever share of the vote—42 percent in the 1977 general election.

In Europe, on the other hand, Alevi emigrants had the chance of early acquaintance with industrial society and culture, that is, the world of class identities, trade unions, large-scale organizations, and democracy. As people who emphasize the progressiveness of their culture, they were quick to adopt the values of the left, which they tried to disseminate among their co-villagers during home visits. Their comparatively higher earnings in Europe enabled them to bring back consumer durables and cars, and to buy real estate in Turkey.[13] Both their assertion of a modern progressive identity and the sudden change in their socio-economic status aroused wide envy and resentment among provincial people who had previously despised the poverty-stricken Alevi. Factors that further aggravated Sunni prejudices against the Alevi were such practices as Alevi women appearing in public, sometimes without even covering their heads.

The industrialization of the metropolitan areas and the rise of the left sparked off a conservative backlash, and in the underdeveloped provincial areas extreme nationalist and reactionary religious groups began to gather strength. The Nationalist Action Party (NAP), which entered Turkish politics in the late 1960s, had rapidly built up an anti-communist paramilitary force. In the eyes of these extreme nationalist militants, communism was defined as anything left of center or closely associated with irreligiousness and moral degeneration. In the provincial setting, the Alevi, both on account of their leftism and the historical Sunni prejudice that they engaged in incestuous and promiscuous sexual relations, were made the immediate targets of propaganda by conservative groups such as the NAP.[14] Furthermore, the Sunni see the Alevi as irreligious on the grounds that they do not observe such rituals as the regular prayers, fasting in Ramadan, and the pilgrimage to Mecca, which are considered the main pillars of the Islamic faith. Indignation and hostility directed towards the Alevi tended to build up especially in the context of Alevi migration from villages to towns and when Alevi workers in Europe bought flats and houses either for family use or to rent out. The Sunni reaction erupted in 1979 in the cities of Çorum and Maraş, where angry mobs roused by reactionary propaganda surrounded the Alevi neighborhoods, killing hundreds, destroying houses and shops, and looting property. The violent clashes continued for several days, during which the police took no significant measures to stop or confine the violence. In both incidents, the army had to intervene to put an end to the turmoil and bloodshed.

In the 1970s, the historical Alevi-Sunni division was reconstituted in the urban context in the form of a polarity of political identities: left and right, communism and nationalism, progressivism and conservatism. In both Maraş and

Çorum, the Sunni crowds had gathered first in the mosques, which in Turkey are operated by the imams, who are salaried state officials. In their political discourse, the angry mobs, which included many students from religious schools, invoked both religious and nationalist themes. The biased attitude of the police, the government's delay in taking action, and the inability of the regime to provide security for the community, all served to turn the Alevi against the state.

The export-led growth strategies of the 1980s, the declining significance of the state in the economy, and the negative consequences of global competition for the workers have dramatically altered the relative positioning of, and relations among, social classes, ethnic groups, and religious communities, as well as the relations of these groups with the state. The political and economic strength of the working class was considerably reduced as a result of repressive legislation, the diminished power of the trade unions, and the destabilization of the labor market. Real wages dropped and living conditions deteriorated for the working people. Public sector employees, too, suffered from privatization, reduced investment and employment, a decline in real wages, and a loss of prestige in the face of heavy criticism from neo-liberals. The increased globalization and privatization of the economy resulted in the erosion of state employment and the decline of union power and leftist political parties. The Alevi felt increasingly threatened by economic, political, and ideological developments which lowered their economic status and social standing. Alevi trepidation was compounded both by the increased Sunnification of the state in the 1980s and 1990s, and by the rise of political Islam.

An event that justified this fear, causing a deep trauma in the collective consciousness of the Alevi, took place in the city of Sivas in July 1993. A group of Alevi poets, artists, and folk dancers were staying in a hotel at the very center of the city that was attacked by Islamic fundamentalist groups who first set the hotel on fire and then provoked a huge Islamist crowd who shouted religious slogans as the hotel burned. Thirty-seven people lost their lives in the fire. Again, since the police were reluctant to interfere, the army was called in to stop the events and disperse the enraged crowd. Later, the Alevi were to criticize the leaders of the Social Democratic People's Party, which was then in power, for their ineffectiveness in preventing the disaster. Those arrested on charges stemming from the incident included members of the local WP, who were defended in court by a group of Islamist lawyers—among whom was an eminent WP politician, Şevket Kazan, later appointed minister of justice in the WP-TPP coalition government. The court initially gave light sentences to the defendants but these were rejected by the supreme court and, at a later trial held amidst the escalating secularist-Islamist conflict, the court imposed 37 death sentences, invoking an image of revenge for the 37 Alevi burned to death in Sivas.

The Alevi population live in small, segregated clusters in the peripheral quarters and districts of big cities. These clusters are surrounded by Sunni neighborhoods. Differences in religious beliefs and values, political affiliations, and lifestyles limit the social intercourse between the two communities. For instance, both groups have strong endogamous practices. Where Sunni groups have radical Islamist or extreme nationalist leanings, intercommunal relations can be particularly tense, carrying the immediate risk of open conflict and violent clashes. Such was the case in 1994, in the Gazi Osman Paşa district in Istanbul, when unidentified gunmen opened random fire on Alevi men sitting in a coffee house, killing two old men. The murders triggered bloody clashes between Alevi youth and the police which lasted for three days; again, the army had to be called in. As the troops walked into the district, they were welcomed by cheers from the Alevi. In the same year, similar violent clashes took place in other peripheral districts in Istanbul.

The response of the Alevi to growing political tension and conflict has been an increased emphasis on communal identity and solidarity, politicization, and, in the case of certain groups, radicalization. Frustration with the performance of social democratic parties led a group of Alevi to found their own party (Peace Party), while others were encouraged to take a more active part in the radical socialist parties. Kurdish Alevi youth leaned towards emphasizing their Kurdishness or rebellious Alevism.[15] Some among the Turkish Alevi youth began to join militant Marxist-Leninist organizations. The Alevi have begun to assert the contrastive and exclusive aspects of their identity rather than what they have in common with others; for instance, in the last few years there has been a proliferation of literature on the religious history, world views, and cultural traits of the Alevi. More striking is the mushrooming of the so-called "congregation houses" in the towns and cities; by and large a new development in Alevi culture, these are counterposed to the Sunni mosques. The Alevi identity, which in the past was well hidden and secretive, now manifests itself in public gatherings and buildings.

What triggered Alevi revivalism was the need for collective defense against the encroachment of Sunni Islam and Islamic fundamentalism upon Alevi identity and community in virtually every aspect of public life. The Alevi fear the police, who indiscriminately label them as "terrorists," schoolteachers, who discriminate against their children, the imams in the mosques, who either ignore the Alevi or accuse them of apostasy and heresy, and the WP and the Islamist movement, which attempt to impose a uniform Sunni way of life upon them. The Alevi are increasingly convinced that they have always been excluded, repressed, and persecuted. The recent groundswell of Alevi radicalism, ready to assume forms of militant action, at least among the youth, can be seen as a response to the politicization of Sunni Islam and its growing influence over the state.

In the multi-party era, the center-right political parties that ruled the country have promoted religion—Sunni Islam—in society, politics, and the state. The police, generally under the influence of the center and extreme right political parties, have developed strong prejudices against the Alevi, while both in schools and state-sponsored religious activities, the Alevi have either been excluded or strongly discriminated against. Increased politicization, first among a section of Sunni Muslims and later among the Alevi, has created a highly explosive situation which threatens not only the security of these two groups but the stability of the state as well.

CONCLUSION

In all three cases examined in this chapter, both inter-collectivity conflict and the conflicts between the individual groups and the state pose important threats for the security of all the parties. In maintaining freedom of belief and religious tolerance, the state's ability to govern and mediate between heterogeneous religious forces is crucial. In Turkey, the absence of a coherent and neutral state policy towards religious dissent, and the increasing influence of certain religious groups and communities over various departments of the state, have emerged as major causes of dispute and conflict. Structural transformations such as massive rural-urban migration, widespread unemployment and poverty in cities, and the difficult conditions that global competition imposes on the domestic economy, bring enormous burdens for the majority of the working people. What often lies at the basis of religious and ethnic politics are the demands, resentments, and hostilities of marginalized, oppressed, and excluded groups, as seen both in the case of the Alevi and the Islamist movement. The instability created by identity politics cannot be easily overcome without the social and economic integration of such groups. Humane, rational, and creative politics can achieve much in the acceleration of economic growth, in increasing the efficiency of administration, in fighting against corruption, in the enforcement of the rule of law, and in the promotion of participation and democracy; all these would mitigate, if not eliminate, existing and emerging tensions and conflicts in society, as well as the multiple threats to the security of both the collectivities and the state.

NOTES

1. David A. Baldwin, "Security Studies and the End of the Cold War," *World Politics* 48 (1995): 117-41.

2. Keith Krause and Michael C. Williams, "Broadening the Agenda of Security Studies: Politics and Methods," *Mershon International Studies Review* 40 (1996): 229-54.

3. Bernard Lewis, *The Emergence of Modern Turkey* (New York: Oxford University Press, 1961).

4. İştar Tarhanlı, *Müslüman Toplum "Laik" Devlet* (Istanbul: AFA Yayınları, 1993).

5. İlkay Sunar and Binnaz Toprak, "Islam in Politics: The Case of Turkey," *Government and Opposition* 18, no. 4 (1983): 421-41.

6. Refah Partisi, 14 Aralık 1995 *Seçimleri Beyannamesi* (Ankara, 1995).

7. Ruşen Çakır, *Ne şeriat ne Demokrasi* (Istanbul: Metis Yayınları, 1994).

8. Ayşe Saktanber, "Formation of a Middle-Class Ethos and its Quotidian: Revitalizing Islam in Urban Turkey," in *Space, Culture, and Power,* ed. Ayşe Öncü and Petra Weyland (London: Zed Books, 1997).

9. Faruk Birtek and Binnaz Toprak, "The Conflictual Agendas of Neo-Liberal Reconstruction and the Rise of Islamic Politics in Turkey," *Praxis International* 13, no. 2 (1993): 192-212.

10. Ziya Öniş, "The Political Economy of Islamic Resurgence in Turkey: The Rise of the Welfare Party in Perspective," *Third World Quarterly* 18, no. 4 (1997): 743-66.

11. Henri Barkey, "Turkey, Islamic Politics, and the Kurdish Question," *World Policy Journal* 13, no. 1 (spring 1996): 43-52.

12. Doğan Avcıoğlu, *Türklerin Tarihi I. Cilt.* (Istanbul: Tekin Yayınevi, 1989).

13. Bahattin Akşit, *Köy, Kasaba ve Kentlerde Toplumsal Değişme* (Ankara: Turhan Yayınevi, 1985).

14. Orhan Türkdoğan, *Alevi Bektaşi Kimliği* (Istanbul: Timaş Yayınları, 1995).

15. Günter Seufert, "Between Religion and Ethnicity: A Kurdish-Alevi Tribe in Globalizing Istanbul," in Öncü and Weyland, *Space, Culture and Power.*

CHAPTER SIX

Ethnicity and Security Problems in Turkey

AYŞE GÜNEŞ-AYATA AND SENCER AYATA

*T*ransnational actors such as ethnic groups are becoming increasingly important in both domestic and international politics. Ethnic groups may challenge the legitimacy of states, instigate action transcending formal boundaries, and be the recipients of international support and as well as the targets of external manipulation. Such action does not necessarily undermine the states concerned but can create significant changes in domestic politics and shifts in the structural setting of international relations.[1] States retaliate by struggling for self-preservation and the maintenance of the status quo.[2] As the dynamics of ethnic activity are external as well as internal, it can constitute a threat not only for national but also for international security. This chapter examines the case of Kurdish ethnicity in Turkey by taking into account the practical and theoretical dynamics of this problem in the domestic context, as well as the complex interplay between the domestic political variables and the international actors and forces involved.

Ethnic studies need to take into consideration both objectively defined primordial solidarities and the situationally created subjective identities.[3] Ethnic tension and conflict tend to erupt when interaction between the previously isolated or socially segregated communities increases as the result of economic development and modernization. Thus, in this paper, changes in agrarian class relationships in Southeast Anatolia, the rapidly changing deployment of labor in the countryside, massive migration to cities, and prospects in the urban labor market, are examined as structural changes that have a significant impact on the formation of a new Kurdish identity. Competition among ethnic groups for economic and political resources, the perception of existing inequalities—in ethnic terms—in everyday life, and the consequent feelings of exclusion and relative deprivation, tend to create and reinforce Kurdish ethnic consciousness and solidarity, which, in turn, provide a basis for collective action. Ethnic tension and unrest is often a result of a complex interplay of economic, social, and political factors. The following analysis of Kurdish ethnicity and activism takes into account all three dimensions. Finally, Kurdish ethnicity is examined within the broader framework of ethnic relations between various ethnic groups in Turkey, and the similarities and differences in the groups' relationships with the state. The ethnic Kurds, despite their internal divisions on religious (Sunni, Alevi), linguistic (Kirmanc, Zaza, Soran), and tribal bases, are by far the largest ethnic group after Turks.[4]

Ethnic action can be economically motivated. Among the migrant Kurds living in western Anatolian towns and cities, economic motives and concerns take precedence over others. Thus, those able to provide for themselves a moderate income and a minimum of job stability and social security are easily integrated into the new society. On the other hand, those Kurds who cannot easily settle in join a familiar community of ethnicity, and become involved in competition for resources with other ethnic groups and the state, which is the main distributor of these resources. This pattern, which tends to politicize ethnicity and engenders conflict with other groups, can be conceived within the framework of legitimate articulation of interests and participation in competitive electoral politics. Ethnic action, furthermore, can be oriented to uphold communal pride.[5] Various Kurdish groups in East Anatolia adopt such an orientation and, as in the case of the separatist Kurdistan Workers' Party, the Partiye Karkeran Kurdistan (PKK), collective action can take a radical militant form. The PKK is analyzed in terms of its origins, ideology, social basis, organizational structure, relationship with the security forces and the state, and its connections with other political forces inside and outside the country. The PKK terror campaign has caused a backlash in the form of a military offensive by the state involving the mobilization of vast numbers of regular troops in addition to the implementation of various counter-guerrilla tactics and strategies. Finally, the tribal-social context in which the PKK operates has had a profound effect on the fate of the Kurdish nationalist movement. Various political and social movements in the region, including the PKK, have attempted to undermine or transform existing tribal loyalties but, in the long run, either were trapped in it themselves or have met with resistance from tribal power centers.

The significance of the international dimension derives mainly from the fact that where borders define the boundaries of a state, ethnic groups often remain divided between two or more states. In regions of the world such as the Middle East, where conquests, colonization, de-colonization, and migration have been frequent throughout history, the existing states were inevitably founded in ethnically diverse societies. The Kurds, for instance, constitute a sizable minority in ethnically heterogeneous countries such as Iran, Turkey, Iraq, and Syria, which face major problems in integrating them. The states in the region often use the Kurds against one another, and this process tends to transform domestic ethnic conflicts into regional ones and thereby aggravate interstate rivalries in the region. A perceived threat is that successful ethnic activity in one country will, either by contagion or imitation, lead to insurrection in others.[6] Thus, the possibility that the Kurds in northern Iraq will gain full autonomy is feared both by Turkey and other Middle Eastern countries. The active involvement of the regional powers in the conflict is another important aspect of the problem. Of primary significance in this context is the status of northern Iraq, the continuing tribal warfare among Kurds in this region, and the support that the Syrian government provides for the PKK. The escalation of the conflict is a major security threat for Turkey, Iraq, Iran, and Syria as these countries face the serious danger of proxy and interstate wars.

The international dimension of Kurdish ethnic activism has become more pronounced since Western states increased intervention in the region in order to promote their own economic and/or security interests, and as the outcome of their increased concern with such issues as human rights, democracy, and pluralism. Discrepancies of power among states, the requirements of international law, and the activities of international organizations make it increasingly difficult for the sovereign states to disregard outside interests and sensitivities. Countries such as Turkey, which are highly committed to the ideal of Westernization and deeper integration with the Western world, become more responsive to, as well as more dependent on, external influences.

The political unrest in the Southeast, and the threat that the Kurdish problem poses for the state and the regime, is approached differently by different political groups in Turkey. The major intellectual and political debate centers around two opposing views: the first urges an immediate political solution to the problem by getting the parties involved in the conflict to negotiate, while the second sees the issue as largely one of terrorism and, consequently, urges the total elimination of terrorism. The last section discusses these as well as other solutions suggested for the Kurdish problem by different political parties and groups in Turkey.

KURDS: OTTOMAN PLURALISM AND REPUBLICAN CITIZENSHIP

Whereas the various states established in Anatolia before the Ottomans were ethnic, in the Ottoman Empire the fundamental distinctions among groups were based on religion. Sense of otherness vis-à-vis people belonging to the same religion remained relatively weak. One important reason was the absence of communication among people, the majority of whom were living in isolated village settlements. This applied to Kurds, as well as to other Muslim groups.

The Kurds were historically and geographically separated from the rest of Anatolia during much of the Ottoman rule. Until the nineteenth century, the Ottomans recognized the autonomy of the Kurdish tribes and landlords.[7] The high mountain ranges where they lived made both transportation and communication among Kurdish groups difficult, thus separating tribes from each other as well as from the rest of Anatolia.[8] Ottoman efforts towards modernization in the early nineteenth century involved the implementation of a centralized administrative structure; this, however, gave rise to a major clash of interests between the Ottoman state and the previously autonomous Kurdish local chiefdoms, which were crushed by the Ottoman army.[9] The weak penetration by modern institutions in the area, however, created a power vacuum which was largely filled by Islamic tarikat (Sufi brotherhood) networks. Islam, from the mid-nineteenth century onwards, has played a uniquely integrative role in this particular region, serving such essential functions as communication, education, and arbitration in disputes among tribes. From this time on, reaction to tightening Ottoman control in the area was mainly expressed in religious terms.[10]

Events assumed a different course with the foundation of the Turkish Republic in 1923. The republican leaders' extreme sensitivity towards issues of national and territorial integrity was a response to the experience of the gradual disintegration of the Ottoman Empire as nations, both Christian and Muslim, succeeded one after the other in claiming their independence. Kurds, too, had uneasy relations with the Ottoman state in its later years, but the absence of an effective leadership and national awareness, combined with their common interests with the Turks vis-à-vis the Russian and Christian communities in East Anatolia, prevented the emergence of an independent Kurdish state.[11] The republican understanding of national unity and cohesion among Muslim peoples had two basic aspects to it. First, Kurds, as Muslims, were denied minority rights because common religious identity among Muslims (Turks, Arabs, Kurds, and Circassians) was taken as a criterion of national unity. In other words, Islam was regarded as the overriding bond among different ethnic groups. Paradoxically, however, the increased emphasis on secularism and the rejection of religion as the basis of legitimacy and citizenship in the new state obliterated what was seen as the fundamental bond between Kurds and other Muslim groups, primarily the majority Turks.[12]

Against this, full citizenship rights were granted to all sections of the population. Aware of the ethnic variety in the country, the Turkish state founded in 1923 was to operate on the basis of territorial nationalism, rather than Turkish ethnicity, in the hope that this would lead citizens to a sense of civic duty and loyalty to the state. The republic has remained essentially loyal to this principle although there have been very important differences in interpretation and implementation.

At times, the state has taken a more impartial stance towards different groups while, at others, Turkish nationalism has been more strongly pronounced by those in power. For instance, following the military coup in 1980, a law was passed banning the use of Kurdish in public.

In Turkey, the collective identities of ethnic groups were never recognized: rights belong to the individual and in this respect there is no legal limitation on any ethnic group. The roads to social mobility have been open to all, at any time, and there has existed no legal discrimination on the basis of ethnicity. The republican ideal was one of repressing communal identities in order to liberate the individual. The denial of a distinctive ethnic identity for the Kurds was thus in accordance with their inclusion in the new society through full citizenship rights and full participation in both society and politics. Eric Rouleau, a leading French journalist and former French ambassador to Ankara who is highly critical of the Turkish government's attitude towards Kurds comments,

> Kurds rarely suffer any discrimination on an individual basis and can reach the highest levels of society. They are senior civil servants, parliamentarians (more than one third of the last parliament was made of ethnic Kurds representing all parties whereas they constitute roughly 20 percent of the population) ministers, and generals. A Kurd was even president of the Republic.[13]

To this one may add that many Kurds have become successful entrepreneurs as well as leading writers and artists. The case of the Kurds in Turkey can thus be seen in terms of two forces operating in completely opposite directions: the centripetal forces of integration and participation based on equal citizenship rights, on the one hand, and the centrifugal forces generated by the rejection of collective ethnic identity in the political system, on the other.

EARLY KURDISH REVOLTS AND SOCIAL CHANGE IN THE SOUTHEAST

Tensions and conflict between Kurds and the state have tended to originate mainly in the southeastern provinces where Kurds constitute the majority of the population. Before the new national borders between Turkey, Iraq, and Syria were drawn, there existed a loosely integrated regional system formed around urban centers such as Aleppo, Mosul, and Baghdad. The economic transactions of the population of Southeast Anatolia, including the Kurds and the other ethnic groups, were oriented mainly to the south, towards Syria and Iraq, rather than to the heartland of Turkey. The new borders imposed new barriers along traditional exchange routes and tribal networks that could only be penetrated by illegal means such as smuggling.[14] In other words, the region was isolated not only from the rest of Anatolia but also from Iraq and Syria, where other Kurdish-speaking people lived.

The Kurdish revolts that took place in 1924, 1926, and 1936-38 had a strong tribal imprint in that they were mobilized by tribal leaders who received support from a few individual Kurdish nationalists.[15] The tribal leaders despised the peasants and were not at all keen on having their help. A second important aspect of the early republican revolts was the predominance of religious themes and concerns over ethnic/nationalist ones in expressing the objectives of the movement.[16] The new republican regime had alienated mainly the religious Kurdish upper classes, for whom the basis of political unity in the Ottoman Empire was Islam rather than language and nationality. A third structural characteristic was that, in suppressing the revolts, the government had effectively mobilized rival Kurdish groups and tribes against the insurgents, such as the Alevi Kurds against the Zaza, and the Sunni Kurds against the Alevi Kurds.[17] The repression of the revolts was followed by the deportation of several thousand Kurdish families to western parts of Anatolia; the majority of deportees were tribal and religious leaders and their relatives.

Tribalism, intra-ethnic divisions among the Kurds, and the deportation of the insurgents by the government forces emerge as elements of the early revolts that recur in the later ones. On the other hand, both the upper-class nature and the distinctively religious character of these early revolts distinguish them from the more recent Kurdish movement, which is more secular in ideology and popular in composition.

In the 1950s and 1960s, Southeast Anatolia was markedly affected by structural changes such as the introduction of multiparty politics, the increased integration of the rural countryside into the market economy, the extension of the road network, and rapid urban growth. The Democrat Party that came to power after winning the general elections of 1950 emphasized the role of Islam as a source of identity and social cohesion among citizens. This new emphasis formed a cultural bridge between the center and the periphery, including the population of the Southeast. The priority given to rural development generally favored landowners, tribal leaders, and rich peasants.[18] The government provided new opportunities for such groups in the form of credit, easy access to new agricultural technologies, and increasing infrastructural investment. Through a mixture of economic and political rewards, the once insurgent, landed upper classes were integrated to a considerable extent into both the market economy and mainstream politics.

Economic change, however, also introduced new divisions in society as the commercialization and mechanization of agriculture created new exploitative relationships in the countryside and caused a mass exodus of displaced peasants into cities, thereby aggravating inequalities between the rich and the poor. Conditions became even more difficult for the laboring poor. For instance, a survey carried out in 1984 shows the rapid increase in the number of landless families: 45 percent of the rural families in the province of Diyarbakır and 47 percent in Urfa were reported to have no land at all.[19] The numbers of unemployed migrants in the cities also began to soar while many who had jobs lived in conditions of abject poverty.

KURDISH NATIONALISM AND THE PKK

The rapid industrialization and urbanization that took place in Turkey in the post-Second World War period and the resultant changes in social class structure in the big cities, fostered in the 1960s and 1970s a vigorous working-class movement and the rise to eminence of leftist political groups and ideologies. In Southeast Anatolia, where a powerful industrial and commercial bourgeois class was largely absent, the enmity of the socialist revolutionaries turned against what was, at that time, called "the feudal remnants," that is, the oppressive landlords, tribal leaders, and reactionary religious forces.[20] These were invariably seen as the agents of imperialism and internal colonialism. The PKK, a Marxist-Leninist revolutionary organization founded in the mid-1970s by Abdullah Öcalan, a revolutionary student then studying at Ankara University, set itself the aim of mobilizing the Kurdish working classes to fight against the feudal landlords in order to eliminate the influence of both Turkish rule and American imperialism in the region.[21]

The PKK's statements of its policy objectives have varied significantly over time according to the context in which they were expounded. These have involved different and contradictory aims: the establishment of a Kurdish state that would unite the Kurds of Turkey, Iraq, and Iran; the full independence of Turkey's Kurds; federal government in a bi-national state where Turks and Kurds would have equal legal status; and political and cultural autonomy for Kurds within the boundaries of a unitary state in Turkey. After the decline of the Soviet Union, however, the organization tended to de-emphasize its socialist revolutionary character.[22] The PKK then began to introduce itself to the West and to international public opinion as a movement seeking a federal solution to the Kurdish problem in Turkey, and voicing the grievances of the Kurds against human rights violations by what it described as a despotic Turkish state. The existence of a highly politicized migrant Kurdish community in Europe has played an important role in this.[23] The growing emphasis on a political solution to the Kurdish problem also reflects the PKK's increased awareness of the immense difficulty of achieving a decisive military victory against the Turkish security forces and the gradual attenuation of its own military muscle in the last few years.

As the socialist fervor in the PKK ideology waned, the organization began to assert more Islamic themes in its propaganda.[24] This can be explained by external factors such as the PKK's improving relations with Iran and its growing immersion in Middle Eastern politics after the Gulf War. More significant, however, have been domestic considerations. The PKK tried to counter the encroachment of the Islamic Welfare Party (WP) on its popular base by appropriating some of the religious themes and symbols that the WP used in its propaganda. Increased emphasis on religiosity also helped the PKK to deny the accusations made by the security agencies that it was being manipulated by the Armenians.

The PKK's military struggle has always had the aim of extending the basis of support among the local population and spreading the Kurdish uprising over a wider geographical area. One specific objective is to demonstrate to the Kurdish people the essential weakness of the feudal landlords and the Turkish military-bureaucratic apparatus. The organization has also aimed at the systematic destruction of the factories, power plants, schools, and infrastructural investments in the region so as to aggravate unemployment, squalor, and poverty among the people, and to increase turbulence, uncertainty, and insecurity in the area.[25] The object of this is to make the local population less dependent on the Turkish government and undermine the legitimacy of the regime and the state. The PKK has kidnapped and murdered engineers and workers and so far has killed 155 teachers. At present, nearly 9,000 schools remain closed in the area.

The PKK has gradually developed a military apparatus, establishing its basis initially in Syria, and then in northern Iraq to exploit the power vacuum created there after the Gulf War. It has also been able to develop a sophisticated political organization involving a number of intelligence and propaganda units, in addition to civilian associations in Turkey and Europe. To operate its military and political apparatus, the PKK draws on multiple sources of finance including voluntary contributions by individuals and organizations both in Turkey and in Europe, extortion from businessmen, armed robbery, aid received from governments supporting the organization, i.e., Syria, and drug trafficking. For instance, in 1992 PKK connections were identified in 23 of the 42 major narcotic operations that took place in the world.[26]

The military muscle and the political power of the organization was at its peak in 1992-93, when it attempted to instigate popular revolts in a number of small towns in Southeast Anatolia. The PKK strategy was to create liberated zones which could then be used as military bases for a regular army in a final war of independence against the Turkish security forces. However, the various revolts initiated by the PKK in towns such as Nusaybin, Cizre, and Şırnak were repressed by the army and this was followed by the forced emigration of the rebels to other towns and cities. These failed urban uprisings marked a turning point in the history of the PKK as many among the local population felt the PKK lacked the strength to resist the security forces in the cities, and saw the practical impossibility of achieving a total military victory against a regular army. In other words, the PKK was unable to succeed in transforming itself from a rural guerrilla force into an organized movement of national liberation. From then on, the organization, while not giving up entirely its usual practice of guerrilla warfare, began to emphasize political propaganda in its campaign, focusing mainly on the theme of human rights violations and, as regards international public opinion, representing its struggle as a search for a political solution to the problem.

THE SECURITY FORCES

Since 1992, the Turkish security forces have mounted their military operations against PKK terrorism using a variety of tactics. Villagers suspected of helping the PKK have been questioned, humiliated, persecuted, and sometimes even tortured, by the security forces. For instance, the so-called Special Teams, made up of nearly 10,000 troops specifically trained for guerrilla warfare, are said to open fire randomly when they meet PKK militants and harass those who they think are collaborating with the PKK. The teams are also held responsible for the several hundred unsolved murders in the region.

The army conscripts who serve in the Southeast are almost all non-Kurds. In the last 15 years, nearly 7,000 troops have been killed in combat and this has aggravated anti-PKK feelings and reinforced Turkish nationalist sentiment among the troops. Furthermore, some members of the Special Teams, as well as some of the civil servants who volunteer to serve in the area, are often ideologically motivated people belonging to the extreme-right National Action Party who abhor those who sympathize with the PKK.

Another military measure taken by the government is the Village Guard system. To counter PKK influence among various sections of the Kurdish population, the government attempted to mobilize local forces into a militia by recruiting poor villagers desperate for an income, providing both weapons and regular salaries for the volunteers.[27] Recruitment on an individual basis, however, has made the Village Guards easy targets for PKK attacks, as evidenced by the massacres of the Village Guards' families, including even suckling babies. Such atrocities, when shown on television, have, as later admitted by Öcalan himself, consolidated in the public mind the image of the PKK as a brutal terrorist organization.

Growing reluctance among rural Kurdish families to join the Village Guards, despite the economic rewards, led the government to look for new arrangements. This new system made possible the recruitment of whole tribes; the government thus began to forge alliances with tribal leaders, who would recruit guards from among their own followers. In turn, the tribal leaders were provided by the government with a lump sum in cash, as well as with guns and ammunition, to distribute to those in their service.

The Village Guard system thus provides scope for membership in the state mediated by corporate bodies, a practice that significantly contradicts the unitary, undifferentiated, and egalitarian republican concept of state membership. By introducing this system, the security forces also aimed to activate the segmentary lineage system, which reinforces divisive tendencies among tribal groups.[28] Sectarian affiliations, as well as religious and linguistic differences, were used to mobilize various groups and tribes against the PKK. Furthermore, the tribal leaders were given easy credit from the state banks and enjoyed preferential treatment in access to government-sponsored projects such as the construction of schools, hospitals, and office blocks. The traditional ruling groups, whose authority was rapidly eroding as a result of changes in the economic structure and the migration of their clientele to cities, thus had the chance to reinstate their power over their tribesmen by using state resources to provide jobs and other opportunities. The collectivization of the Village Guard system, by providing the guarantee of collective defense, immediately caused families belonging to the same tribe to flock to join the Village Guards.[29] The number of Village Guards reached 70,000 by 1997, several times the number of PKK militants. In many villages and towns, the Village Guards have effectively eliminated the PKK. Since the Village Guards know the topographical conditions in the area well, they have been asked to join the military operations carried out against the PKK in both Turkey and northern Iraq.

The same system, however, has created many problems for the government, as well as for the prospects of long-term peace in the region. In the first place, a sizable number of guards have actively collaborated with the PKK, as indicated by nearly 20,000 dismissals for undisclosed reasons. Secondly, many have been convicted of committing ordinary crimes such as robbery, sexual harassment, intimidation, and illegal appropriation of property. Furthermore, some tribal leaders and their followers have become involved in illicit activities such as international drug trafficking. As evidenced by the recent scandals, organized crime has been perpetrated by Mafia-type organizations including the police, politicians, and tribal leaders. Corruption in government and society, largely emanating from the political disorder and turbulence in the Southeast, now poses a major threat to the stability of the political regime in Turkey.[30]

Another drastic policy adopted by the government has been the evacuation of villages, the numbers of which, according to different sources, vary between 2,000 and 3,000. In the main, these villages are those situated along the porous border through which the PKK militants infiltrate Turkey from northern Iraq, or isolated hamlets seen as vulnerable to PKK attacks, influence, and propaganda, or villages actively collaborating with the PKK militants. The evacuation of the villages has deprived the PKK both of the support it used to receive from the local population and of the possibility of hiding its militants among villagers. In the evacuated areas, the security forces have been able to treat all those they come across as suspects, a major deterrent to the easy movement of the guerrillas.[31]

However, tens of thousands of families have been forced to migrate to the cities without being provided with either jobs or houses. Many continue to live in appalling conditions of poverty on the outskirts of cities without receiving any significant help from the government.[32] Diyarbakır, for instance, has become a city of the unemployed: in 1996 the rate of unemployment was as high as 21 percent, while 43 percent of the city's population was casually employed in marginal activities. Only one-third of the workforce had access to social security. Two-thirds of the recent migrants were in search of jobs. Nearly one-half of household heads were earning only the minimum wage while the average family had more than five children. Eighty-seven percent of the city's population was estimated to be living below the poverty line.[33] Such problems create wide resentment among the population as indicated by very high levels of electoral support for radical parties such as the Kurdish nationalist Halkin Demokrasi Partisi (HADEP) and the Islamist WP.

In 1996 and 1997, the PKK suffered heavy losses in a series of military operations carried out by the security forces in Turkey and, particularly, in northern Iraq. In many towns and cities, its military strength was considerably weakened: some of the previously more turbulent settlements now enjoy considerable peace and order. PKK attacks on civilian and military targets have decreased drastically; the militants have retreated to high mountains where conditions are difficult enough for survival, let alone guerrilla warfare. Furthermore, the organization seems to have lost ground in the western parts of Southeast Anatolia where it initiated its struggle, i.e., Antep, Maraş, Adıyaman, and, particularly, in Abdullah Öcalan's hometown of Urfa.

Thus, despite such achievements as its tenacious resistance to a massive military campaign, the building of a body of support in both Turkey and Europe, and the successful internationalization of the Kurdish problem, the PKK cannot be said to have realized its major military objectives. There are several explanations for this. The international context is more favorable for the state in that the collapse of the Soviet Union and declining Russian influence in the Middle East have deprived the PKK of superpower support, while the tribal divisions and continuous warfare among the rival Kurdish factions in northern Iraq have aroused doubts in the Western world as to the viability of an independent Kurdish state. Furthermore, Turkey's increased military control over its borders, coupled with its active collaboration with the Kurdistan Democratic Party (KDP) to confine the PKK in northern Iraq, has worked to the PKK's disadvantage. Also significant have been changes in the military situation: the massive deployment of 250,000 regular troops and 70,000 Village Guards, as well as improvements in the military equipment used in guerrilla warfare and as logistic support for the security forces. The assertion of the supremacy of the security forces over the PKK has won the support of the silent majority, while the state-directed retribalization process has mobilized traditional power groups in the region against the PKK. Moves made by the security forces to deplete the organization's financial sources should also be mentioned; of most significance in this context have been efforts to cut the PKK's revenues from international drug trafficking.

In the short term, the PKK benefited significantly from the increased political instability and economic deterioration that swept across East and Southeast Anatolia; it used this as an opportunity to extend its popular support, and to recruit new militants from the vast pool of unemployed Kurdish youth. In the long term, however, factors such as the flight of capital and qualified manpower, the deterioration in employment conditions and infrastructure, and, most significant of all, the absence of peace, order, and political stability in the area caused massive migrations in which millions of people escaped to either more secure places in the same region or, in even greater numbers, to the prosperous cities and metropolitan centers in western Turkey. The desperate and poverty-stricken population that remained became ever more dependent on the tribal leaders and the security agents. All this has been of little or no benefit to the PKK.

ETHNIC IDENTITY AND SOLIDARITY IN THE URBAN CONTEXT

The majority of the Kurdish population, who now live in the western provinces, remain largely outside the PKK's sphere of influence and tend to integrate with the urban economy and culture at a more rapid pace than in the underdeveloped parts of the East and the Southeast. Place of birth analysis of the 1985 census data shows that 22.8 percent of Istanbul's population is from East and Southeast Turkey—a substantial number, but certainly not all, of whom are Kurds. By 1990, this had reached 25 percent for Istanbul, 24.4 percent for Izmir, and 12 percent for Ankara. Furthermore, the three major Mediterranean cities of Adana, Mersin, and Antalya have also emerged in the 1990s as major destinations for migrants from eastern provinces.[34]

Studies indicate that metropolitan life has a profound impact on the lives, attitudes, and values of Kurds, leading towards both increased integration and the assertion of cultural distinctiveness. For instance, the majority of the migrants, and almost all of their children, know and speak Turkish. Here the implication is that there is no communication barrier between Kurds and other groups. More significant is the fact that sizable numbers of Kurds achieve upward social mobility through education and, particularly, entrepreneurship; by emulating middle-class values and styles, such groups integrate with urban society and institutions with greater ease.[35] The absence of negative discrimination in such areas as the labor market, business, housing provision, education, and politics all seem to contribute to this. A recent survey carried out amongst the migrant Kurds indicates that slightly more than half of these migrants were able to become home-owners, albeit often in squatter housing areas. The rate of unemployment among the migrant population is 12.4 percent, a figure that compares favorably with the figures in the economically backward southeastern and eastern provinces. Moreover, 64 percent of the respondents stated that they have access to social security. Thus, the vast majority tend to evaluate their living conditions in the city as superior to that in the rural areas they left and to which they do not consider returning.[36]

Despite close relations among migrants of the same origin and the maintenance of ties of solidarity among co-ethnics, Kurds tend to have considerable intercourse with other sections of the population, taking part in a wide range of urban and public activities. In the first place, religion, specifically Sunni Islam, is a powerful source of identity and solidarity for all devout people, irrespective of their ethnic backgrounds. Thus, the migrant communities living in the squatter housing areas frequently come together around mosque-centered activities such as funerals, prayers, sermons in the mosques, and voluntary associations initiated by leaders and authorities. These activities reinforce feelings of belonging and common identity among the participants. Secondly, the migrants have many common interests such as gaining authorization for land and infrastructural services. These require a common stance vis-à-vis local authorities. Third, in the squatter housing areas, neighbors tend to establish relationships with each other; women especially, whose freedom of movement is restricted to a narrow locality, tend to become good friends with their neighbors without taking social background differences into consideration. The sharing of similar experiences in urban life, as well as common work experience, also facilitates intercourse among diverse ethnic and religious groups.[37] Furthermore, intermarriage among Sunni groups is an extremely widespread practice: in the country as a whole, there are reported to be well over one million marriages between Kurds and Turks.

Kurds, however, also emphasize their differences. First, traditional cultural traits that can be traced back to the tribal society, such as strict submission to authority, patriarchal relations, and absolute loyalty to the kinship group, are redefined and reproduced in the urban context. The state-supported retribalization process and the emergence of a Kurdish business stratum have reinforced primordial relations among superiors and subordinates under new linkage systems. Some examples include patronage networks in party politics, cooperation in Mafia-type organizations, ethnic monopolization of economic activities, and the employment of poor migrants as cheap laborers by Kurdish contractors.

Communitarian tendencies are quite marked among migrant Kurds, who tend to establish monopolies to exclude others from entering particular sections of the market. Similarly, ethnic communities encourage voting for familiar candidates and political parties that keep strong Kurdish representations in local and general elections. The emphasis on identity on the part of some ethnic groups tends to stimulate the assertion of ethnic identity and group solidarity among rival groups that compete for similar resources. Ethnic networks are highly useful as sources of knowledge and points of contact in the case of such urgent matters as finding jobs and housing, and dealing with the bureaucracy. People tend to trust and depend on their relatives, co-villagers and co-ethnics even more so in the urban context. In all these, the segmented lineage system, according to which all individuals are regarded as members of the tribe and are assigned specific obligations to their lineage group as opposed to the "other side," emerges as an essential source of social cohesion and solidarity.

Ethnic relations between the Kurds and other groups in the cities can involve tensions and conflict. Some Kurds feel that they are victims of the system and cannot get their share of the cake. Some tend to perceive exclusion in cultural rather than economic terms, asserting that institutional recognition of Kurdish identity is indispensable for achieving improvements in the material situation of the Kurds in Turkey. Such politicized Kurds are highly critical of the attitude of the security forces in the Southeast, as well as of the state towards the Kurds in general, arguing that the only way to end the ongoing conflict is to give Kurds cultural autonomy. Paradoxically, however, these tend to be the most urbanized Kurds, who often do not speak Kurdish and categorically reject the idea of going back to their home towns. In the survey mentioned above, only 15 percent of the respondents complained about negative discrimination by Turks and other ethnic groups. The picture that emerges is one in which the longer the length of time spent in the city and the higher the level of income and education, the happier the Kurd. Finally, only 4.8 percent said that they find maintaining a Turkish identity —in the non-ethnic sense—humiliating, while the majority mention that they enjoy having both Turkish and Kurdish identities.[38]

There are a number of identifiable political attitudes among Kurds living in western Anatolian cities. In the 1995 general elections, the Kurdish nationalist party HADEP, generally considered by many foreign observers and liberal intellectuals in Turkey to be the representative party of the Turkish Kurds, took only 4.1 percent of the vote nationally. Furthermore, nearly half of their votes were cast for the socialist parties in electoral alliance with HADEP. These results led foreign observers especially to question whether the PKK, or even HADEP, could really represent the majority of Kurds in Turkey. Electoral support for HADEP was concentrated in a few provinces in the Southeast, while the majority of the Kurds living in the western provinces voted for the WP and other mainstream political parties on the left and right. The election results indicated that the majority of the Kurds did not aim for secession, but aimed to consolidate their position in urban society, preferring not to be involved in radical nationalism.

The obvious contrast between the migrant Kurds in the west and those living in the conflict ridden areas in the Southeast shows that the popular basis of radical Kurdish nationalism tends to erode rapidly with the increased urbanization and economic integration of the Kurdish population.[39]

THE INTERNATIONAL DIMENSION

The Kurdish ethno-nationalist activity that gained vigor and momentum in the 1980s and early 1990s was deeply affected by changes and developments that took place in both the regional and the wider international context. Of primary significance here was the Gulf War and its extremely heavy cost to Turkey. Turkey is estimated to have lost at least $35 billion as a result of the closure of the oil pipeline and the economic embargo imposed on Iraq: these events deprived Turkey of the pipeline revenues, cheap Iraqi oil, and a major trading partner. Trade with Iraq was the major income source for millions of families living in the Southeast. As trade came to a sudden halt in 1991, poverty and unemployment began to soar in the region, a development from which the PKK benefited enormously. Another negative impact of the Gulf War on Turkey was the power vacuum that emerged in northern Iraq. This enabled the PKK to establish new military camps in the region and to infiltrate units involving ever growing numbers of militants through the Turkish-Iraqi border—hence the enormous increase in PKK activity in the aftermath of the Gulf War.

The Kurdish problem increasingly became a regional and international problem after the Gulf War as new regional actors and international powers began to interfere in the affairs of Iraq. Iran, Syria, Iraq, and Turkey all tried to mobilize rival Kurdish factions in the area against each other, thereby causing a number of proxy wars, the most serious of which took place in September 1996 between the Baghdad-supported KDP and the Patriots' Union of Kurdistan (PUK) supported by Iran. The clashes ended with a clear victory for Mas'ud Barzani, chairman of the KDP and, as a consequence, the Talabani PUK forces retreated to Iran. The growing links between Iran, the PUK, and the PKK have also contributed to a deterioration in diplomatic relations between Iran and Turkey.

In 1997, the Turkish security forces organized two major offensives, backed by heavy air activity, to destroy the PKK camps in northern Iraq. Several thousand PKK militants were killed and the major guerrilla camps in the region were destroyed. In both operations, the KDP gave its active support to the Turkish military. Such intrusions by Turkey and Iran into Iraqi territory were protested by the Baghdad government, which described the situation as a violation of its sovereign rights. Western, and specifically the United States, intervention in northern Iraq to implement the UN sanctions and the no-fly zone also had the aim of providing support for Kurds struggling for autonomy in Iraq. This policy changed after the second Gulf crisis in 1996, when the fighting between rival tribal groups ended with the KDP inviting support from Iraqi forces against the rival factions, precipitating the withdrawal of United States forces from northern Iraq.[40]

Turkey has several policy objectives with regard to northern Iraq.[41] In the first place, it does not consider the annexation of northern Iraq. Secondly, the top priority has always been the prevention of the establishment of a fully autonomous Kurdish entity in northern Iraq. Thirdly, Turkey aims to minimize all outside intervention and influence in this area by both regional and Western powers. All three aims converge with the maintenance of the territorial unity of Iraq. Within this broad framework, however, there are also a few tactical and strategic considerations. One is to prevent the escalation of the conflict between the KDP and the PUK, which has given increased scope for maneuver to the PKK. Turkey does not seem supportive of the idea of Baghdad establishing full control over northern Iraq, for the reason that it may, like Syria, lend support to the PKK to instigate political unrest in Turkey. Despite this, Turkey has fully supported efforts to reopen the oil pipeline, which would enable Iraq to export its oil and reintegrate into the world economy, on the assumption that increased trade with Iraq would generate more employment and greater prosperity in the Southeast.[42]

The main source of external support for the PKK has, since its very beginning, been from Syria. Sources close to the PKK indicate the vital importance of this support in such areas as its maintenance of a military basis in the Bekaa Valley, financial aid, the issue of passports and identity cards for the leaders of the organization, and the establishment of links between the PKK and the representatives of other countries. A widely held view in Turkey is that Syria, without any serious economic costs or military risks, has instigated political instability in Turkey by giving active support to the PKK, in retaliation against Turkey building dams on the Tigris and the Euphrates, a process that is gradually increasing Turkey's control over the water supplies in the region.[43]

A very important international dimension of the Kurdish problem is the growing emphasis on Kurdish identity and the rapid spread of Kurdish nationalist organizations in Europe, where several hundred thousand Kurds from Turkey live.[44] Although the majority went there as migrant workers, in the 1980s and 1990s the PKK began to smuggle Kurds desperate for jobs and money into European countries as refugees seeking asylum, and was thereby able to build a popular base among the Kurdish community. The PKK also benefited considerably from the attitudes and policies of European governments towards the promotion of multiculturalism. Attempts by countries such as Sweden to incorporate migrants, not as individuals but as collectivities based on ethnic and religious origin,[45] have created and reinforced Kurdish national awareness and nationalist activities. The official emphasis on the national identities of the immigrant communities is often a compensation for the relatively low level of welfare among these groups and their denial of full citizenship rights. In other words, political exclusion or incomplete incorporation by the host countries tends to strengthen both ethnic solidarity and relations with the home country and its problems. One highly visible outcome of this policy is that, while the Kurds easily intermingle with other ethnic groups in the western cities of Turkey, in Europe they tend to separate themselves from other immigrant communities from Turkey.

The PKK organizes demonstrations, meetings, conferences, and various lobbying activities in Europe to communicate its views to political parties, governments, and non-governmental organizations. Due to the absence of guerrilla activity and the potential for articulating their interest in democratic platforms, the PKK has been able to introduce its aims in primarily political terms, stressing human rights violations and the demands of the Kurds for political autonomy within Turkey. As a result of these developments, the center of gravity for Kurdish nationalism has increasingly moved towards Europe and away from the Kurdish heartlands.

POLITICAL ATTITUDES TOWARDS THE KURDISH PROBLEM

The Turkish government's attitude towards solving the PKK problem has tended to follow a few established patterns. A political solution that involves a dialogue with the PKK, and a federal system of government based upon official recognition of two different nations with equal constitutional rights, is categorically rejected. Successive governments have emphasized that their target is the complete elimination of the military power, political support, and the ideological influence of the PKK. The policy implications of this approach have consisted of extending military mobilization in the area, protecting the borders against infiltration, weakening the organization's logistic support, and diplomatic efforts to break its ties with other countries.

The government's attitude to the wider Kurdish problem, however, has changed significantly over time. Until the 1990s, the approach was either one of silence or open denial of the existence of a Kurdish population in Turkey. Against mounting pressure both from inside the country and from the Western world, the official view, which asserted that Kurds were actually ethnic Turks, was replaced by one that did accept the existence of a Kurdish ethnic group as only one among a total of 27 ethnic groups in Turkey. The new approach also emphasizes that these groups have lived peacefully together for centuries, the Turks and Kurds having for instance fought the war of independence against imperialist powers side by side. Similarly, the diversity of ethnic origins among the people of Anatolia is stressed in order to show that people of diverse stocks and backgrounds have mixed to such an extent that any claim on ethnic and racial purity is totally unjustified. The corollary of this statement is that

Turkishness needs to be defined not in ethnic but in constitutional terms, to refer to a common political bond among the citizens of the Turkish Republic.

In the last few years, the government has begun to show increased sensitivity towards the social and economic problems of the local population and the issue of the economic development of the region. The $32 billion GAP project involves building of 17 hydroelectric power plants and 17 irrigation schemes, which will cover 9.5 percent of Turkey's total land area.[46] Future governments are likely to concentrate on socioeconomic policies to complement what has so far amounted to an essentially military campaign against the PKK.

Gradually, the state, political parties, and public opinion have begun to recognize the existence of some form of Kurdish ethnicity and identity in Turkey. The issue has been discussed on private television channels and in the leading newspapers. Books published in Kurdish, studies on Kurds, and journals and newspapers propagating Kurdish nationalism and even the PKK point of view, have begun to appear in increasing numbers on the shelves and in windows of bookstores and shops in the big cities. HADEP, well known for its close associations with the PKK, participated in the 1995 general elections. Throughout the 1990s, liberal attitudes to matters of Kurdish identity have become more widespread. Indeed, only several years ago a bare mention of Kurdish ethnicity in public was interpreted by the authorities as a major offense against the law and the state. The use of the Kurdish language and discussion of Kurdish issues is increasingly, albeit quietly, tolerated by the authorities. What still remain as major problems, however, are various clauses in Turkish law that restrict freedom of speech and expression, and the arbitrary decisions and practices of government officials and security agents that involve human rights violations.

The views of politicians and intellectuals on the Kurdish problem vary. The nationalist parties on the extreme right and conservative politicians in the center-right parties tend to reject the notion of a Kurdish ethnic entity in Turkey and attribute the ongoing turbulence to mainly external factors.

The WP had a radically different approach to the problem, one essentially based on subsuming all ethnic identities (including both Kurdish and Turkish) under a broader Islamic one. This concept is particularly inspired by the Ottoman notion of a supra-ethnic and supra-nationalist Islamic community. The republican secularization reforms that eradicated the common religious bond among Muslim groups of diverse ethnic backgrounds in Turkey are believed to have reinvigorated primitive tribal instincts engendering inter-ethnic rivalry and conflict. The WP had a wide constituency among the Kurds. The party's efforts towards providing social security, jobs, and services for the poor proved highly effective in winning the support of some Kurds. Historically, Islam was the primary source of identity among the Kurds and the axis around which the everyday life of the Kurdish culture was organized. In the present context, Islamic ideology becomes a safe haven for Kurds who want to retain their distinctive identity under the protective umbrella of a superior one. As such, the WP was able to survive even in the turbulent provinces in the Southeast, challenging the electoral base of HADEP.

Bülent Ecevit, the leader of the Democratic Left Party (DLP), also has a distinctive interpretation of the problem. According to his view, the underlying reason for what is supposedly a Kurdish problem is actually one of social inequality generated by oppressive landlordism and tribalism in the Southeast. The priority in the DLP approach is immediate and comprehensive land reform to undermine the political and economic power of the landlords and to redistribute the land among the needy peasants. The abolition of the Village Guard system is seen as a necessary step towards the dismantling of the hierarchical tribal structures. Ecevit argues that had the problem really been one of Kurdish ethno-nationalism, then the same Kurds who live in the western parts of the country would also have revolted against the state. The political quietism of Kurds in the West is seen as sufficient proof for the argument that extremes of class inequalities and class polarization, that is, the historically and geographically specific aspects of the social structure in the Southeast, are the major reasons for Kurdish unrest. Thus, the emphasis in this perspective is on social class and economic reform rather than ethnicity and national self-determination.[47]

The social democratic Republican Peoples Party (RPP) adopts a liberal approach to the Kurdish problem, underlining institutional reforms aimed at the recognition of Kurdish identity. The RPP also advocates, with other liberal intellectuals, a set of measures that would enable Kurds to exercise cultural and political autonomy, such as decentralization to strengthen local participation in politics. The party also shows great sensitivity to the issue of human rights violations.[48] The RPP view is very close to what various political groups and parties on the left, as well as liberal intellectuals and writers, call a "democratic solution." In this view, the emphasis is laid on political reforms that would enable the regular participation of moderate Kurdish groups in mainstream politics. The set of policy measures advocated would include devolution of power to local authorities, the strengthening of local representative institutions, teaching Kurdish —at least as an optional language course—in schools, and the establishment of a Kurdish institute of languages and history. Such measures are assumed to create a new Kurdish leadership that would be an alternative to the PKK.[49]

The Kurdish problem and the turbulence caused by the PKK continue to generate multiple security threats for Turkey. First, the clashes between the security forces and the PKK militants has had a huge human cost, involving tens of thousands of deaths and casualties. Secondly, the conflicts make the country highly vulnerable to manipulation by outside forces. Thirdly, the Kurdish problem places ever increasing strains on Turkey's relations with the Western world and the European Union (EU) in particular, especially with regard to human rights. Fourth, political unrest causes political radicalism in the country, which, in turn, tends to erode the legitimacy of the regime. Finally, the huge military cost, added to deteriorating relations with some neighboring countries, becomes a major bottleneck for the economy, causing ever-growing budget deficits, high inflation, and reduced capacity for investment in education, health, and infrastructure.[50]

Why, then, has it proved so difficult for the government and other political actors to come up with a working solution? One explanation put forward by the government is the political instability in the region and the external support that the PKK obtains from rival states such as Syria, Greece, Iran, and Russia. Liberal intellectuals writing in the press blame the insistence on a military solution to the problem, which they say rules out political initiatives. To understand the present state of deadlock in politics, at least two other factors need to be considered.

To begin with, the vast majority of the political elite, from almost all political parties, tend to identify the PKK as a terrorist organization and, very much in accord with the military, they refuse to negotiate peace terms with the PKK leadership. Furthermore, the political parties fear that they may lose votes if they enter a negotiation process that involves the PKK.

Secondly, the problem is linked with the class structure in the east and the nature of political leadership among the Kurds. In East and Southeast Anatolia, there is, on the whole, an absence of powerful social groups that can play a leadership role in mobilizing the people, gain respectability in the eyes of the government authorities, and take initiatives in proposing sound democratic solutions to the existing problems. The tribal leadership stratum that moved to the cities is either too corrupt or too dependent on the state to be trusted by all the parties involved and, thus, play a mediating role. Religious leaders have wide legitimacy among the Kurdish people but their activities are always viewed with suspicion by the secularist state. The new middle class, as represented by a small stratum of politicized professionals such as lawyers and doctors, is as yet too weak to establish itself as a dominant group. As a result, in many small towns and cities in the region, the local people often find themselves torn between two combating forces, the security agents and the PKK. There is a profound lack of intermediate groups and associations.

Can this power vacuum be filled? The acceleration of economic development in the western provinces of the Southeast might provide a chance. The intensification of the GAP process has already set in motion such processes as an increase in agricultural productivity, a transfer of wealth from primary to other sectors of the economy, and a rapid growth in agro-businesses and industries. Industrialization in the region has also gained pace as a result of the relocation of export-oriented manufacturing from the coastal parts of the country to the peripheral areas, among which southeastern provinces such as Antep, Urfa, Adıyaman, Maraş and Malatya are prominent. Agricultural and industrial development have an important impact in terms of the alleviation of such problems as poverty and unemployment, but the political implications are even more profound. The newly booming towns are witnessing the emergence of new entrepreneurial and professional groups that are gradually consolidating their power and influence. Their expectations and interests are different from those of the old power groups and, in their relations with the government and other groups in society, they have different approaches and use different styles of negotiation. Thus, their demands tend more to the economic, they emphasize dialogue, and their relations with other parts of the country are complementary in nature. With the advent of industrialization, the economies of some provinces in the Southeast are, for the first time in history, rapidly integrating with the western parts of Turkey. Meanwhile, the entrepreneurial classes are increasingly marginalizing the *tarikat* shaykhs, tribal leaders, professional politicians, and rural guerrillas. In the coming years, the new industrial elite can play a more active role in negotiating peace, in which it has a big stake, with the political parties and other influential groups in Turkey.

CONCLUSION

The threat to the security of the state that emanates from a separatist ethno-nationalist movement is an extremely complex one, involving a multitude of dimensions, factors, and processes. In the first place, the problem has domestic, regional, and international aspects, none of which are less important than, and therefore not immediately reducible to, the others. Furthermore, developments taking place in one sphere have a marked impact on others. For instance, a new crisis in the Gulf might easily change all parameters of the conflict. Secondly, the debate that centers around the question of whether the PKK and the ongoing turbulence in the Southeast stem from socioeconomic or politico-cultural factors is equally futile since, again, the two are closely intertwined. Kurds do have full citizenship rights in Turkey and structural discrimination against them does not exist. However, the vast majority of the Kurds who have recently migrated to towns and cities do not have access to proper jobs, decent houses, or social security—although, in this respect, their situation is not very different from that of other migrant communities. In other words, citizenship exists on paper only, as it does not, in reality, guarantee certain basic rights. As trends in the big cities of western Anatolia indicate, those Kurds able to attain a reasonable level of economic and social security tend to integrate into society more easily. In the case of the excluded groups the manifestation of ethnic identity and solidarity, alongside the demand for the recognition of collective ethnic identity, becomes an integral means of demanding citizenship rights that are essentially socioeconomic in nature. However, while both tend to fuel and aggravate this activity, neither the assertion of ethnic identity nor the socioeconomic problems of the Kurds provide immediate and sufficient explanation of the intensity of the guerrilla warfare. This requires taking into account such aspects as class inequalities, the nature of the confrontation between the security forces and the PKK, and the role of international actors.

The Kurdish unrest also has a contextual dimension to it. In the media and in popular use, the reference is almost always to the "Southeastern Problem." Indeed, the low intensity war, which has been going on for years, does have strictly territorial boundaries. However, the greatest proportion of the Kurds now live in the western parts of the country and several hundred thousand more live in Europe. Furthermore, especially since the Gulf War, northern Iraq has emerged as a new and significant factor. Although a Kurdish identity is a common denominator, the ways the Kurds reveal their identities, as well as their relations with other groups and states, are considerably different in all the four different contexts mentioned above. For instance, the Kurds have peaceful relations with other groups and the states involved both in western Turkey and in Europe, but in the case of the former locus they tend to emphasize their similarities with other groups, whereas in Europe the stress is on distinctive elements of their identity and Kurdish ethno-nationalism. Such divergent tendencies influence the Kurdish population living in the Southeast in different ways. Thus, although the separatist guerrilla activity is a regionally specific phenomenon, the Southeast, where proportionately greater numbers of Kurds live, cannot be conceived in isolation from the other parts of the country and the world. It needs to be emphasized that even the Southeast is far from being a socially, economically, and politically homogeneous area; the more prosperous and populous provinces towards the west of this particular region have already begun to enjoy peace, stability, and order as they industrialize, urbanize, and economically integrate with the other parts of the country. The implication is not only that there is a decline in the intensity of military conflict but that it is becoming confined to a narrower locality.

Both the problem of separatism and the ethnic problems of the Kurds in Turkey need to be perceived in their full complexity, involving the domestic and international, politico-cultural and socioeconomic, and contextual dimensions. This requires moving a step beyond a single-minded focus on terror and its external manipulation and state-centric accounts of security problems, to conceptualizations and analyses that take into account the whole multitude of social, economic, and political aspects and variables.

NOTES

1. John F. Stack, *Ethnic Identities in a Transnational World* (Westport, Conn.: Greenwood Press, 1981).

2. Bennett, "Security Bargaining and the End of Laterstate Rivalry," *International Studies Quarterly* 40, no. 2 (1996): 157-84.

3. B. Bobrow, "Complex Insecurity: Implications of a Sobering Metaphor," *International Studies Quarterly* 40, no. 4 (1996): 435-50.

4. Peter Alford Andrews, ed., *Ethnic Groups in the Republic of Turkey* (Weisbaden: Reichart, 1989); Mehrdad R. Izady, *The Kurds* (Washington, D.C.: Taylor and Francis, 1992).

5. Cynthia H. Enloe, *Ethnic Soldiers: State Security in Divided Societies* (Harmondsworth, U.K.: Penguin, 1980).

6. Ted Robert Gurr and Barbara Harff, *Ethnic Conflict in World Politics* (Boulder, Colo.: Westiew, 1994).

7. Martin van Bruinessen, *Agha, Shaikh, and State: On the Social and Political Organization of Kurdistan* (Utrecht: University of Utrecht, 1978).

8. Dr. Fritz, *Kürtlerin Tarihi* (Istanbul: Hasat Yayınları, 1992).

9. Celile Celil, *XIX Yüzyıl Osmanlı Imparatorluğunda Kürtler* (Ankara: Öz-Ge Yayınları, 1992).

10. Bruinessen, *Agha, Shaikh, and State.*

11. Kemal Kirişçi and Gareth M. Winrow, *Kürt Sorunu; Kökeni ve Gelişimi* (Istanbul: Tarih Vakfı Yurt Yayınları, 1997).

12. J. Brown, "The Turkish Imbroglio: Its Kurds," American Academy of Political and Social Science, *Annals* (September 1995): 541.

13. Eric Rouleau, "Turkey: Beyond Ataturk," *Foreign Policy* 103 (1996): 76.

14. M. Yeğen, "The Turkish State Discourse and the Exclusion of Kurdish Identity," *Middle Eastern Studies* 32, no. 2 (April 1996).

15. Uğur Mumcu, *Kürt Islam Ayaklanması* (Ankara: Tekin Yayınevi, 1991).

16. Philip Robins, "The Overland State: Turkish Policy and the Kurdish Issue," *International Affairs* 69, no. 3 (1993): 657-76.

17. P. J. Bumpke, "The Kurdish Alevis: Boundaries and Perceptions," in Andrews, *Ethnic Groups,* 514.

18. David McDowall, *A Modern History of the Kurds* (London: I. B. Tauris, 1996).

19. Mustafa Sönmez, *Doğu Anadolu'nun Hikayesi: Ekonomik ve Sosyal Tarih* (Ankara: Arkadaş Yayınevi, 1992).

20. Martin van Bruinessen, "Gerilla Savaşı ve Siyasi Cinayet Arasında: Kürdistan İşçi Partisi," in *Kürdistan Üzerine Yazılar* (Istanbul: İletişim, 1992), 361.

21. İ. İmset, PKK: *Ayrılıkçı Şiddetin 20 Yılı (1973-1992)* (Ankara: Turkish Daily News Publications, 1993); Michael M. Gunter, *The Kurds in Turkey: A Political Dilemma* (Boulder, Colo.: Westview, 1990).

22. S. Button, "Turkey Struggles with Kurdish Separatism," *Military Review* (December 1994/January 1995): 70-79.

23. Gunter, *Kurds in Turkey.*

24. Ömer Vehbi Hatipoğlu, *Bir Başka Açıdan Kürt Sorunu* (Ankara: Mesaj Yayın, 1992).

25. İmset, PKK.

26. Ibid.

27. M. A. Kışlalı, *Güneydoğu Düşük Yoğunlu Çatışma* (Ankara: Ümit Yayıncılık, 1996.

28. L. Yalçın-Heckmann, "Kurdish Tribal Organization and Local Political Processes," in *Turkish State, Turkish Society,* ed. Andrew Finkel and Nükhet Sirman (London: Routledge, 1990).

29. Kışlalı, *Güneydoğu Düşük Yoğunlu Çatışma;* McDowall, *Modern History of the Kurds.*

30. Türkiye Odalar ve Borsalar Birliği (TOBB), *Doğu Sorunu: Teşhisler ve Tesbitler, Özel Araştırma Raporu,* Stratejik Araştırmalar Dizisi: 1 (Ankara: TOBB, 1995), 93.

31. Kışlalı, *Güneydoğu Düşük Yoğunlu Çatışma.*

32. Atilla Göktürk, "Zorunlu Göç ve bir Kent: Van," in Devlet İstatistik Enstitüsü, *II Ulusal Sosyoloji Kongresi: Toplum ve Göç, Sosyoloji Derneği Yayın no. 5,* T. C. Başbakanlık Devlet İstatistik Enstitüsü Yayın no. 2046 (Ankara, 1997); Ahmet Bilgili and Feramuz Aydoğan, "Doğu Anadolu Bölgesinde Zorunlu Göç Olgusunun Sosyolojik Çözümlemesi: Van Örneği," in ibid.

33. Türk Mühendis ve Mimar Odaları Birliği (TMMOB), *Bölgeiçi Zorunlu Göçten Kaynaklanan Toplumsal Sorunların Diyarbakır Kenti Ölçeğinde Araştırılması,* (Ankara: TMMOB, 1996).

34. Günay Anadolu Projesi (GAP) Research Team, *Population Movements in the Southern Anatolia Project Region* (Ankara: Middle East Technical University, Department of Sociology, 1994), 173-77.

35. Ayşe Güneş-Ayata, "Geleneksel ve Modern Dayanışma," in *Gecekondularda Ailelerarası Geleneksel Dayanışmanın Çağdaş Organizasyonlara Dönüşümü,* T. C. Başbakanlık Kadın ve Sosyal Hizmetler Müsteşarlğı Yayınları no. 75 (Ankara, 1993).

36. Ü Özdağ, *Güneydoğu Anadolu Bölgesi'nde Doğu ve Güneydoğu Anadolu'dan Batı'ya Göç Edenlerde Kültürel Yapı ve Kültürel Kimlik Sorunu* (Ankara: Türk Metal-İş Sendikası Yayınları, 1995).

37. Birsen Gökçe, "Doğu ve Güneydoğu Anadolu'da Göç Konusunda Yapılmış Çalışmaların Metod Açısından Değerlendirilmesi," in Devlet İstatistik Enstitüsü, *II Ulusal Sosyoloji Kongresi: Toplum ve Göç, Sosyoloji Derneği Yayın no. 5,* T .C. Başbakanlık Devler İstatistik Enstitüsü Yayın no.2046 (Ankara, 1997).

38. Özdağ, *Güneydoğu Anadolu Bölgesi'nde Doğu.*

39. Murat Şeker, "Survey on Ethnic and Religious Identity in Turkey," (Mimeo, 1998).

40. McDowall, *Modern History of the Kurds.*

41. Nur Bilge Criss, "The Nature of PKK Terrorism in Turkey," *Studies in Conflict and Terrorism* 18 (1995): 17-37.

42. Balı Mahmut Aykan, "Turkey's Policy in Northern Iraq, 1991-95," *Middle Eastern Studies* 32, no. 4 (October 1996): 343-66.

43. Bruinessen, "Gerilla Savaşı ve Siyasi Cinayet Arasında," 367.

44. Paul B. Henze, *Turkey toward the Twenty-First Century* (Santa Monica, Calif.: Rand, 1992).

45. Yasemin Nuhoğlu Soysal, *Limits of Citizenship: Migrants and Postnational Membership in Europe* (Chicago: University of Chicago Press, 1994).

46. Gün Kut, "Burning Waters: The Hydropolitics of the Euphrates and Tigris," *New Perspectives on Turkey* 9 (fall 1993): 1-19.

47. Demokratik Sol Parti, *Demokratik Sol Parti Program* (Ankara: Sistem Ofset, n.d.).

48. Sosyaldemokrat Halkçı Parti, *Güneydoğu Raporu* (Ankara: Sosyaldemokrat Halkçı Parti, 1989).

49. Metin Sever, *Kürt Sorunu: Aydınlarımız ne Düşünüyor* (İstanbul: Cem Yayınevi, 1992).

50. Henri Barkey and Graham Fuller, *Turkey's Kurdish Question* (Lanham, Md.: Rowman and Littlefield, 1998).

PART III:
ECONOMIC CAPABILITIES

CHAPTER SEVEN

Economic Improvement in the Middle East: A Genuine Move Forward or Preservation of the Status Quo?

SOHRAB SHAHABI AND FARIDEH FARHI

*U*ncertain times demand a rethinking of categories to which one has become accustomed. The recent eruptions in the established international order and traditional practices of statecraft have given an air of nostalgia to many customary modes of analysis used in international politics. Even basic concepts in international relations such as the state, security, war, danger, and sovereignty are being questioned and alternative conceptualizations of these categories put forward. One area receiving much attention is related to national security. As has been repeatedly noted, during the Cold War superpower competition underscored the definition of security in military terms. Security was said to have been determined by the requirements of a preexisting sovereign state and war or military competition was conducted in its name as a response to an objective danger—something that was presumably easily identifiable, if not evident, and almost always related to threats to the territory, society, or governmental functions of the threatened state.

In the Middle East, such an understanding of security is, of course, bound to continue as an important element of state relationships. Boundary conflicts and memories of very recent wars assure the predominance of a territorially-based and military-directed definition of security. Furthermore, the problem of political legitimation assures the continued reliance on the use of external threats as a means to secure domestic peace and control. Nevertheless, there are important signs that such a limited understanding of security is no longer deemed sufficient, even in the Middle East. The concept of regional security is gaining ground over the traditional concept of national security and economic issues are receiving more attention as "critical" mechanisms through which the security of individual states and regimes, as well as the region, can be realized over the long run. In other words, ideas such as increase of productivity, economic reform, the integration of regional and international markets, and protection of income sources are becoming part of the national security lexicon. Accordingly, in the past few years, several proposals have been put forth from a variety of corners, calling essentially for an economic overhaul of the Middle East, a region which is generally considered to be not very well integrated and facing a dark future if something is not done to deal with its economy-related problems.

The purpose of this chapter is to unpack these recent proposals in the light of the changing political and socioeconomic environment of the Middle East. The concerns of these proposals will be deciphered and the solutions offered will be critically evaluated. It will be argued that these proposals tend to ignore certain political facts about the region, consciously or unconsciously. They tend to be either impossible to implement or essentially a recipe for the maintenance of the current balance of power within countries as well as the region in general. The chapter will end with several suggestions as to the kind of considerations a viable plan for economic improvement in the Middle East must take into account.

THE CHANGING ENVIRONMENT OF THE MIDDLE EAST

Today the study of the Middle East must begin by looking at four dynamic processes that are actively changing the political and socioeconomic map of the region: the end of the Cold War, the so-called peace process, the revival of Islam, and the deteriorating economic position of the region vis-à-vis other regions of the world.[1] How are these four processes related and in what ways do their interplay affect the security of the region and the possibility of economic improvement in the future?

The Cold War and the Arab-Israeli conflict closed off the possibility of fundamental political change in the region for almost half a century, creating a situation in which most Middle Eastern governments could safely deny their people participation in the running of their countries. Cold War rivalry could be manipulated by individual rulers in a variety of ways to guarantee credible foreign support. The Arab-Israeli conflict could be used to arouse public emotion and sympathy against outsiders and divert it from domestic concerns. Finally, the oil boom of the 1970s had a spillover effect throughout the Middle East, creating yet another favorable resource for those in power. All these worked hand in hand to allay any perceived need for the modernization of political structures and institutions in individual countries.[2]

Since the 1980s, however, conditions in the Middle East have changed drastically. The Islamic revolution in Iran unleashed a wave of popular demands in the region. Middle Eastern rulers have been notorious for using supranational sentiments to consolidate their power. In other words, supranational sentiments were a means to buttress state power. Now, though, these sentiments are being used to contest the manner of the state's hold over society and, as such, rather than being a source of legitimation, ways are being sought in which they might be asserted independently of the state, even in those societies in which these sentiments have been part of the state's ideological apparatus.

On another front, the Camp David Accords effectively eliminated the possibility of another Arab-Israeli war, and the initiation of the peace process, even if ultimately unsuccessful, has taken away from the Arab rulers the ever-present alibi or political asset they had for gaining the emotional and political support of the Arab masses. Indeed, as will be argued later, increasingly the rulers in the Middle East are in need of new political assets in order to neutralize the anger, dissatisfaction, and disillusionment of their aspiring citizens.[3]

The end of Cold War rivalry has also eliminated yet another space in which Middle Eastern rulers could maneuver. Joining the peace process, and hence the Western camp, is presented as the only positive alternative available to individual countries, effectively undermining the kind of legitimacy that accrued to individual Middle Eastern leaders through their acumen and ability to play one superpower against another. Finally, the reversal of the oil boom in the 1980s, especially since 1985, and the staggering cost of the two Gulf Wars have disrupted not only the spillover effect of the oil boom (via movement of labor and worker remittances) but also the economies of the oil-rich states, once considered to run so smoothly. Instead of peace and prosperity, balance of payments problems accompanied by indebtedness, runaway inflation and consequent dislocations in domestic production, and the state's evident incapacity to extract revenues from its citizens through taxation, have become hallmarks of the "new" Middle East.

This gloomy economic prospect, coupled with perceived painful political compromises made with Israel, constitute a serious challenge to the internal stability of most countries in the region. This is perhaps why attention has moved somewhat away from external threats to security to threats from within. With the deteriorating economic conditions and the loss of externally-generated political assets, the Middle Eastern rulers are finding it difficult to maintain balance and security within their societies without initiating change.[4] The dilemma is that this change must necessarily address the deteriorating economic conditions of the individual countries and the region precisely at a time when the political rulers of the countries have lost access to political assets they have historically relied upon. The peace process does of course benefit countries of the region from an external security perspective and can potentially enhance the political standing of individual leaders, providing the foundation for the initiation of economic change. But there is a difference between a long-term positive vision of the future and the implementation of means that assure the realization of that long-term vision. The success of the peace process is itself dependent upon the implementation of certain necessary economic and political steps. In other words, the reliance on the peace process as a cure-all, when the success of the process itself is contingent upon reforms within the individual countries involved, is at best a fantasy and at worst a recipe for political disaster.

This dilemma of the peace process has not gone unnoticed. Various discussions, debates, and proposals concerning the future of the Middle East tend to acknowledge the necessity of enhancing the political assets of governments or rulers in the region as well as bringing a degree of economic prosperity to a region certainly not lacking in resources but sorely in need of economic reform. Stated differently, in a fashion reminiscent of post-Second World War debates regarding newly independent Third World countries, questions related to political development (even if the term itself is not used) and economic reform, and their interplay, have come to the fore, but this time they are firmly located within a framework attentive to the national security of individual countries in particular and regional security in general. The next section will deal with the way these questions are generally posed in current discussions and some of the proposals for enhancing the economic security of the region.

PROPOSALS FOR REFORM IN THE MIDDLE EAST

A cursory look at some of the proposals and attempts to come to grips with the question of security in the Middle East suggests that, although the necessity for political adjustments is acknowledged, the tendency has been to emphasize economic reforms first. Several projects, including those initiated by Harvard University, the United Nations Institute for Disarmament Research (UNIDIR), and the World Bank, come to mind in this regard, all bearing suggestions for the improvement of the economic situation in the Middle East.

The Harvard project was initiated with the involvement of Palestinian, Jordanian, Israeli, and American economists in order to accelerate the peace process by designing and proposing economic programs that would ultimately create a suitable environment for economic activities, creation of employment, and economic development in the whole region.[5] Relying on the strength of each of the participating countries (i.e., Israel's strong economy and technological know-how, Jordan's relatively skilled labor, and the Occupied Territories' unskilled labor), the project proposes increased reliance on the private sector and the creation of a free economic region beginning with the three countries mentioned but allowing for the involvement of Egypt, Syria, and Lebanon by the end of the century. For linking the very different and unequal economies of Jordan and Israel, a variety of immediate and medium-term projects are proposed, extending from expansion of tourist services and construction of joint airports in the short term to the establishment of the Middle Eastern Bank for Cooperation and Development in the medium term, the latter being the mechanism through which investment can be brought and distributed in the Middle East. In short, the idea is to move the separated and state-supported economies of the region towards a system of free trade and ultimately an economic environment in which products, services, capital, technology, and labor power are exchanged freely.

The UNIDIR project on confidence building and arms control in the Middle East is organized around the strategic principle of cooperative security, "to enhance peace and security through institutionalized consent rather than physical coercion."[6] The emphasis is reportedly

> less on preparations to counter threats than on the prevention of threats in the first place . . . Militarily, the basis for cooperation is mutual acceptance and support for defence of home territory as the exclusive national objective, and the subordination of power projection to the constraints of international consensus. There is a close relationship, therefore, between cooperative security and non-offensive defence. Finally, a fully developed cooperative security framework would include provisions for collective security as a residual guarantee in the event of aggression.[7]

Although the project's emphasis is on arms control and nonproliferation of weapons of mass destruction, it demonstrates the firm belief that, with the freeing of resources previously spent on military build-up and competition, economic improvement will ensue and confidence in the region will be enhanced. As for the strengthening of security in the region, it proposes concurrent progress along three parallel tracks: a political track, an arms control track (with confidence building measures forming a web of connections between the two), and a track along which "the governments of the region demonstrate their ability to cope with their internal problems and satisfy the aspirations of their peoples."[8]

Finally, as is to be expected, the World Bank proposal is the most comprehensive of the three projects in terms of geographical coverage as well as economic programs.[9] At the same time, the World Bank recommendations for the Middle East offer very few surprises in so far as most of them have already been proposed for other parts of the world. As is the case for other regions, the recommendation for "credible and consistent trade liberalization" leads the way, together with the creation of a "high return, nimble investment environment." Governments are asked to "make privatization a priority," "get on the international financial map," "integrate reduction and the economy," "use natural resources sustainably," and "rely on growth and targeted interventions to reduce poverty." These general recommendations, of course, come with a series of more specific suggestions: support for non-oil exports, elimination of burdensome licensing requirements, provisions for clear, simple, and credible rules for foreign investors, elimination of subsidies of natural resources (energy and water) and environmental services, and reassessment of regulations developed to protect workers, such as minimum wage and restrictions on firing and temporary contracts. In short, promotion of non-oil exports, efficiency of the private sector, creation of more flexible and skilled workers, and reduction of poverty through faster growth constitute the familiar objectives of the World Bank proposal for the Middle East.

These three proposals are in many ways different in terms of emphasis as well as particular suggestions and there may be other proposals to which we have not given attention. Nevertheless, put together, they seem to hint at three sets of recommendations that would presumably enhance regional security in the long run: 1) implementation of structural adjustment programs and privatization; 2) creation of laws and regulations intended to attract foreign capital; and 3) adoption of arms control measures as a means to enhance regional cooperation, release more funds for economic development, and build confidence of foreign investors in the region. These three sets of recommendations, although coming from different perspectives emphasizing different dimensions of sustainable economic security and development, together seem to constitute a "plan" for revitalizing the Middle East, preparing it for astounding changes that are to come. We will deal with each set separately.

Structural Adjustment Programs

Structural adjustment programs (SAPs) have been in vogue for quite a while now. Our intent here is not to question whether or not these programs could improve the economic situation in the Middle East or to evaluate the performance of certain Middle Eastern countries, such as Morocco, Tunisia, and Jordan, which have adopted the recommended policies more vigorously than others. Whether we like them or not, SAPs and the so-called liberalization policies have become an integral part of the international environment, mostly inspired by the failure of previous development policies and the success of the so-called economic miracles of the East Asian Tigers. Hence, today, despite the mixed performance of liberalization policies in the Third World,[10] the question cannot be whether SAPs are good or bad for the Middle East or any other part of the world. They are here, entail difficult and politically costly adjustments (in terms of unemployment and lower consumption to allow for greater investment) for the countries involved,[11] and are in many ways forced upon countries throughout the world. Perhaps a more useful question that needs to be reflected upon concerns what it takes, specifically in terms of structure of power and authority, for these programs to work in particular countries of the Middle East and the region in general. Then, in view of the kind of answer given to this question, one can speculate about their chances of success in contributing to regional security. As the World Bank report itself admits, in other parts of the world reforms have been possible where leaders have successfully marshaled domestic political support, technical expertise, and external financing to provide the basis for effective reform.

But how can the leaders marshal political support, and within what political framework? Like everything else about SAPs, the question of political preconditions for its success is a contested one as well. Some, like Samuel Huntington, believe that, in the light of Gorbachev's experiment in the Soviet Union, an "authoritative" government (be it authoritarian or democratic but most likely the former) with "both the will and the power to put through reforms" is needed to assure success.[12] Others go further and argue that chances of success are enhanced if an authoritative structure is efficient and can attract popular participation in the later stages when privatization and private investments need to be encouraged. Indeed, democratic governments are generally recommended for the final stages of adjustment policies. Others, including some in the World Bank itself, shy away from the choice between democracy and dictatorship and argue that the concept of a "people friendly government" is a better one to use.[13] In such a government, the manner in which power is exercised in the management of a country's economic and social resources must involve accountability, rule of law, strong administration, and transparency and predictability.

The obvious question here is how can one be assured that a government with the above characteristics will be initiated in the Middle East when the prerequisite checks and balances and popular participation do not exist and interest groups that profit from the old regime are deeply entrenched. The proponents of SAPs believe that competitive pressure from the world economy, combined with domestic pressure for new and better job opportunities, is most likely to trigger change in the Middle Eastern countries. But the reality is that there can be no such assurance and indeed evidence in the Middle East suggests that for those countries that have been forced to go through economic liberalization, parallel political liberalization has not necessarily come about.[14] Lack of political liberalization would, of course, not be a problem if the political leaders of the Middle East did not have to rely on a broad-based consensus to carry out the reforms, that is, a broad-based consensus on the legitimacy of government and national unity based on much explanation and debate within the country and among the people. Simply put, the successful implementation of initially destabilizing SAPs is only possible if the initiators of these programs have accumulated enough political assets to spend during the difficult adjustment period. But as mentioned before, the political stock of Middle Eastern regimes is quite low at this time and the expectation that SAPs might be used as a mechanism to increase their political assets seems a bit unrealistic, to say the least. This is perhaps why, instead of moving towards fundamental structural transformation of the economy and its management, reforms have generally stopped at limited opening up of trade and investment opportunities and have aimed more at political survival than economic efficiency. Any further moves would probably require changes in the structure of political authority in the countries involved, something not envisioned or desired by the formulators of liberalization policies. At this point, for most governments of the Middle East, the dilemma consists of the futility of trying, through budget cuts, to convince people to take on more responsibility for their own well-being, while the government itself continues to maintain unquestioned authority. Equally futile, of course, is the bid by the private sector monopolies to inherit, under the guise of economic liberalism and privatization, the productive assets of the public sector without assuming any of the social burden.[15]

Foreign Capital

The second component of policies geared to the economic improvement of the Middle East is the creation of an environment attractive to foreign capital. Ironically, the Middle East, especially the Persian Gulf sub-region, has been a surplus area in terms of capital. According to World Bank estimates, capital from Middle Eastern countries held abroad is about $350 billion, more than any other region in the world as a share of gross domestic product (GDP).[16] Hence, perhaps a better way to think about generating investment is through means that would help the region retain its own capital. It has been argued that capital does not remain within the region because there are not enough investment opportunities. Alan Richards cites over-regulation of capital markets and lack of institutional infrastructure and skilled labor as constraints on private investments.[17] A comparison of the Middle East with other regions, however, may give us other clues. To be sure, it is true that foreign direct investment (FDI) inflows to the Middle East have been very low (only 3 percent of the total inflows to the developing countries in 1993, equal only to Africa and less than all other regions). But the reasons for such a low inflow are not as clear as Richards and many others would have us believe. The infrastructural and regulatory limitations in the Middle East are not particularly worse than other regions and the Middle East is in fact comparatively rich in terms of skilled human resources, energy, and infrastructural development. According to the World Bank, because of the largest transfer of income in world history during the 1973-85 period, the Middle Eastern countries were able to engage in massive public investment in excess of the already high levels prevailing since the 1960s:

> The state invested heavily in both human and physical capital . . . Most MENA [Middle East and North Africa] countries could afford generous social expenditures during this period. Enrollments increased rapidly and expenditures per pupil as a share of national income rose to some of the highest levels in the world . . . Middle East and North African governments were also effective in reducing poverty. By 1990 only 5.6 percent of the population in MENA lived on less than $1 a day, compared to 14.1 percent in East Asia and 28.8 percent in Latin America.[18]

We are not suggesting here that the limitations listed by Richards and others have not adversely affected the rate of investment in the Middle East. But since more or less the same limitations exist in other developing regions, they cannot be sufficient explanations for the difference in the rate of foreign investment that, for instance, exists between the Middle East and Latin America (FDI inflows to Latin America were 23 percent more than the inflows to the Middle East in 1993). This difference becomes even more puzzling when one considers the fact that Latin America had to attract capital from the outside while the Middle East merely needed to reduce the outflow of capital, certainly an easier task given the familiarity of the capital owner with the environment, language, regulations, etc., and the degree of nationalistic feelings that may work in favor of the Middle East.

As has been argued elsewhere,[19] low rates of domestic and foreign investment in the Middle East cannot be traced to mere economic or administrative constraints. Political impediments (low level of governmental legitimacy and stability, uncertainty about the future, etc.) must also be seriously considered. In other words, the same impediments that prevent the SAPs from going beyond the status quo inhibit not only foreign investment but also the investment of domestic capital. Not only are the gross savings rates in Middle Eastern countries about ten percentage points of GDP lower than those in, for instance, Indonesia, Malaysia, or Thailand, but a large sum of what is saved is not put to good use. Changed into gold or foreign currencies, the savings essentially remain outside the formal economic system. Our bet is that none of the policies intended to attract foreign capital and re-energize domestic capital will even begin to be effective unless the governments in the Middle East recognize the need to redefine their role away from unquestioned authority and towards guarantors of the rule of law. Even then, an important distinction must be made between steps needed to secure the movement of capital and those required for securing the owner of capital. Because of the overemphasis on attracting foreign capital, little attention has been paid to the latter. The owner of foreign capital, after all, derives his or her security from residence in another country. It is the owner of domestic capital who is constantly in search of a feeling of security, only enhanced or developed with the demarcation of state authority. Lack of attention to this delicate distinction entails an implicit encouragement of foreign capital and a continued neglect of means of activating domestic capital.

Arms Control and Regional Cooperation

The third set of policies intended to improve economic conditions and enhance security is arms control. It is argued that arms control in the Middle East will improve the process of confidence building and regional cooperation. It will also lead to economic improvement as much needed funds are released to pursue non-military activities.

Comparatively speaking, defense expenditures per capita are indeed quite high in the Middle East, with some countries, such as Oman and Saudi Arabia, having a per capita expenditure of between five and six times more than the European members of North Atlantic Treaty Organization (NATO) and more than 2.5 times that of the United States.[20] The Middle East also wins the military game in terms of highest global levels of public spending on the military and the highest world ratio of soldiers to its total population. There are a number of reasons for all this, including small populations, political tension in the region, and low levels of confidence. But the fact that the countries of the region could afford such high levels of expenditure has played a very important role.[21] In addition, the interest of the military-industrial complex and a whole series of intermediaries that are engaged in the business of armaments should not be overlooked either. Together with their connections in various global governments, they constitute a web of interlinkages that engages in deals which receive very little publicity, does not involve much accountability, and procures very handsome profits for the sellers as well as those who "make the deal" in the form of commissions, bakshish (gift of money), or bribes, or whatever is suitable at the moment of transaction. To be sure, political tension and lack of confidence has fueled quite a bit of the military competition in the Middle East but, put very simply, military build-up in the area, particularly in the Persian Gulf subregion, is also closely linked to oil money, the political structure of the countries involved, and the political influence of arms merchants in arms producing and arms consuming countries. All this suggests that even if there is arms control in the region and the level of military expenditure is reduced, the money saved is not necessarily spent in the economic improvement of the region. As mentioned before, scarcity of funds has never been the source of underdevelopment in the region. The money saved can only become a source of economic improvement if governments become more accountable and transparent in their expenditures.

SOME SUGGESTIONS AND CONCLUDING REMARKS

The point of this article is really rather simple and perhaps something quite familiar to almost all the parties interested or involved in the Middle East. The main problem of the region is political. A secure Middle East of the future can only be a possibility if these political problems are not only recognized (we think they are) but also addressed, if not immediately, at least in a piecemeal fashion. The peace process has ironically, but not unexpectedly, made these political problems blatant, hence the urgency for doing something to reduce them without "losing control." Indeed this fear of losing control, according to Vahan Zanoyan, has led to the conventional wisdom (interestingly in both the Middle East and the West) that to prevent a disruptive change the status quo must be preserved and buttressed.[22] Privatization and liberalization policies promoted by the World Bank may indeed bring about fundamental changes in Middle Eastern societies, but for now, and for a while to come, they lead to the tipping of the balance towards the rich and, paradoxically, towards a large number of state-supported entrepreneurs who are making money in a thoroughly rigged market and are not necessarily compelled for economic or non-economic reasons to invest their money in productive activities. The least that can be said about these policies is that they are not very conducive to the creation of a free market. At this point, they simply concentrate wealth further in the private sector (or ruling family) monopolies with either direct or indirect presence in various ministries, enabling them virtually to guarantee that no competition enters the market.

Similar problems exist around the question of foreign investment. Foreign investment may indeed be attracted to a few Middle Eastern countries who are marked as "favored" but, enclosed in a region not marked as favored, they will not be conducive to regional integration and will ultimately reinforce the old unequal patterns. Finally, confidence building measures are of really no use if the political systems involved, both inside and outside of the region, still feel the need to create enemies in order to maintain the status quo.

Criticisms abound; however, it is not very clear what else can be done about the Middle East. Wholesale political change is of course utter fantasy but lack of political change will also doom the region to the most feared outcome. What can be done? Several steps come to mind that seem very general and this generality works against efforts to figure out ways to implement them. But figuring out mechanisms for implementing them is precisely what is needed. And what are these steps?

First and foremost is the recognition of the stakes involved for those inside and outside of the Middle East. The Middle East is not a region out of the planet earth. It is an extremely important area of the world, and the events within it drastically affect the world economically, political, culturally, and environmentally. Decision-makers, inside and outside of the Middle East, must come to understand the long-term stakes a prosperous and humane world has in a thriving and calm Middle East. They must begin to see that short-term political expediencies cannot be allowed to detract from the urgency for fundamental political change in the direction of more proper state-society and state-state relations. They must come to understand that policies that rely on old recipes in the form of pursuing economic growth in the hope of achieving controlled economic reform, coupled with the old tactics of creating and demonizing enemies in order to maintain the status quo, will have serious consequences for the not very distant future (that is, for our children or even ourselves) not only in the Middle East but also the world. In other words, there has to be a clear recognition by all the parties involved that not only are things bad, but that they might well get worse. How to communicate this message is itself a project that needs serious thinking and planning.

The second task also involves thoughtful consideration of how to improve state-society relations in order to enhance the legitimacy of various existing polities, not merely leaders or even governmental institutions. To be sure, there has been a certain amount of thinking about this, mostly in the form of debates on civil society. Even economically-oriented institutions such as the IMF and the World Bank have talked about the need to promote "effective government and strong civil society."[23] A good public sector, it is said, can only be generated based on rule of law, protection of legitimate economic activities and interests, a government's accountability to its citizens, effective measures to curb corruption, a participatory approach to development, easy access to information and services, and sound decision making reflecting the actual needs of people. All this, of course, sounds well enough, but very little is said about exactly how, given the vested domestic and foreign interests, these foundations for a good public sector can come about, taking on forms that suit the idiosyncrasies of Middle Eastern societies. Furthermore, at times one gets the impression that all the talk about civil society is yet another effort by the state to construct a docile society, composed of layers of patronage networks. In the midst of all these reforms one can detect merely an assumption, or more properly a wish, that the policies of economic adjustment and liberalization will ultimately "fix" everything. In other words, economic efficiency will create a good civil society which will, in turn, assure the continuance of an efficient economic system.

This one recipe for all approaches, reminiscent of the failed attempts of the 1960s, must end. If the arguments of this paper are to be taken seriously, economic reform is not a proper vehicle for increasing the political assets of governments in the Middle East. If anything, the reverse is true. We all know what the problem is. In order to become secure, the Middle Eastern polities need to rely on a supportive society in concrete and formulated ways (hence so much talk about civil society). But this support will not come about unless the state begins to seem less arbitrary in day-to-day life. Accordingly, any genuine discussion of economic improvements must begin here. In other words, attention must turn towards state structures and internal and external forces that inhibit the reforms of these state structures. Put bluntly, an increase in the political assets of the state, required for enacting genuine economic reform, can only come about with the reform of the state itself.

We know that state policy in most countries of the region is aimed first and foremost at the maintenance of state power. As such, it is unlikely that most of the regimes currently in power will voluntarily institute genuine and long-term political or even economic reforms, for to do so would fundamentally jeopardize their political survival. In their recalcitrance, they are aided by external forces which see anything but the status quo as disruptive. Almost by definition, this logic of political survival will subvert economic rationality and prevent comprehensive reform. At the more institutional level, concerns over servicing the regime's core constituency in the public sector prevent the state from reforming its inefficient industries. Very rapidly, then, stabilization or selective liberalization, essentially meaning policy improvisation and incoherence, becomes the name of the game. Clearly this disposition must change, creating an international environment and context in which the maintenance of the status quo both inside the countries and at the interregional level becomes too costly, and making a process of critical self-examination mandatory for rulers and ruled alike (more so for the rulers since there are ample signs that the ruled have already begun this process).[24] If the sacredness of the status quo begins to vanish in the minds of insiders as well as within the international community, alternatives may begin to be speculated upon and the costs of abandoning it may not seem so overwhelming.

As so aptly pointed out by that eminent champion of civil society, Vaclav Havel, effective change towards a more humane society cannot come in the form of some new collection of dogmas and rituals. There is indeed no "special recipe to awaken the mind of man to his responsibility to the world and for the world."[25] What is needed is a space to breathe and an acknowledgment that the radical changes occurring throughout the world cannot leave the region, and its regimes in particular, untouched.

Notes

1. Comparison with other regions, especially East Asia, has been one of the main motivating factors for increased attention to the economic question in the Middle East. According to Caio Koch-Weser, vice-president of the World Bank for the Middle East and North Africa region, "The region, in spite of its good resource endowment, has failed to keep up with development elsewhere in the world. A telling example, in 1960, South Korea and Egypt had approximately the same per capita income. Today, Korea's is almost ten times as high as that of Egypt. At the same time . . . GDP growth has failed to keep up with the population growth of the region as a whole." See Caio Koch-Weser, "Economic Performance and Regional Cooperation: A Development Agenda for the Middle East and North Africa," *Middle East Policy* 2, no. 2 (1993): 28.

2. Avoiding the discussion concerning the high number of authoritarian regimes in the region, which can be very heated as to which one is more authoritarian, it can still be confidently said that almost all governments in the region have found it difficult, or have refused: to improve the allocation of responsibility between the central government and local administrations, to develop improved accounting and auditing standards, to modernize their legal systems, to give greater clarity and integrity to their public administration, or to develop better public communications.

3. The peace process itself cannot constitute a political asset, at least for now, since it is itself a contested process at the level of public opinion. In fact, support for the peace process may require reliance on political assets already accumulated.

4. This is not to say that the reliance on the notion of externally generated threat has vanished from the political map of the Middle East. Several states in the Middle East continue to use the possibility of external military threat as the justification for their military build-up and foreign presence in the region. The main foreign player in the region also identifies support for the friendly countries in the region as one of the justifications (apart from the protection of Israel and security of oil flow) for its overwhelming military presence in the area. See Department of Defense Office of International Security Affairs, *United States Security Strategy for the Middle East* (Washington, D.C., May 1995).

5. For a discussion of the Harvard project see S. Fischer et al., eds., *Securing Peace in the Middle East: Project on Economic Transition* (Cambridge, Mass.: MIT, 1994).

6. James Leonard et al., *National Threat Perceptions in the Middle East,* United Nations Institute for Disarmament Research, research paper no. 37 (New York: United Nations, September 1995).

7. Ibid.

8. Ibid., 7.

9. See World Bank, *Claiming the Future: Choosing Prosperity in the Middle East and North Africa* (Washington D.C., 1995).

10. According to Singer, using the four indicators of rate of real GDP growth, ratio of domestic saving to GDP, ratio of investment to GDP, and ratio of exports to GDP, the countries adopting SAPs show improvement in terms of ratio of exports to GDP. The rate of GDP growth suggests a partial picture of success and the other two indicators show the opposite in the sense that the adjusting countries did worse than the non-adjusting countries. Singer's conclusions are based on the World Bank's own studies. See Hans W. Singer, "Are the Structural Adjustment Programmes Successful?" *Pakistan Journal of Applied Economics* 11 (summer and winter 1995): 4-6. For analysis of economic liberalization policies in the Middle East, see Tim Niblock, "Economic Liberalisation in the Arab World: The Social and Po-

litical Significance," RUSEL working paper 1 (Exeter: Research Unit for the International Study of Economic Liberalisation and its Social and Political Effects, University of Exeter, 1991), and Gerd Nonneman, "Economic Liberalization in the Developing World: The State of the Debate, and the Case of the Middle East," RUSEL working paper 12 (Exeter: Research Unit for the International Study of Economic Liberalisation and its Social and Political Effects, University of Exeter, 1993). See also Iliya Harik and Denis J. Sullivan, eds., *Privatization and Liberalization in the Middle East* (Bloomington: Indiana University Press, 1992) and Henry Barkey, ed., *The Politics of Economic Reform in the Middle East* (New York: St. Martin's Press, 1992).

11. The World Bank itself acknowledges the costs of SAPs in their early stages: "The costs result because a substantial share of existing capital—both human and physical—must be restrained, converted, or simply retired, to allow for the accumulation of more appropriate types of capital. These costs translate into higher unemployment and lower consumption (to allow for greater investment) during the transition. Estimates of the magnitude of these short-term adjustment costs in MENA countries are about a 1-2 percent loss in per capita consumption and a 3 percent rise in the rate of employment relative to the no-reform scenario." See *Claiming the Future,* 77.

12. Samuel P. Huntington, "What Cost Freedom? Democracy and/or Economic Reform," *Harvard International Review* 15, no. 2 (winter 1992/93): 12.

13. See Rainer Tetzlaff, "Good Governance and Structural Adjustment Programs: The World Bank's Experience in Africa South of Sahara," *Pakistan Journal of Applied Economics* 11 (summer and winter 1995): 167-86.

14. This does not mean that there have been no parallel moves towards political liberalization. These moves, however, have been mostly tactical, that is, aiming to broaden responsibility for the adoption of policies which will harm the interests of the poorer part of the population.

15. For a clear exposition of this point see Kiren Aziz Chaudhry, "Economic Liberalization and the Lineages of the Rentier State," *Comparative Politics* 27 (October 1994). To cite just one example, Chaudhry argues that in Saudi Arabia during the 1980s reforms allowing local businessmen to engage in activities previously in the hands of the state did not lead to more efficiency and competition. Influenced by these businessmen, the government ended up further restricting and even eliminating foreign competition.

16. World Bank, *Claiming the Future,* 6.

17. Alan Richards, "Beyond Islamic Extremism: The True Causes of Instability in the Middle East," paper presented at the Center for Strategic and International Studies, Georgetown University, Washington, D.C., 7 September 1995.

18. World Bank, *Claiming the Future,* 34-38.

19. Sohrab Shahabi, "Investment Policy in Iran," *Iranian Journal of International Affairs* 7, no. 4 (winter 1996): 764-79.

20. See the table on world military expenditure as a percentage of GDP, 1983-93, in *SIPRI Yearbook 1995: Armaments, Disarmament and International Security,* (Oxford: Oxford University Press, 1995).

21. According to Calabrese, "The Gulf has been a subregion in which the appetite for weapons and their availability have converged. It is also an area where, political antagonisms aside, other circumstances have favored the continuation of the arms race; namely the economics of petroleum." John Calabrese, *Revolutionary Horizons: Regional Foreign Policy in Post-Khomeini Iran* (Basingstoke, U.K.: Macmillan; New York: St. Martin's Press, 1994): 10.

22. Vahan Zanoyan, "After the Oil Boom," *Foreign Affairs* 74, no. 6 (November/December 1993): 2-7.

23. Task Force on Multilateral Development Banks, "Serving a Changing World," *World Report* (Washington, D.C., 15 March 1996).
24. See Kanan Makiya, "A Turning Point in Arab Politics?" *Journal of Democracy* 6, no. 1 (January 1995): 90-103.
25. Vaclav Havel, "Transcending the Clash of Cultures," *Journal of Democracy* 6, no. 2 (April 1995): 9.

CHAPTER EIGHT

The Economic Component of
Middle East Security:
Twenty-First Century Options

ROGER OWEN

INTRODUCTION

*T*he aim of this chapter is to examine the economic component of Middle Eastern security at both the regional level and the level of individual states. To do this it will pose the following questions:

1. Is the Middle East a coherent economic unit and, if so, how has it been affected by both the centrifugal and centripetal forces set in train by the second Gulf War, the end of the Cold War and the breakup of the Soviet Union?
2. What have been the main features of the traditional approach to Middle Eastern economic security and are they still relevant?
3. What are the options for the future?
4. What are the most likely patterns if present trends continue?

In what follows I will attempt to address these questions in two stages, first by looking at the way such questions have been treated in the past and then by asking how they present themselves now in the new global economic circumstances of the later twentieth century.

HISTORICAL APPROACHES TO ISSUES OF MIDDLE EASTERN ECONOMIC SECURITY

The Middle East as a Coherent Economic and Political Unit

The term Middle East was originally a geostrategic concept applied first to the area between the Gulf and what is now Pakistan and then, during the Second World War, to the whole region from Egypt to Iran and from Syria and Iraq to the Sudan which was placed under the control of a single agency for its economic management, the Anglo-American Middle East Supply Centre (MESC) in Cairo. Its continued use in the postwar period was further justified by the various cross-regional links provided by Arabism and Islam, as well by the close involvement of Israel and Iran with the Arab state system for geographical, military, and some (generally oil related) economic reasons. As a rule, the states of the Maghrib were excluded from the conventional economic or political definitions of the region but this began to change in the 1980s with the coining of a new term, the Middle East and North Africa (MENA), by the World Bank and International Monetary Fund (IMF).

The defining features of the Middle East system have been examined many times by academic scholars, almost all of whom have based their analysis on the assumption that it constitutes a distinct political and strategic unit. Nevertheless, most would also agree that it has been subject to a number of important centrifugal tendencies in recent years, particularly since the end of the second Gulf War. These include the growing divisions between the Gulf states grouped together in the Gulf Cooperation Council (GCC) as well as the growing rift between the Gulf states and their Gulf War allies, Syria and Egypt. To this might be added the uneasy relations between those states who have started to normalize their relations with Israel since 1993 and those who still hold back, together with the new divisions imposed from outside by the Euro-American diplomatic isolation, first of Libya, then of Iraq and, to a more limited extent, of Iran and the Sudan. We may also note similar tendencies in North Africa where initial efforts to use the Maghrib Union (MU) as a vehicle both for economic integration and negotiation with the European Union (EU) have foundered on the rock of Libya's isolation and Algeria's political troubles, leaving Morocco and Tunisia to try to obtain a privileged association with Europe on their own. Finally, parts of the region have begun to explore stronger links with certain outside forces and institutions, notably the EU, the newly independent states of the former Soviet Central Asia, and the rapidly growing energy-importing countries of East Asia.

What has received less attention, however, is the relationship between these centrifugal forces and certain other centripetal forces also at work in the Middle East. One of these is the peace process, which many still hope will serve to break down existing barriers between Israel and its Arab neighbors. A second is the continued salience of Arabism, if not as a unifying force at the political level, at least as the animator of a whole variety of cultural and other cross-border links throughout the region. The third is the greater degree of cohesion within the Organization of Petroleum Exporting Countries (OPEC) as far as questions of price and supply are concerned.

To this might be added two more forces with both centrifugal and centripetal tendencies. The first is the return of Turkey as an important regional actor as a result of its increasing economic and, latterly, strategic and military interests involving its Arab neighbors, Israel, and Iran. The second is the overall cohesion given to the region by a shared interest in questions of military security, notably nuclear proliferation and cross-border terrorism. It is factors such as these that demand that questions of Middle Eastern economic security be analyzed in regional as well as national terms.

Historical Approaches to the Question of Economic Security in the Middle East

Twentieth-century approaches to the question of Middle East economic security can be summed up under three headings: independence, development, and schemes for Arab integration. It should also be noted that the weights given to these factors not only varied over time but also differed considerably according to whether the subject was being approached from within or outside the region.

For the leaders of the first post-independence Middle Eastern regimes, economic security was seen, first and foremost, as an essential underpinning for their political independence. If colonialism represented financial exploitation and enforced backwardness, then the first duty of a post-colonial government seemed to be to get rid of the previous barriers to national development—such as foreign ownership or the neglect of industry—while being firmly on guard against attempts either to preserve or to seek to reestablish former positions of power in a neo-colonial form. Hence, in spite of the ability to use their new sovereignty to nationalize foreign assets and to refuse loans and agreements that they saw as continuing the old ties of dependence, such governments continued to remain fearful of intrusive forces from within the international economy and to do their best to protect themselves against them.

Such ways of thinking led most regimes to stress those policies of development which held out the possibility of reducing dependency through import substitution, supported by a growing repertoire of barriers and controls. Meanwhile, more and more areas of activity were defined as essential not just to economic, but also to national and military, security—e.g., military production, energy, transport—and so placed off-limits to foreign investment. Even in states with relatively open economies, like many of those in the Gulf, new categories of threat were constantly being identified. These included reliance on a growing army of foreign labor, which in turn produced a defensive response in terms of the creation of protected positions for local nationals, for example by creating local monopolies over the ownership of property or insisting on a majority local interest in any business enterprise.

Two implications of this defensive approach to economic security are significant. First, with political and economic considerations so closely intertwined, it was the political which almost always took precedence. A good example is the appearance of the notion of food security as a result of the Arab world's heavy dependence on imported meat and cereals in the 1970s. Fear of possible political pressures from the major wheat and barley exporters, notably the United States, led a number of regimes, such as those in Syria and Saudi Arabia, to encourage the growth of domestic production at whatever cost. Second, the dominance of the political hardly provided a context in which economic cooperation was likely to flourish. Not only was the Arab boycott of Israel a clear use of trade for political ends but the two major attempts at creating an institutional mechanism for greater integration—the free trade area project of the 1950s and the common market approach of the 1960s—were also defeated more by considerations of national sovereignty and the incompatibility of rival systems of management and control than they were by more purely economic reasons such as the sameness of each country's mix of industrial products.[1]

One important result was a move towards the creation of less ambitious subregional groupings during the 1970s and 1980s: the Gulf Cooperation Council, the Maghrib Union, and the short-lived Arab Cooperation Council (ACC) linking Egypt, Iraq, Jordan, and Yemen. But even here political considerations made the achievement of economic goals highly problematic. The ACC, for example, was designed largely to contain Iraqi expansionist tendencies and collapsed with Saddam Hussein's occupation of Kuwait. Futhermore, following the second Gulf War, GCC plans for moving towards a Gulf common market were put under great strain by the decision to base its military security not on mutual cooperation but on bilateral agreements with the United States and its Gulf War partners, as explained below.

Paradoxically perhaps, it needed this further political fragmentation of the Middle East in the early 1990s, as well as the debt crisis and the move towards structural adjustment including deregulation and export promotion, to open the way for a discussion of new patterns of cooperation based on less defensive, more globally minded, notions of what is meant by economic security. One possible new pattern originated from the argument concerning the need to underpin the Israeli-Palestinian peace process either with the establishment of an Israeli/Palestinian/Jordanian economic union or, in some formulations, with a much larger Middle Eastern common market. The latter was loudly touted by Shimon Peres, the former Israeli foreign minister, in his book, *The New Middle*

East, which appeared shortly after the Oslo agreements. It has also received encouragement from the present United States administration in terms of its support for the successive Middle Eastern business conferences held in Casablanca, Amman, Cairo, and Doha between 1994 and 1997. There have also been moves to create a permanent Arab-Israeli institutional structure by means of such initiatives as the establishment of a Middle Eastern Development Bank.

A second pattern, presented at the Barcelona conference of November 1995, is that of a Euro-Mediterranean Free Trade Area in manufactured goods to be put in place by the year 2010. Here, what was clearly a politically-based initiative by the Europeans, designed to discourage instability on their southern border, was met by a fundamentally economic response from those Middle Eastern states that initially signed the treaty —Turkey, Israel, Mauritania, Morocco, Tunisia, Egypt, Jordan, Syria, Lebanon, and the Palestine National Authority (PNA)—in the hope of obtaining solid economic advantage in the shape of financial and technical aid.[2]

Meanwhile, all the states of the region began to experience strong pressures to join those organizations and institutions which now played a central role in managing the global economy, such as the World Bank and the new World Trade Organization (WTO), with their strong emphasis on deregulation, lower tariffs, and the introduction of rules and regulations exhibiting good international commercial practice. Suddenly it seemed to become more dangerous to national economic welfare to stay out than to join in.

ECONOMIC SECURITY IN THE PRESENT AND FUTURE

In a situation in which policies aimed at independence and self-sufficiency no longer seem the be-all and end-all of economic security, the first priority for Middle Eastern states is to define how they wish to relate to the outside world, whether to their own Middle Eastern neighbors or to the larger regional and international organizations which already regulate trade and investment regimes over substantial parts of the world.

There are various possibilities to explore. The Middle Eastern states could attempt to create a new regional or subregional economic grouping which would then negotiate its own special form of association with the EU. They could join the Euro-Mediterranean scheme complemented by their own bilateral treaty with the EU. They could confine themselves to membership of a global institution like the WTO. They could engage in a mix of such bilateral and multilateral initiatives.

However, before discussing these various options in greater detail it would be useful to indicate some of the general features of Middle Eastern economic life that will have a direct bearing on future discussion. These are as follows:

1. The Middle East is very underendowed with natural resources except for oil and its associated gas. Few of the Arab countries have deposits of other minerals. There is also a general scarcity of water, made worse by a considerable variation in the annual rainfall needed to produce the bulk of the crops in Syria, Jordan, and northern Iraq. This, in turn, increases the importance of irrigation and, therefore, of water-sharing agreements between the riparian states along the major rivers such as the Nile, the Tigris, and the Euphrates.

2. As is often pointed out, the Middle East and North Africa currently account for the lowest proportion of intraregional trade in the world, less than 10 percent.[3] Nevertheless, like all generalizations, this particular one hides a number of significant differences and issues. One is the fact that, in value terms, the whole picture is dominated by the export of oil. Another is that the proportion of intraregional trade varies enormously from country to country, with Jordan, Yemen, and Lebanon at the high end with some 20 to 25 percent, and Egypt and most of the oil producers at the lower end with no more than 5 or 6 percent.[4]

3. The existence of economic, or proto-economic, unions can act to encourage competition rather than cooperation among neighboring states desiring closer economic association. This can already be seen in the case of the Euro-Mediterranean initiative in which putative members have to sign bilateral treaties with the EU in which each is encouraged to try to obtain special privileges for its own industries. The same tendencies can be seen to be coming into existence with relation to Israel as a result of the peace process. The peace process has both encouraged competition among some Arab states for favorable treatment by the Israelis, and also driven a wedge between those—like Qatar and Morocco—who have established both diplomatic and economic relations with Israel, and those—like Syria and Saudi Arabia—who have not.

4. Schemes currently exist for a great variety of specific, but non-institutionalized, forms of Middle Eastern cross-border cooperation concerning, for example, oil and gas pipelines, international highways, tourism, and shared electricity grids. Similar types of schemes are also required to allocate the water to be found in major rivers including the Tigris, the Euphrates, and the Jordan.

Present Options

Present options for closer regional association can be classified (logically) under five headings: regional, subregional, multilateral association with the EU, bilateral, and global. It is also possible to imagine some combination of the above as well as the more general process of harmonizing national trade and investment regimes through common processes of IMF and World Bank-inspired structural adjustment or some common association within the WTO. Let me look at each of these in turn.

Regional

It is difficult, if not impossible, to imagine a regional scheme for economic co-operation which is not preceded by one for political, and perhaps military, coop-eration, including peace treaties between Israel and all its Arab neighbors, and the end of the Arab trade boycott. This is just the reverse of the situation which ob-tained in Western Europe in the 1950s when integration began with the creation of various economic mechanisms such as the Franco-German Iron and Steel Community. While the possibility of a comprehensive Arab-Israeli treaty cannot be ruled out, the 1996 victory of Benjamin Netanyahu's Likud coalition has made such a scheme very much less likely in the near to medium term. To give only one of a large number of possible examples of the negative impact of the Netanyahu government, the 1997 Doha economic conference, once seen as a vi-tal facilitator of further Arab-Israeli cooperation, was boycotted by major states such as Egypt, Saudi Arabia, and Morocco, leaving it with only low level repre-sentation from Oman, Kuwait, Yemen, Jordan, and Tunisia.

Subregional

One subregional group already exists (the GCC) and one is just beginning to come into existence (Israel/Palestine/Jordan). Both face difficult problems. The GCC lost much of its political momentum as a result of the second Gulf War when its member states decided to base their military security not on mutual co-operation but on bilateral agreements with Western states, notably the United States. This, in turn, helped to slow down efforts to create a customs union with common laws, common currency, and a common external tariff. Hence, by the end of 1997, while agreement had been reached on one thousand common clas-sifications for the new tariff, 300 still remained under negotiation.[5] Only when this is complete will the GCC be able to sign a long-delayed free trade deal with its major trading partner, the EU. Other plans, for example, the linking of elec-tricity grids and granting the right for one state's banks to open branches in an-other state, have been agreed but not yet implemented.[6]

The second of the subregional groups (Israel/Palestine/Jordan) is also experi-encing obvious political difficulties which are hampering economic progress. Moreover, in spite of the economic agreements signed in 1995 between Israel and the PNA, and between Israel and Jordan, there is also still no general consensus on what a future economic union between the three entities should consist of. As of early 1998, the only organization that has exhibited a direct interest in giving a further push to such a scheme is the EU. In cooperation with the United Nations Development Programme, the EU plans to launch a joint project in May 1998 to promote cooperation in trade-related services between Israel, Jordan, and the PNA. However, it should also be pointed out that the EU has become increasingly frustrated by its inability to engineer progress as far as the Palestinians are concerned. In spite of the customs union established between Israel and the PNA-controlled territories in 1994, and of subsequent deals expanding this union's access to Arab, European, and North American markets, Palestinian exports have continued to decline well below the levels they attained in the early 1980s, while plans to open both Gaza airport and Gaza port as a conduit for Palestinian trade remain stalled.[7]

Given the magnitude of these problems, not to speak of the widening gap between the policies of the Israelis, the Jordanians, and the PNA, it seems unlikely that cooperation can progress beyond some form of free trade area with at least two currencies, separate national legislation, and considerable internal barriers to the movement of labor. Meanwhile, earlier hopes that such a union could act as a catalyst for a larger grouping including Egypt, Syria, and Lebanon are inconceivable under present political circumstances.

Finally, the deterioration in Arab-Israeli relations since May 1996 has provided an opportunity to revive schemes for purely intra-Arab cooperation. This has led to an agreement to form a Free Trade Zone consisting of 18 Arab countries, beginning with mutual tariff reductions of 10 percent as of 1 January 1998, and then proceeding in stages to the complete elimination of all such tariffs over the next ten years.[8] Meanwhile, efforts are being made to revive progress towards implementing the main provisions of the Arab common market which came into existence in 1964 between seven member states (Egypt, Iraq, Jordan, Libya, Mauritania, Syria, and Yemen) but has remained largely moribund. Whether such ambitious schemes will be any more successful than those of their many predecessors still remains to be seen.

Multilateral (with Europe)

There is obvious concern inside the EU to establish closer relationships with the states of the southern Mediterranean within some overall framework for mutual cooperation. This is based on the recognition (felt most keenly by the Mediterranean members of the EU) that they have a variety of economic interests in common (energy, tourism, labor migration, pollution) as well as the larger political interest of preventing the establishment of extremist governments along the North African coast. In addition, there is a European acceptance of the advantages of something like the North American Free Trade Association (NAFTA) formula in which United States investment in the region to the south of the Rio Grande is encouraged in the interest of raising Mexican standards of living and thus reducing the temptation of Mexicans to try to migrate north.

As far as the countries of the southern and eastern Mediterranean are concerned, the long-term advantages of cooperation with the EU are twofold. First, it provides the framework for greatly increased European investment both in upgrading these countries' industrial plants and in creating new ones. Second, it holds out hopes of greater access to the growing European market. This is particularly the case for those countries that follow the EU's advice to enter into agreements to produce goods jointly, an obvious attempt to nudge the Arab states and Israel towards the creation of their own regional market which, it is supposed, would stand a much better chance of attracting international investment than at present.

The more immediate significance of such schemes should also not be overlooked. For one thing, they engage the EU in a process of continuous dialogue and so ensure that there is some equivalence between the types of arrangements on offer to the Mediterranean states and those the community is negotiating with the countries of Central and Eastern Europe. For another, these same proposals can act as a set of blueprints providing general guidance as to the direction in which all states should be trying to move. And yet, as is obvious, the problems that stand in the way of the successful implementation of these proposals are also immense. Politically, they depend on further progress in the troubled peace process. Economically, they require an enormous amount of complex negotiation and bargaining given the wide variety of interests involved and the particular problems posed by competition in such areas as agriculture and fishing.

Bilateral

As mentioned above, various Mediterranean states are also pursuing bilateral arrangements designed to take advantage of certain geographic economies of scale that come from linking pipelines and electricity grids and systems of transport, particularly between Israel and its Arab neighbors. Such an approach has the great attraction of allowing agreements to be negotiated on a project by project basis without involving the establishment of a more complex, and perhaps politically embarrassing, institutionalized politico-economic relationship. Similar considerations may well apply to the types of water-sharing arrangements which may emerge between Turkey, Syria, and Iraq.

Global

As of early 1998, nine Arab states were members of the WTO, while six more are negotiating to join. A number of these—for example Egypt, Qatar, and the United Arab Emirates (UAE)—previously belonged to the General Agreement on Tariffs and Trade (GATT) but have not yet completed the substantial number of extra policy and institutional changes that the move from the old to the new organization involves, i.e., signature of the revised GATT as well as the two new treaties involving trade in services (GATS) and trade-related intellectual property rights (TRIPS). In addition, some are in the middle of a drawn out process of structural adjustment with important consequences for their foreign trade regimes and the legal arrangements designed to encourage and to protect foreign investment. It is thus possible to discern a movement towards standardization and harmonization that is proceeding independently of any formal intraregional arrangements.

Multiple Memberships

Lastly, a number of states have already taken initiatives which combine, or plan to combine, two or more of the above levels of economic arrangement. Some members of the Euro-Mediterranean scheme are also members of the new Arab Free Trade Zone; others, such as Israel, Jordan, and Palestine, are linked together by their own local economic arrangements, while the Israeli/Palestinian customs union has trade treaties with the EU and NAFTA. More recently, most of the GCC states have agreed to join the Free Trade Zone as well.

PROBLEMS AND POSSIBLE FUTURE PATTERNS

Progress in any of the directions just indicated poses real problems for all the countries concerned. To begin with, the decision to join this or that scheme has to be taken against a background of the larger political context, in which the United States, Europe and, to a lesser extent, Russia, China, and Japan compete for power and influence in the Middle East. An important component of this competition will still be the struggle for privileged access to Middle Eastern oil and gas. So too will be the on-going tension between the United States policy (supported by Israel and some of the Arab regimes) of using trade sanctions to isolate outlaw states like Libya and Iraq, and the more commercially-driven European approach.

Then again there are particular problems for the Middle Eastern countries in carrying out the basic preliminary task of trying to form some general picture of their own present balance of economic advantage and disadvantage, of their op-timal future direction, and then of the types of relationships—with their Middle Eastern neighbors, the EU, and the world economy in general—that might best bring this about. But, as we know, it is difficult for modern states to undertake such a task, the more so when the political future is so difficult to predict and when there are important domestic constituencies involved. In addition, many Middle Eastern regimes remain authoritarian and so deprive themselves of use-ful public opinion and debate. Furthermore, not all possess the expert personnel either to draw up such a policy or to suggest ways in which it might be imple-mented. Finally, most of these countries contain powerful vested interests that are willing to use the appeal to national interest to protect their local institutions from one type of foreign competition or another. Such pressures are bound to increase at least in those countries where the impact of liberalization, allied with the impact of global economic forces, will create even larger pools of unemployment and relative deprivation than there are at present. All this makes the transition from the traditional emphasis on political diplomacy, to one that places greater emphasis on economic aims, a particularly difficult one, making huge demands both on leadership and bureaucratic resources.

Finally, as I have noted above, there is no institutional architecture in place that would allow Middle Eastern economic problems and possibilities to be discussed in either a regional forum or *vis-à-vis* important external actors outside the region itself.

In these circumstances, it is possible to see a number of general tendencies working themselves out over the next few decades:

1. Given its superior strength and coherence, the EU will set the agenda for cooperation with the Middle East with very little input from the Middle Eastern states themselves as a group.
2. For much the same reasons, Israel will continue to set the terms for movement towards the establishment of a local Israeli/Jordanian/ Palestinian free trade area, a situation that can only increase the present unwillingness of both the Egyptian and the Syrian regimes to join with it in a more institutionalized form of subregional economic cooperation.
3. The GCC will make only slow progress towards a common market, a situation that will give its members an incentive to join other associations as well, notably the new Arab Free Trade Zone.
4. The members of the new Arab Free Trade Zone will experience great difficulty in keeping to their timetable of regular tariff reductions, the more so if their present unity is threatened by the return of a different Israeli government with a more positive approach to the peace process than the present one.

CONCLUSION

In this paper I have presented four main arguments for further discussion. First, the Middle East, as traditionally defined, still constitutes a coherent framework for questions of economic security. Second, if economic security is to mean anything in a Middle Eastern context, it means both political agreement and growth promoted by institutionalized patterns of cross-border exchange. Third, in the absence of any forum for regional discussion, the most likely form of future cooperative arrangements will be of a partial, scheme by scheme, type. Fourth, and finally, Middle Eastern involvement in larger, internal, schemes will be shaped largely by extraregional forces, notably the EU.

NOTES

1. For an interesting alternative approach to the question of the lack of Arab unity, see Ian S. Lustick, "The Absence of Middle Eastern Great Powers: Political 'Backwardness' in Historical Perspective," *International Organization* 51, no. 4 (autumn 1997): 653-83.

2. The two other Mediterranean states that attended the Barcelona meeting, Malta and Greek Cyprus, are candidates for a closer form of association with the EU than that offered to the Arab states and Israel.

3. See, for example, World Bank estimates of intra-MENA trade as 5.6 percent for 1980, 8.9 percent for 1990, and 7.6 percent for 1993. International Economics Department, Analysis and Prospects Division, "The World Economy and Implications for the Middle East and North Africa Region, 1995-2010," by E. Mick Riordan et al., unpublished (Washington D.C.: June 1995), table 23. Note, however, that the bank's definition of the MENA region excludes the Arab Gulf states.

4. Rodney Wilson, "The Economic Relations of the Middle East: Towards Europe or within the Region?" *Middle East Journal* 48, no. 2 (spring 1994): 281, table 2.

5. Ashraf Fouad, "Gulf Arabs Move Closer to Unity," Reuters quoted in *Daily Star* (Beirut), 18 December 1997.

6. Faris Glubb, "The GCC: Important Steps Forward," *Middle East International,* 5 December 1997.

7. Shada Islam, "Santer Slams Israel," *Middle East International,* 27 February 1998, p.13 and Frances Williams, "Palestine Trade Hit by Stalemate in Mideast," *Financial Times* (London), 13 March 1998.

8. Hassan Ibrahim, "The Arab Common Market," *Newsletter of the Economic Research Forum for the Arab Countries, Iran and Turkey* (Cairo) 3, no. 4 (December 1997-January 1998): 5.

PART IV:
NATURAL RESOURCES

CHAPTER NINE

Water and Security in the Middle East: The Israeli-Syrian Water Confrontations as a Case Study*

HILLEL I. SHUVAL

INTRODUCTION: WATER WARS IN THE MIDDLE EAST—REALITY OR RHETORIC?

The men of Isaac dug in the dry riverbed and found a well of living waters there. The herdsman of Gerar quarreled with the herdsman of Isaac saying "This water belongs to us." Isaac called the well Eshek [quarrel] since they had quarreled with him . . . then he dug a new well at another place and they did not quarrel over that, so he called it Rehovot [spacious]. "Surely," he said, "the Eternal has made space for us now, so that we can all prosper in the land." Gen. 26: 19-22

*T*his reference in the Bible to an event that took place some 4,000 years ago may well be among man's oldest accounts of conflict and feud over water. In the past, countries have engaged in conflicts over water or used the control of water resources to dominate an adversary. This chapter will try to examine the question of whether this history of conflict and wars over water still applies to the Middle East of today, or whether the modern technology of dams, pipelines, and desalination, together with regional cooperation, and the ease and low cost of the importation of "virtual water" in the form of food staples, has fundamentally changed the nature of water conflicts. Today, water is, after all, an economic good, available in unlimited quantities at the price of desalination; thus there is an upper economic bound on the value of water.[1]

Dr. Boutros Boutros Ghali, former foreign minister of Egypt, and former secretary-general of the UN, has said that "the next war in the Middle East will be over water." Other Middle Eastern leaders, including King Hussein of Jordan, have in the past made public statements containing similar dire predictions about future wars over water in the Middle East. Journalists, political scientists, and veteran water experts have quoted, requoted, and reformulated the "water wars" hypothesis so often that it has become accepted by many laymen and politicians as part of the conventional wisdom of Middle East geopolitics.[2]

According to the study of Population Action International[3] many countries in the Middle East now face or will be facing severe water shortages as their populations grow and their water resources remain fixed. The intensity of the water conflicts in the Jordan River basin appear to be particularly grave since three of the five partners to the disputed waters—Israel, Jordan, and the Palestinians—face serious long-term water problems, particularly when considering the expected doubling of populations within the next 30 years. Israel's estimated current water resources are about 300 cubic meters/person/year,[4] with somewhat less available to Jordan. This estimate includes some waters historically used by Israel within its borders which are disputed by the Palestinians, since they are derived from the shared Israeli/Palestinian aquifer. Without an increase in water resources and with a doubling of population in some 30 years, these per capita numbers will be cut in half. I have also estimated that the 1997 figure for the Palestinians is 92 CM/P/Yr, based on the 1997 census of the Palestine National Authority (PNA), which reports a total Palestinian population of 2.4 million persons. This will go down to some 45 CM/P/Yr by 2025, assuming a doubling of the population and that they continue having available to them only the water resources that they are currently using. Of course, the Palestinians are presently in the process of negotiating for a larger share of the transboundary ground and surface water from their neighbors, Israel and Jordan.

However, the two other Jordan River riparians, Syria and Lebanon, currently have much more copious water supplies at their disposal and will not face the same sort of conditions of extreme water scarcity in the future that will be faced by their three less fortunate downstream neighbors. The potential total water resources available to Syria on a per capita basis was about 2,000 CM/P/Yr in 1990 or more than six times as much as available to Israel and 12 times as much as available to the Palestinians on a per capita basis. The water resources available to Lebanon were similarly large on a per capita basis.

From the above analysis, with all of its tentative estimates of the availability of water resources some 25 to 30 years in the future, one thing is clear: Jordan and the Palestinians will be extremely short of water by the year 2025, with fewer than the 125 CM/P/Yr considered by many as the Minimum Water Requirement (MWR)[5] for human survival to meet all the needs of domestic/urban/commercial and industrial uses at a reasonable standard of living, while Lebanon and Syria will still have available to them significantly more water than the absolute minimum. Israel, too, will be hard-pressed for water, and will be just on the borderline of the MWR.

This chapter is devoted mainly to an analysis of the water conflicts of Syria, Lebanon, and Israel, who share the transboundary waters of the Jordan River basin (see Map 9.1). These nations will, it is hoped, attempt to reach an accommodation over their conflicts in the peace process initiated by the United States and Russia at the Madrid Conference in 1991.

Map 9.1: Major Water Projects in the Jordan River Basin

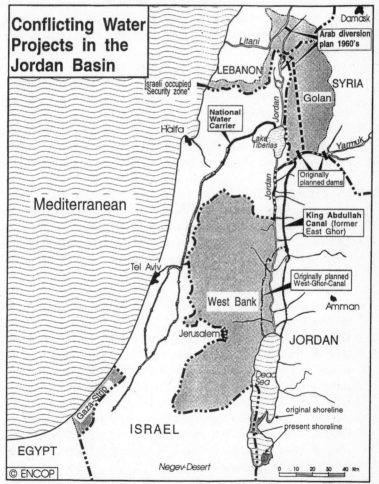

Source: From Stephan Libiszewski, Water Disputes and Their Role in the Resolution of the Arab-Israeli Conflict, ENCOP. Occasional Paper No. 13 (Berne: Center for Security Studies and Conflic Research/Swiss Peace Foundation, August 1995), p. 8.

Jordan and Israel reached a comprehensive peace agreement, signed in October 1994, which included a mutually accepted agreement on water. In November 1995, Israel and the PNA reached a new stage in their peace efforts which resulted in the interim agreement, called the Oslo II Agreement, which includes a preliminary, mutually agreed, formulation concerning the recognition of the water rights of the Palestinians in the West Bank and Gaza, although they are still far from a final agreement on water.

Looking at the Middle East water conflicts, particularly those associated with the five confrontational nations, it is possible to discern the following shared series of important social, economic, and national issues associated with them, some of which may have security implications. They are not necessarily listed in their order of importance.

1. A need to maintain, regain, or expand national water/property rights;
2. Irrigated agriculture to assure independence in essential food supply and so-called food security;
3. National and ideological commitments to agriculture as a way of life: traditional Arab rural lifestyle of the *fallahin* (village farmers); the Zionist ideological goal of return to the soil, pioneering and greening of the desert;
4. Irrigated agriculture as a low-cost social policy to assure employment/ livelihood for a sector of the population, including returnees, who have insufficient education and training for industry or commerce;
5. Agricultural settlements as a way of staking claims to land/borders;
6. Need for fresh potable water supplies for present and future urban and industrial development and economic prosperity;
7. Reserve resources for future population growth: Return of the Diaspora, an ideological commitment, which has deep emotional significance for the Jews of Israel and the Palestinians;
8. The strategic and political advantages and sense of power and well-being resulting from a nation's having control over its own water resources and having control over the water resources of its neighbors, and, conversely, the fear and anxiety that might result if water resources were controlled by a neighbor;
9. The fear of transboundary water pollution, e.g., that a neighbor will pollute a downstream country's water resources through negligence or inadequate environmental regulations, monitoring and control of urban, industrial, and agricultural wastes.

HAVE CONFRONTATIONS OVER WATER
SINCE 1948 LED TO WARS?

We shall examine examples of the series of limited military confrontations over water between Israel and Syria that occurred during the period between 1948 and 1966 in an effort to determine whether or not the water issues involved could or did lead to war in the Middle East as claimed by some.

The First Military Confrontation: 1953

Although there had been earlier local military confrontations between Syria and Israel over the al-Hamma springs (Hamat Gader), the first major, but localized, military confrontation over water between Israel and Syria took place in the fall of 1953. On 2 September 1953, Israel began work on a canal at Gesher B'not Yaakov in the Israeli/Syrian demilitarized zone along the Jordan River to divert water from the Jordan. This was the first stage of the Israel National Water Carrier (NWC) which was planned to transport Jordan River water to the south and to the Negev for Israel's major agricultural irrigation development projects.

The initial Israeli plan for the diversion works on the Jordan River and the NWC, drawn up by the American engineer G. B. Hays, was conceived in the immediate pre-state days. It was based on the 1923 international border between mandatory Palestine and Syria which also was the recognized international border established under the UN partition plan for Palestine which had provided the international legitimacy for the establishment of Israel as an independent state in 1948. According to the international borders of mandatory Palestine and the UN partition plan, the site of the diversion works at Gesher B'not Yaakov was on the Israeli side of the Jordan River, and Israel felt it had every right to carry out civilian water works there (see Map 9.2).

In 1948, Syria rejected the UN decisions and—together with the armies of a coalition of Arab states, including Jordan, Lebanon and Egypt together with Palestinian irregulars—attacked the newly created state of Israel. Israel survived and overcame the massive joint attack and in 1949 signed armistice agreements with its adversaries, negotiated by the UN intermediary, Dr. Ralph Bunche. The armistice agreement signed between Israel and Syria established cease-fire demarcation lines and a number of demilitarized zones along the borders between Israel and Syria, based on the de facto situation of troops on the ground at the end of the war.

In a number of places, the Syrian invasion forces crossed the former international borders of mandatory Palestine and, at the time of the cease-fire agreement, were left in control of critical water source areas to the west of the international border which never had been part of Syria but had been included in mandatory Palestine. These areas included a section of the canals from the Banias springs, which is one of the three main tributaries of the Jordan River, sections of the

Jordan River, the eastern shores of Lake Tiberias, portions of the Yarmuk River, and the strategic al-Hamma mineral springs contiguous to the Yarmuk River. The area of Gesher B'not Yaakov on the Jordan River was now in one of the demilitarized zones. In those early years, Syria continuously made efforts to broaden its foothold and increase its control in the demilitarized zones and areas west of the international borders which it had occupied during the war of 1948.

Map 9.2: Internatinal Border between Israel and Syria and the 1949 Truce Line

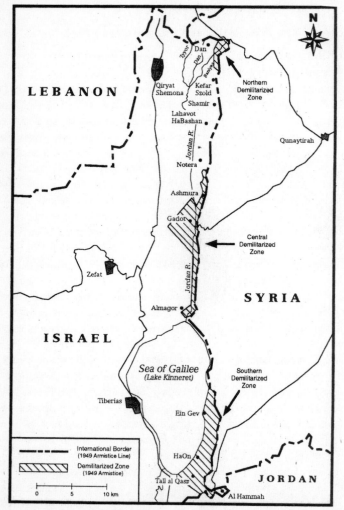

Source: From Peace with Security: Israel's Minimum Security Requirements in Negotiations with Syria by Ze'ev Schiff, Policy Paper No. 34 (Washington, D.C.: The Washington Institute for Near East Policy, 1993), p. 8.

In 1951, Syria had challenged an earlier project concerning Israel's plans to drain and reclaim some 10,000 hectares of the malarial Hula swamps. The swamp lands, which had been purchased by a Jewish company, the Palestine Land Development Company in 1934, were also partially in the demilitarized zone. UN Truce Supervision Organization (UNTSO) chief of staff, General Riley, ruled in June 1951 that "civilian land conservation was permitted in the Demilitarized Zone under the terms of the Armistice Agreement."[6] The Hula drainage and land reclamation project was carried out as planned and completed in 1956.

The Israeli canal construction operations at Gesher B'not Yaakov were carried out under the protection of Israeli tanks and there were exchanges of fire between Syrian and Israeli tanks, with the Syrians citing illegal Israel military activities in the zone. Syria deployed its armed forces along the border and opened fire on the canal construction site and the earth-moving equipment operating there. In October 1953, Syria protested to the UN Security Council that the Israeli diversion works infringed upon the rights of the Arab inhabitants of the demilitarized zone. Syria claimed the works had deprived it of Jordan water, and that Israel had conducted military operations in the zone. Israel's ambassador to the UN, Abba Eban, argued in 1953 in support of Israel's project at Gesher B'not Yaakov, maintaining that it was a civilian agricultural irrigation and desert reclamation project. He further argued that the 1951 UN decision in support of Israel's drainage scheme for the Hula provided a precedent since the schemes were similar, and that there should be "continuity in principles."[7] Syria countered that the project violated the 1949 Armistice Agreement because it would increase Israel's military capability and deprive Syria of water resources derived from its territory.

On 23 September 1953, the UN chief of staff, General Bennike, called on Israel to cease work on the canal. Israel ignored the clear call by the UN peacekeeping force to stop the excavation of the canal and to cease all military activities in the demilitarized zone. Syria called up more armored forces to the area, and Israel and Syria were on the verge of a potentially serious military conflagration.

The United States government realized the seriousness of the situation and decided to intervene. United States secretary of state, John Foster Dulles, declared on 20 October 1953 that the United States government would withhold foreign aid funds earmarked for Israel unless Israel heeded the UN directive.[8] The American economic aid funds to Israel were at that time a major source of support in Israel's efforts to resettle and absorb some 600,000 new immigrants who had arrived in the country as Holocaust survivors and refugees from Middle Eastern and North African Arab countries. This was the first publicly announced use of United States economic sanctions against Israel and the effect was dramatic, with Israel deciding to cease work on the canal on 27 October 1953, within a week of the American declaration. On the same day, as Israel announced its temporary discontinuance on the Gesher B'not Yaakov canal project, "without prejudice to rights, claims, or position in the matter," President Dwight Eisenhower announced resumption of economic aid to Israel.[9]

The power of intervention by the international community and economic sanctions were clearly demonstrated in this case and were effective since, apparently, the strategic and economic value of the water project for Israel was less important than the possible strategic and economic advantages of continued American support. This was particularly true in this case, since the Israeli government was aware of the fact that there were alternative ways of achieving the same water project development goals without a direct military confrontation with Syria. Israel was eventually able to continue the project with a diversion on the shores of Lake Tiberias located 212 meters below sea level. This move of location was very costly for Israel, since it involved a greater investment, greatly increased pumping costs, and poorer quality of water. The water had to be pumped up some 400 meters; the lake water was also saline and presented serious problems for agricultural use compared with the Jordan River water at the upstream site. However, the change in site avoided any political or military entanglements with Syria and gained important economic and diplomatic support for Israel from the United States.

Simultaneously with the ending of the potential military confrontation between Israel and Syria, President Eisenhower appointed Eric Johnston as his personal envoy and roving representative. Johnston's task was to seek a comprehensive program for the development of the Jordan River water resources "on a regional basis." He skillfully avoided discussions of water rights and succeeded in achieving consensus among Israeli, Jordanian, Syrian, and Lebanese water experts at the technical level as to the amounts of water each of the riparians could reasonably use for agricultural development schemes, with particular emphasis on promoting refugee resettlement projects for both sides. G. G. Stevens[10] reports that the result was the proposed apportionment of the Jordan River waters under Johnston's final form of the "Unified plan" which later became known as the "Johnston plan" (see Table 9.1). It must be stated at this point that there is no official document called the Johnston plan and there are a number of different interpretations as to the final water allocations included in the Johnston proposals. It is worthwhile noting that the amount of water allocated by these proposals to Syria (132 millions of cubic meters/year)[11] and Lebanon (35 MCM/Yr) were exactly the amounts recommended by the Technical Committee of the Arab League which, under Egyptian leadership, formulated the "Arab plan" for allocation of the Jordan basin waters. Apparently these are the amounts of water that Lebanon and Syria themselves demanded, and claimed that they needed and could reasonably use in the limited agricultural areas in the vicinity of the Jordan sources. The figures were accepted by Eric Johnston, and Israel as well, in 1955.

TABLE 9.1

Volume of the Jordan River System's Flow Apportioned between States in the Final Form of Johnston's Unified Plan, in millions of cubic meters/year (MCM/Yr)

Jordan	480
Syria	132 (42 from Banias-Jordan)
Lebanon	35
Israel	466[a]
Total Annual Flow	1113

[a]The residual flow is Israel's share of the total flow, given that the above listed amounts were claimed as necessary by the other states. Israel's share would vary according to the flow conditions of the river system.
Source: G. G. Stevens, Jordan Water Partition (Stanford, Calif.: Stanford University Press, 1965).

Israel was ambivalent, at first, about the Johnston proposals since it was allocated a much smaller share of the Jordan waters than it felt it should rightfully have. It maintained it needed more water to meet its growing demand for irrigated agriculture to satisfy the increasing requirements for food supply for the rapid influx of immigrants. Israel had more than doubled its population from its founding in 1948 and anticipated that the flow of refugees would continue, resulting in major demands on its limited water resources. Israel was also deeply concerned that Johnston proposed that it receive only the residual flow, with the other states being given priority and allocated a fixed amount of water each year. This meant that at times of severe drought Israel might receive no water from the Jordan. Israel was also very troubled about the nature of the neutral authority, proposed by Johnston, which was to be established to oversee the allocation of Lake Tiberias waters. Israel feared loss of its sovereignty and strategic control over the lake.

According to the State Department's internal documents, United States negotiators used the "carrot and stick" technique to bring Israel to agreement. The United States, on the one hand, warned that the aid program to Israel might be jeopardized in Congress unless Israel came to terms with Johnston. Abba Eban reported that the United States once again threatened Israel with economic sanctions.[12] On the other hand, the United States promised generous financial support for Israel's major water development projects, and other technical assistance, as well as an attractive security agreement, if Israel would accept the Johnston plan.

David Wishart quotes recently declassified internal United States State Department documents which indicate that in June 1955 Israel agreed to the basic terms of the plan that Johnston had drawn up, including the controversial joint water storage in Lake Tiberias and neutral "water master" proposals.[13]

According to Wishart, the State Department reports show that "Israel displayed an apparent willingness to permit joint storage of Yarmuk waters in Lake Tiberias for use by Jordan, to allow withdrawals from the lake to be supervised by a neutral water master, and to permit Jordan to withdraw 100 MCM/Yr from Lake Tiberias over and above the amount stored there from the Yarmuk."

In Michael Brecher's study of documents and the minutes of cabinet meetings, it is revealed that in the final internal Israeli debate, which approved the Johnston plan, Foreign Minister Moshe Sharett, the head of the Israel water negotiating team, Levi Eshkol, as well as David Ben Gurion who had just returned to the government as Defense Minister, after his self-imposed "retirement" in Sde Boker, all supported the comprehensive view that acceptance of the Johnston plan would, in the long run, bring Israel major political, economic, and strategic advantages, including a potential opening of cooperation, de facto recognition, and ultimately peace agreements with its Arab neighbors—Syria, Lebanon, and Jordan.[14]

On the other hand the technocrats, water experts, and water engineers, and the agricultural lobby led by engineer Simcha Blass, Israel's veteran water planner, took the narrow view and bitterly opposed the plan on the grounds that Israel would be deprived of vital water resources. Once again the broader view of economic, strategic, and security advantages of cooperating with the United States and the Arab neighbors outweighed the disadvantages concerning the exact amount of water that might be available to Israel under the Johnston plan and the potential limitations of security and sovereignty over Lake Tiberias. Without the massive financial support from the United States and the world community, Israel would not have been able to develop its water resources and it opted for potential strategic advantages and political realism rather than the narrow view of the water technocrats which would have led to confrontation and stalemate. From Israel's point of view it appears that war over water was not a realistic option at that time.

Wishart has produced a report on the breakdown of the negotiations over the allocation of the Jordan waters, based on recently declassified United States State Department records of the negotiations.[15] The Johnston plan was accepted by Israel and the official Arab representatives at the technical level, but on 11 October 1955, the technical committee of the Arab League forwarded it to the political committee of the Arab League where it failed to win approval.[16] Thomas Naff and Ruth Matson maintain that the Arab "non-adoption" of the plan was not total rejection.[17] Miriam Lowi puts it more bluntly, citing Arab concern "that their agreement would imply indirect recognition of the Zionist state."[18] In a letter written in 1955, the Arab Higher Committee for Palestine explained its opposition to the Johnston plan: "The scheme is another step made by the imperialists and Zionists to attain their ends, territorial expansion in the heart of the Arab homeland, under the attractive guise of economic interest."[19]

Wishart concludes that at the political level, "the Arabs were reluctant to accept the plan that involved acquiescence to Israel's development goals, abandonment of traditional principles of water rights assignment, and the possibility of a United States security pact with Israel."[20] Wishart reasons that the Arabs apparently opted to break off the water negotiations with the United States, since they did not feel serious water needs or pressure regarding water development and felt that they had more to lose politically than they would gain economically, particularly since each one of the Arab states felt that they could eventually develop their water resources on their own and were not in need of any regional cooperation projects.

On the practical level, however, informal agreement to comply with the Johnston formula by Israel and Jordan did provide the basis for major American financial assistance to Israel in the construction of the NWC. This enabled Israel to develop important irrigation projects in the south and in the Negev, as well as to give assistance to Jordan in the construction of the Eastern Ghor canal (now known as the Abdullah canal), providing for major irrigation development projects along the previously barren eastern banks of the Jordan River (see Map 9.1). Both countries have cooperated informally ever since in allocation of Yarmuk water, along the lines of the Johnston proposals.

Israel continued to plan and work on construction of the NWC but, as mentioned earlier, it shifted the point of water diversion from the controversial site in the demilitarized zone at Gesher B'Not Yaakov to one at Eshed-Kinerot (near Tabcha) on the shores of Lake Tiberias, thus avoiding the issue of construction in the demilitarized zone and a direct military confrontation with Syria. However, the problems of water allocation with Syria and Lebanon remained unresolved. They were to come to the fore with new military and strategic confrontations a few years later.

The Second Military Confrontation: 1965

On 11 June 1964, Israel's NWC was completed after five years of uninterrupted work. In January 1965, the Syrian and Lebanese initiated projects, approved and financed by the Arab League summit conferences at Alexandria in September 1964, to build canals to divert the headwaters of the Jordan River, with the stated intention of preventing Israel from utilizing a major portion of its waters. The waters of the Banias, in the Golan Heights in Syria, were to be diverted by a canal to the Yarmuk River, and the Hasbani River, rising in Lebanon, was to be diverted to the Litani in Lebanon (see Map 9.1). The motivation was mainly political; this was to be a punitive action against Israel's construction of the NWC which was pumping water from Lake Tiberias to southern Israel and to the Negev for new agricultural irrigation projects there. Neither Syria nor Lebanon had much to gain by the diversionary canals. In the case of Lebanon, most of the diverted flow would go directly to the sea, while the canal being constructed by Syria would carry the water to the Yarmuk where it could possibly be used by Jordan. It should be noted that some Middle East experts felt that the Arab League diversion plan was partially an outgrowth of the internal power struggles between Egypt and Syria and only indirectly related to the specific Israeli-Syrian water conflict.

Israel protested to the UN Security Council, declaring that these "diversions of vital water sources were an infringement of its sovereign rights." The approach to the UN to intervene brought no results. In March, May, and August 1965, Israel launched localized shelling from tanks and air attacks against the Syrian and Lebanese works and threatened more serious military interventions; this was because the diversions could potentially reduce Israeli water resources by some 260 MCM/Yr which represented more than 50 percent of the waters available to it from the Jordan River.

Israel felt that such a drastic reduction in its vital water supply would present a very real and serious economic and security blow as well as a threat to its sovereignty. For Syria and Lebanon, the amount of water to be diverted was insignificant in comparison to their relatively large water resources potential. For Syria, the amount to be diverted from the Banias, some 120 MCM/Yr, at best, was only 1 percent of its potential national water resources. If Syria and Lebanon had any possibility of utilizing the waters of the Banias and the Hasbani locally they would have done so rather than carry out the expensive and basically useless diversion. Due to the topography of the area—with little flat agricultural land available in the vicinity of the sources of the Jordan River—Syrian and Lebanese farmers could only have had marginal agricultural benefits from the Arab League diversion project. Pumping the water to other, higher agricultural land in Syria would be prohibitively expensive, since the upper plateau areas of the Golan Heights are some 800-1,000 meters above the Jordan basin water sources. Jordan would have gained the major benefit from the water diversion project.

After the initial Israeli military interventions Lebanon, which had nearly completed its portion of the diversion works, discontinued the project, but Syria continued. Israel launched further serious air attacks against the Syrian works and localized border fighting broke out; the Syrian works were severely damaged and eventually destroyed. In 1966 the project was abandoned.[21] Syria was obviously not prepared to go to war over the diversion canal, since few if any vital economic or security issues were at stake. Israel may have been concerned about a possible renewal of the diversion project but proved to itself and to Syria that, with very limited military intervention at the local level, the problem could be dealt with effectively without a major military confrontation.

The Six Day War

Naff and Matson wrote that "some say that these events led to the June 1967 War."[22] In a later paper, Naff was even more specific in claiming that "water was an important factor in the outbreak of the 'Six Day War.'"[23] There were indeed a number of Israeli-Syrian border incidents followed by air battles involving Israeli and Syrian fighter planes during the period between the Israeli military action to destroy the Jordan diversion project and the Six Day War. However, it is moot whether there is a clear case that the water issue was a central factor or even a factor of any significance in the outbreak of the war.

Most historians and military experts agree that the June 1967 war with Egypt, Jordan, and Syria, known as the Six Day War, would not have started had not Egypt forced the withdrawal of UN peace-keeping observers from the Sinai Peninsula and declared a closure of the Straits of Tiran, thus effectively blockading the port of Eilat and Israel's sea link to Asia. This unilateral action by Egypt was in clear violation of the 1957 agreement concerning Israel's withdrawal from Sinai after the 1956 war, and challenged Israel's vital oil supply lines and threatened her freedom of the seas. Egypt's action was perceived by Israel as the casus belli that precipitated the war, rather than the issue of Syrian diversionary works on the Banias, which meanwhile had been abandoned. There is also a question as to whether Israel would have attacked Syria in 1967 if Syria had not initiated attacks on the Hula Valley settlements from its positions on the Golan Heights, in anticipation of an imminent Egyptian victory in the south.

It appears more judicious to assume that Syria did not continue the work on diverting the headwaters of the Jordan River, when faced with a serious but local, military confrontation with Israel, for the simple reason that the project was mainly political and punitive in nature and Syria as well as Lebanon had very little to gain economically or strategically by the diversions.[24] It is not unreasonable to conclude that the Syrian military authorities were not prepared for a major military confrontation with Israel's full armed forces over the waters of the Jordan, which neither Syria nor Lebanon had ever used to any great extent and which were apparently seen as non-essential or minor water projects of little economic or strategic importance. There was no real basis for a water war over Israel's use of force to stop the Syrian-Arab League project to divert the tributaries of the Jordan. However, since talk of water wars makes good newspaper copy, the press has continued to promote the story.

Once the war between Israel and Egypt got under way, and following Egypt's assurance to Syria that Israel was about to collapse, Syria joined in by attacking Israel from the north. The leaders of the Israeli communities in the Hula Valley under the Golan Heights brought pressure to bear on the Israeli government to retaliate against the heavy Syrian attacks. In response, Israel's counter-attack led to the capture of the Golan Heights from Syria. There is no doubt that once the battle against Syria had started, the strategic importance of the Banias springs, the al-Hamma springs, and the eastern shores of the Jordan River and of Lake Tiberias was a factor in assuring their early inclusion within the areas occupied by the Israeli armed forces. However, there is very little evidence or logic to suggest that the counter-attack against Syria in June 1967 and the capture of the Golan Heights was motivated mainly by the water issues or the Syrian diversion project which, by that time, presented no imminent threat.

The Six Day War completely changed the hydro-politics of the Jordan basin. The tributaries and springs of the Jordan all fell under Israeli control. Israel's share of the Yarmuk alignment grew, as did its share of the route of the Jordan River from south of the Beit Shean Valley to the Dead Sea. This advantage was exploited by Israel, and the use of water from the Jordan River in Israel increased, amounting to 550-600 MCM/Yr, in contrast to the Johnston plan's estimated allotment of about 400 MCM/Yr.[25]

Arnon Sofer points out that one of the reasons some Israelis have given to justify the increased use of Jordan basin water by Israel after the 1967 War was "the fact that it now rules over the areas of Judea and Samaria (the occupied territories of the West Bank) and the waters intended in the Johnston plan for this section now belong to Israel."[26] However, the Palestinians query this argument and ask if under the Oslo agreement—and with the creation of the PNA in most of the Occupied Territories according to the second phase of the Oslo agreement approved in September 1995—Israel should now forego its claim to the 100-150 MCM/Yr of additional water it has drawn from the Jordan basin since 1967. The PNA argues that this additional water should be reallocated for use by the water-short PNA in the West Bank, as was intended by the original Johnston plan. While there is a final peace treaty between Israel and Jordan, which includes a settlement of all of the outstanding water issues on the Jordan between the two nations, the Palestinian, Syrian, and Lebanese claims on the Jordan waters remain to be settled.

Over the past two decades, the Syrians have begun an independent project for capturing the flood flows of the Yarmuk in its territory and drilling deep wells to capture a major portion of its base flow. By doing this they have increased their diversions of the Yarmuk River water above and beyond the amount allocated to it under the Johnston plan (see Map 9.3). Under the Johnston plan, and according to the Arab plan sponsored by the Arab League with Syrian acquiescence, Syria was to be allocated 132 MCM/Yr from the Jordan basin, 90 MCM/Yr from the Yarmuk and 42 MCM/Yr from the Banias and from downstream flows of the Jordan. The current Syrian plans include building 27 dams on the Yarmuk tributaries with a storage capacity totaling 200-250 MCM.

Map 9.3: Existing Syrian Dams on the Yarmuk River and the Site for Proposed Jordan-Syrian Al-Wahda Dam and the Hydroelectric Station

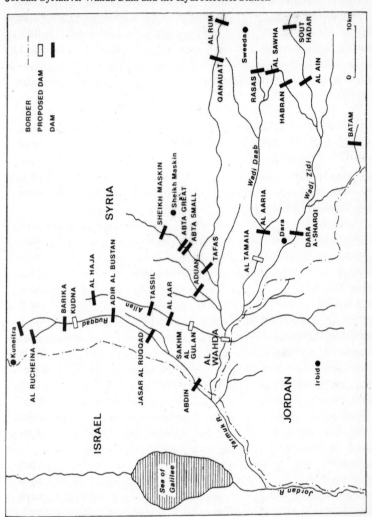

Source: From Arnon Soffer, "The Relevance of the Johnston Plan to the Reality of 1993 and Beyond," in Water and Peace in the Middle East, edited by J. Isaac and H.I. Shuval (Amsterdam: Elsevier Press, 1994), p. 121.

Most of these dams have been completed and can be seen clearly in aerial photos.[27] In 1992 their capacity came to 153 MCM/Yr.[28] In such a situation, Jordan will be left with some 200 MCM/Yr of the 480 MCM/Yr that was promised in the Johnston plan (see Table 9.1). Some Jordanians fear that the joint Syrian-Jordanian al-Wahda dam (Unity dam) project, which was to have been built at Maqaren on the Yarmuk River (see Map 9.1) according to the 1987 treaty between Syria and Jordan, is hardly feasible any longer. This is because the major Syrian diversions along the Yarmuk River have in effect undermined the project, leaving Jordan with only limited amounts of water from the Yarmuk. A smaller dam project may, however, still be feasible. This issue of conflict between Syria and Jordan, over the waters of the Yarmuk, remains to be settled.

A MARKET APPROACH AS A BASIS FOR JOINT WATER MANAGEMENT

The Harvard Middle East Water Project (HMEWP) was initiated in 1992 by a group of faculty members from Harvard University and the Massachusetts Institute of Technology, headed by Professor Franklin Fisher, under the auspices of the Center for Social and Economic Policy in the Middle East of the John F. Kennedy School of Government at Harvard University, together with a group of Israeli, Palestinian, and Jordanian water scientists and economists.[29]

The HMEWP proposes a rational economic method for analyzing water issues that may help the parties to perceive the conflict and approaches to its resolution in a new way. The project's main goal is to adopt an economic approach to regional water management that will lead to optimal social use of the limited water resources of the region, through water sales and transfers between areas and economic sectors, within nations and between nations. In addition it is one of the goals of the project to help the parties to the conflict to calculate the real economic value of the waters in dispute, and in this way gain some sense of proportion concerning the size of the conflict. Thus, the project will, it is hoped, facilitate a resolution to the conflict.

While water may in some ways be unique in terms of the depths of the historic, national, and emotional roots of the conflict over it, it is nevertheless, in the final analysis, an economic good which can be purchased/manufactured in unlimited quantities at a price, e.g., by desalination of sea water. In many cases new, yet untapped, water resources can be developed: recycled wastewater, dams built to store previously wasted floodwaters or water transported from one source to another and purchased for much less than the cost of sea water desalination. Particularly under conditions of peace, it is possible to visualize cooperation in regional water management and development to the benefit of all the partners; an economic approach, including regulated water marketing, might well become feasible.

The HMEWP is based on the following approach:[30]

1. Water is a scarce resource. Scarce resources have value. In the case of water, however, that value is not merely the price that water would ob-

tain in a free market. National aims, including agriculture, employment, and social policy are involved in the value of water.

2. The project seeks to calculate the value of water in the region at the present and in the future up to the year 2020. It first examines the cost of supplying water, from different sources at different points, and transporting it. Next, it estimates private demand curves for water from different sectors including domestic/urban, industry, and agriculture. Finally, it incorporates national water policy expressed as additional demand for water at different prices. Equilibrium prices for water are calculated—prices that equate supply and demand.

3. With the full value of water calculated, the value of the property rights at issue can be assessed. Since water cannot be worth more than the cost of replacing it, an upper bound for that value can easily be obtained. In preliminary runs of the mathematical simulation model developed by the HMEWP, Professor Fisher has made a tentative estimate which suggests that the money value of the water/property rights dispute between Israel and the Palestinians is most likely no greater than some U.S.$50m to $60m/year. He concludes that "the property rights dispute is one over a sum sufficiently small that nations can negotiate about it."[31] By monetizing the dispute, the HMEWP hopes to contribute to facilitating its resolution.

While the HMEWP has not yet had an opportunity to study the possibility of a market approach involving Israel, Syria, and Lebanon, my own very preliminary look at the possible outcome of monetizing the value of their dispute over the Jordan River waters will be presented below.

ISRAELI-SYRIAN SECURITY ISSUES

At the time of writing, very little progress has been made in the current Israeli-Syrian peace negotiations and there is no indication that water issues per se have been discussed directly or indirectly. However, one critical water issue has emerged indirectly in connection with the opening Syrian and Israeli positions on the question of the final borders. The stated policy of the Israeli government under Prime Ministers Yitzhak Rabin and Shimon Peres, concerning the Golan, was that "the depth of the peace will determine the depth of withdrawal." However, press reports had suggested that—based on the precedent of its peace agreements with Egypt and Jordan, where a return to the international borders provided the basis for the agreement—Israel would insist that in the case of Syria as well, the international borders that existed between Syria and mandatory Palestine in 1948 provide the point of departure for the negotiations. The full position on this issue of the new Israeli government under Prime Minister Benjamin Netanyahu, who was elected in May 1996, is not yet known. However, according to public statements made by Netanyahu since his election, it appears that the position of the previous Labor Party/Rabin-Peres government, on withdrawal from the Golan Heights and final borders, has been rejected. On the other hand, Syria has insisted that the cease-fire lines determined in the Armistice Agreement of 1949 become the permanent borders between Israel and Syria.

The cease-fire demarcation lines of 1949 included within Syrian control several strategic water sources including the Banias springs, portions of the Jordan and Yarmuk Rivers, the al-Hamma mineral springs and the eastern shores of the Sea of Galilee (see Map 9.2). These elements were not allocated to Syria according to the 1923 officially recognized international border that existed between mandatory Palestine and Syria. Israelis point out that the cease-fire lines of 1949 were the result of aggression and military conquest and that Syria cannot logically demand that Israel relinquish the Golan Heights captured during the 1967 war while Syria is allowed to hold the strategically important areas on the western side of the international border that it captured in the 1948 war. Some Israelis claim that the very same international border of mandatory Palestine provided the basis for the peace agreements with Jordan and Egypt. Furthermore, they claim that only by a return to the international border with Syria will there be symmetry and therefore adherence to the principle that land taken in war by either side be returned as part of the peace agreement. While there are other important strategic considerations in the debate about the return to the international border, the water issue is one of the most critical.

BORDERS BASED ON STRATEGIC WATER SECURITY CONSIDERATIONS

There are a number of groups and political parties in Israel who oppose giving up part or all of the Golan Heights to Syria as well as the cession of most areas of the West Bank and Gaza to the Palestinians in return for peace. These groups differ greatly in motivation and ideology. With some, security considerations are of uppermost importance, while with others religious/nationalist/ideological considerations dominate. The Greater Land of Israel Movement, for example, holds that Israel cannot return any of the areas it now occupies since, according to the Bible, God allocated the Land of Israel to the Jewish people. Such groups oppose giving up "a single inch" of territory. Most of this support is based on religious/ideological rationale. However, some extreme right-wing secular groups also support this position, but for nationalist/ideological reasons.

Other, more mainstream right-wing groups base their opposition to giving up all or parts of the Golan Heights mainly on strategic and defense considerations, claiming that giving up the Golan Heights would expose Israel to inordinate security risks, such as a surprise attack from the dominating Golan Heights by a future Syrian leader.

Another approach has been motivated by concerns over water security and protecting Israel's water sources that arise in the Golan. This approach has motivated a study of the possible alternative borders with Syria which would provide Israel with complete control over its current water resources, thus assuring Israel of water security on its border with Syria. These resources, which total some 170 MCM/Yr, include the flow of the Banias of about 120 MCM/Yr and surface flow to the Jordan from the side wadis of the Golan Heights which can contribute some 50 MCM/Yr in rainy years. In 1991, a study was made of this question by the Jaffee Center for Strategic Studies of Tel Aviv University, under the direction of General (Reserves) Aharon Yariv, former head of intelligence of the Israel Defense Forces, in cooperation with Tahal Water Planning for Israel, Israel's leading quasi-governmental water resources planning agency.

The study was never released to the public for what were originally claimed as security considerations, but which according to Ze'ev Schiff were apparently mainly politically motivated reasons. A fairly detailed report, leaked to the press, has revealed that the Jaffee Center/Tahal study evaluated the possibility of drawing up water security borders with Syria that would ensure that all the strategic water elements—both ground water and surface water—that Israel is currently utilizing would remain in Israeli control.[32] Map 9.4, which is based on the newspaper version of the Jaffee Center/Tahal map,[33] shows these proposed water security borders. This water security map would include within the borders of Israel the tributaries of the Jordan River, the al-Hamma springs, the side wadis of the Golan Heights which can be dammed up for water storage and could divert water from the Jordan watershed, as well as the entire area contiguous to the Sea of Galilee. According to this map, Israel would not have to hold on to most of the Golan from a water security point of view. However, the area defined by the international border, which according to unconfirmed press reports was apparently proposed by the previous government of Israel as a basis for an agreement, covers a good part of these water security areas, except for the drainage areas of the side wadis in the Golan which at best would yield some 50 MCM/Yr in good years and little or nothing in draught years. A similar water security map was drawn up for the West Bank which also showed that, strictly from the water resources point of view, most of the West Bank areas could be given up.

It is interesting to note that at the time the report was completed, the then minister of agriculture, General (Reserves) Raphael Etan, leader of the right wing Tsomet Party, is reported by Schiff as having quashed the release of the report

Map 9.4: Suggested Possible Lines of Israeli Withdrawal from the Golan Heights Based on Water Security Considerations

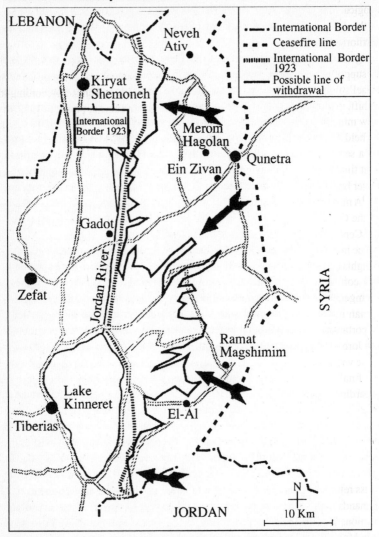

Source: From Ha'aretz Daily Newspaper Ltd., October 8, 1993, Part 2.

claiming security considerations.[34] However, Schiff revealed that Etan, who held a major controlling influence over Tahal, prevented the agency from releasing the report since it clearly indicated that it would not be necessary to hold onto all of the West Bank or the Golan Heights to ensure water security, and from a water security point of view alone, a territorial compromise was feasible. General Etan, one of the leading right-wing opponents of giving up any territories for both ideological and security reasons, had previously published full-page advertisements in the *Jerusalem Post* in 1991 claiming that Israel could never give up any of the territories it occupied based on water security considerations alone. The right wing accused the Jaffee Institute and Tahal of presenting the water security map to support a dovish ideology that favored the approach of achieving peace with Israel's neighbors based on the concept of territorial compromise. According to Schiff, when the Labor government of Yizthak Rabin came to power in 1992, the new minister of agriculture, Yaakov Tzur, requested that the release of the report be held up temporarily since it might reveal Israel's tactical negotiating positions on a sensitive water security issue in the peace negotiations, which had for the first time begun to be held in a serious manner.[35] To this day the full report has never been officially released.

A number of political groups in Israel who favor maintaining major portions of the Golan, based mainly on considerations of security, have revived the Jaffee Center/Tahal "water security" map in support of their position opposing any peace initiative with Syria based on almost complete withdrawal from the Golan Heights up to the international border. Others groups, who favor a major territorial compromise with Syria in return for full peace with adequate security arrangements, point out, however, that by returning to the recognized Israeli-Syrian international border, Israel will be able to assure control of most of the important water sources including the Banias and will prevent Syrian access to the Jordan River and Lake Tiberias. Thus, it can be seen that the water security issue with Syria is very much alive, and still must be confronted and resolved in the final peace negotiations in which it may play an important role, especially regarding the final borders.

THE WATER DISPUTE AMONG ISRAEL, SYRIA, AND LEBANON

Press reports, to date, have not provided a clear picture of Syrian expectations or demands for a settlement concerning water. It has been reported that Syrian publications have presented different descriptions of the water sources of the Jordan (see Map 9.5).[36] In some cases the Syrians have referred to the Jordan as a Syrian river and on others as an international river. In other cases the Syrians have divided sovereignty over the Jordan according to its three main sources: Banias (Syria), Hasbani (Lebanon), and Dan (Israel). In one Syrian report it is stated that once the Golan is returned and the Syrian residents return, there will be a "need for greater water supplies."[37]

Map 9.5: The Jordan River Basin Watershed Boundaries, Tributaries, and Mean Annual Discharges

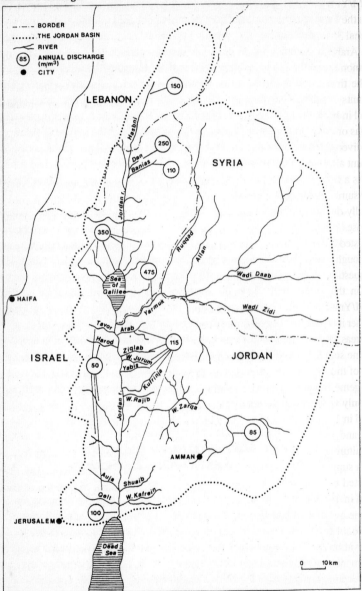

Source: From Arnon Soffer, "The Relevance of the Johnston Plan to the Reality of 1993 and Beyond," in Water and Peace in the Middle East, edited by J. Isaac and H.I. Shuval (Amsterdam: Elsevier Press, 1994), p. 120.

According to the Johnston Unified plan, Syria was to be allocated 20 MCM/Yr from the Banias, 22 MCM/Yr from the Jordan River, and 90 MCM/Yr from the Yarmuk for a total of 132 MCM/Yr.[38] Lebanon was also allocated an additional 35 MCM/Yr from the Hasbani. These figures were based on an independent Arab League evaluation of the amount of agricultural land that Syria and Lebanon could economically irrigate with waters taken at those low elevations. At the time of the Johnston negotiations in 1955, Syria demanded that those amounts of water be allocated for its use. Johnston included the Syrian demands in full in his final plan. While prior to 1967 Syria had not utilized the flow of the Banias or the Jordan to any great extent, during the period from 1974 to 1987, it has diverted far more from the Yarmuk and its groundwater sources than the amount allocated under the Johnston plan.

As a first rough estimate of possible Syrian and Lebanese demands, it could be assumed that the minimum amount of water that Syria could claim it could usefully divert from the Jordan sources, and economically utilize for agricultural purposes within the lower reaches of the Golan Heights, would be the 42 MCM/Yr requested by Syria in 1955 and included in the Johnston Unified plan. That would be enough water to irrigate some 5,000-10,000 hectares. There is, however, a serious question over whether that much flat irrigable agricultural land is actually available in the lower Golan. Lebanon might also be expected to demand the 35 MCM/Yr allocated to it under the Johnston plan although here too, it is questionable whether it could effectively use the water without major pumping to other more distant areas. Thus the total of possible Syrian and Lebanese demands is 77 MCM/Yr.

One scenario assumes that, under a peace agreement, Israel will return all or most of the area of the Golan Heights to Syria, in exchange for adequate security arrangements, full diplomatic relations, and peaceful cooperation. While there was only very limited Syrian irrigated agriculture on the Golan prior to its occupation in 1967, Israeli settlements with the help of the Mei Golan Water Cooperative and the Mekorot Water Company have meanwhile developed irrigated agriculture on the Golan, mainly through the construction of 15 small dams which supply some 30 MCM/Yr of water in good years. Practically no water is collected by these dams in drought years. Prior to the Israeli occupation of the Golan in 1967, most of this water would normally drain into Lake Tiberias and become available for use by the Israeli NWC. In addition, a well field pumping some 6.5 MCM/Yr has been developed at Alonie Bashan in the central Golan at an elevation of 600 meters above sea level.[39] It can be assumed that under a peace agreement these water works in the Golan Heights would revert to Syria and that Israel would view the 50 MCM/Yr of Golan water as part of the Jordan River basin waters allocated to Syria under the original Johnston plan.

Pumping water up from Lake Tiberias, which is 210 meters below sea level, or from the Banias springs at 350 meters above sea level, to the agricultural areas on the central Golan Heights at levels ranging from 800 to 1,000 meters above sea level, is expensive. It has been estimated that the energy costs alone are about U.S.$0.20 on the average for a cubic meter.[40] Including capital cost the total cost of the water might come to about U.S.$0.25-$0.30/CM. While water at this price is too expensive, and totally unfeasible for Syrian agriculture, it might eventually be feasible for urban use. The Syrians may have in mind a project supplying Jordan water for domestic purposes to Damascus, which suffers from serious water shortages. Considering the distance and height to which the water would have to be pumped the cost would be high; however, it might not be more expensive than the Yarmuk-Amman pipeline in Jordan.

The maximum Syrian claim might include the entire flow of the Banias of 110 MCM/Yr and the flow of 50 MCM/Yr from the Golan side wadis for itself, and the entire flow of the Hasbani, 150 MCM/Yr, for Lebanon, for a total of 310 MCM/Yr. The two countries might justify these claims based on the argument that the sources of these tributaries to the Jordan River rise in Syria and Lebanon and thus are fully their property. However, prior to the occupation of the Golan in 1967 and prior to the establishment of Israel in 1948 neither Syria nor Lebanon actually used much water from these sources, which have always flowed downstream in the Jordan River and for the past 40 years or so have been fully exploited by Israel.

The Syrians would have difficulty in justifying such a claim under modern precepts of international water law which do not recognize upstream source countries as the sole and absolute owners of all water flows in an international river basin. On the contrary, international law gives considerable weight to the rights of downstream users to continue their use of that portion of an international water basin that they have previously used for human and economically productive purposes.[41] The recently approved water convention of the International Law Commission of the UN also gives priority to the rights of historical, or prior, users and considers depriving a riparian who currently uses the water for economic and social uses to be unacceptable since it will result in "appreciable damage" to that user. The outstanding example of such a situation is the undeniable rights of Egypt to the waters of the Nile River which it currently uses and has used for thousands of years, despite the fact that essentially all of its flow emanates from upstream countries. Syria itself derives most of its waters from rivers that emanate in the territory of its upstream neighbor, Turkey.

Another factor in international water law that would weigh heavily against such a Syrian claim would be the fact that Syria's overall water resources potential per capita was in 1995 some 2,000 CM/P/Yr, or six times that of Israel's 300 CM/P/Yr. Syria would have a difficult time proving that it has an overriding objective need for the water. It appears that even if Syria and Lebanon make such claims, great costs would be involved in pumping the water to agricultural areas at higher elevations. Syrian and Lebanese agriculture can hardly justify the development of water sources which involve pumping costs of between U.S.$0.20 and $0.30/CM. The return on such an investment would most likely be negative. As pointed out previously even the 1955 Arab League water plan accepted by Syria and Johnston only claimed for Syria 20 MCM/Yr from the Banias and 22 MCM/Yr from the upper Jordan, with only 35 MCM/Yr for Lebanon from the Hasbani.

Monetizing The Water Dispute

It is beyond the scope of this paper to anticipate the outcome of the direct negotiations among Israel, Syria, and Lebanon on the peace agreement in general and the issue of borders and a water agreement in particular. However, it would not be unreasonable to assume, as suggested above, that Syria and Lebanon will, in the first instance, stake a maximum claim to the full estimated 310 MCM/Yr from the upper Jordan headwaters which are derived from sources in Syria and Lebanon (160 MCM/Yr from the Banias and side wadis of the Golan and 150 MCM/Yr from the Hasbani), even though they never used significant amounts of that water themselves.

While the water argument may be used to gain leverage on other points in the negotiations, the economic motivation and objective needs for Lebanon and Syria to gain major water allocations at the sources of the Jordan would apparently not be great. A pragmatic compromise proposal on the Syrian-Lebanese side would not be so unlikely if this analysis is correct. Such a Syrian-Lebanese compromise might be the demand that they be allocated their share as defined under the Johnston plan, that is, 35 MCM/Yr for Lebanon and 42 MCM/Yr for Syria. The Syrians have already taken more than their share of the Yarmuk as defined by the Johnston plan. It should be pointed out that the Israeli-Jordanian agreement used the allocations of the Johnston plan as the point of departure for their negotiations.

I take no position on the feasibility or justification of such a proposal but present it as one possible example we can use to examine the economic implications for Israel of such a compromise settlement. As stated above, the Harvard project has not yet made a study of the economics of a water market approach between Israel and Syria, so that my own very tentative analysis presented here can only be considered as a most preliminary attempt to illustrate the type of thinking involved. Let us assume that Syria and Lebanon propose to reduce Israel's use of the headwaters of the Jordan River sources by about 80 MCM/Yr, which is the volume of water that theoretically would have been allocated to them under the Johnston plan. This represents some 5 percent of Israel's current annual renewable fresh water resources of some 1600 MCM/Yr. Previous studies by the

HMEWP have shown that the maximum current value of the Jordan River water for Israeli agriculture has been estimated roughly at about U.S.$0.20/CM.[42] Thus the net current loss to Israel of foregoing 80 MCM/Yr of Jordan water for agricultural use in the central or southern regions of Israel would be about U.S.$16m/year. This is a relatively small amount of money.

However, let us assume that at some time in the future, say in the year 2020, the 80 MCM/Yr of water that hypothetically Syria and Lebanon demand would be needed for domestic/urban/ industrial use along the coast of Israel at Tel Aviv and would have to be replaced by sea water desalination in the south of Israel. The maximum replacement cost to Israel for that amount of water, by desalination along the Mediterranean coast, would be about U.S.$.85/CM, minus the transportation cost of water from the Jordan to the areas in the south of about U.S.$.20/CM. This would result in an effective cost or loss to Israel of U.S.$0.65/CM or, some U.S.$52m/year. Some experts predict that the cost of desalination of sea water will be significantly lower in 20 to 30 years. Even this amount of money, which might be forfeited at some distant date in the future, is not great. In this way, using the Harvard approach, the approximate size of the dispute in monetary terms can be estimated. Many refinements to the actual economic simulation model used by the HMEWP are needed to obtain a more accurate estimate, but as a rough first guide, Professor Fisher agrees that the above figure is reasonable.

In conclusion, this approach would suggest that when the water dispute is converted to financial terms, the annual amount of money involved is hardly enough to justify bringing an end to the peace negotiations or starting a "water war." As Professor Fisher puts it: "Such a sum of money is small enough for countries to negotiate over rather than to go to war over!"[43] Of the 1996 GDP of Israel of about $80b, the maximum current value of the water in dispute in the case of Syria and Lebanon represents some 0.065 percent. It might be argued that this would be a relatively small price to pay to achieve an overall peace and security settlement. It must be emphasized that water is, after all, an economic good which can be replaced and purchased in unlimited quantities by sea water desalination at the current price of about U.S.$0.85/CM, which is more or less the price that Israelis now pay for urban water supply.

Even if in economic terms such a compromise would have an insignificant impact on Israel's overall economy, it would, however, result in about a 10 percent reduction in the amount of water available to Israel's highly subsidized agriculture, which plays such an important role in the country's national identity and ideology. This would inevitably raise opposition from agricultural circles and the water establishment. It is not clear that Israel's agriculturally oriented water negotiators are ready at this stage to accept the economic point of view as presented here. However, whatever final agreement is reached on the division of the waters of the Jordan River basin, it will be essential to include mutual inspection and monitoring on both sides of the final borders to ensure not only that all parties to the agreement take no more than their agreed share but that agreed pollution control measures to protect the quality of the water sources be strictly enforced.

ISRAELI, JORDANIAN, AND PALESTINIAN WATER ISSUES

The approach developed by the HMEWP has clearly shown that in the case of Israel, Jordan, and the Palestinians, economic cooperation within the context of a limited water market approach, among the riparians sharing the water resources, is more beneficial to all parties than going it alone. Other studies on the economic approach have reached similar conclusions. Peter Rogers has shown, based on the experience in the India-Pakistan water dispute and others, that in most situations cooperation by the riparians in the development of water resources can benefit all parties to the river basin dispute.[44] He proposes approaches based on game theory concepts that provide solutions for economic cooperation on international river basins "based on maximizing the total net benefits that could be derived from the utilization of the basin, given the total resources available for the development."

It is beyond the scope of this chapter to discuss in detail possible advantages to be gained by all parties, through the development of regional water projects, under conditions of peace in the region. These have been described elsewhere[45] and might include:

1. Purchase of water from Lebanon and the construction of pipelines from the Litani and Awali Rivers that could supply water directly or indirectly to Jordan, the PNA, and Israel. Lebanon might be able to supply as much as 500 MCM/Yr from these sources for a period up to 25 to 30 years, which would cover the economic life of the projects.
2. The construction of a dam or dams on the Yarmuk which could supply electrical power to Syria and Jordan and water to Syria, Jordan, and the PNA. This project might make possible the construction of the Western Ghor canal, which was originally planned by Jordan to transport Yarmuk water across the Jordan River for the benefit of the water-short Palestinians on the West Bank.
3. The construction of a pipeline from the Jordanian portion of the Yarmuk River to divert excess winter flow into Lake Tiberias where it would be stored, by agreement with Israel, for later use by Jordan. In order to increase the potential storage capacity of the lake—to make this joint management option feasible—Israel would divert the flow of the Jordan

River directly into the Israeli NWC at a high point, well upstream of Lake Tiberias, near Kfar HaNasi. This diversion would in principle be a return to the initial concept of the diversion at Gesher B'not Yaakov which was blocked by Syrian opposition and military action in the fall of 1953. It would allow gravity flow of Jordan River water into the NWC and result in a major saving in pumping costs for Israel. There would be other major benefits for Jordan, Israel, and even possibly the Palestinians. The shared use of Lake Tiberias for storage of winter flood flows was one of the important and controversial elements of the Johnston plan. An Israeli press report indicates that Israel and Jordan have reached a secret agreement on this project, despite Syrian objections.[46] However, at this time, Syria is not in a position to block the project by local military action, as it did in 1953, since it is no longer in control of the area. Syria's concern about this project might provide it with the impetus to renew peace negotiations with Israel over the fate of the Golan Heights since it may now perceive that, without an overall peace agreement with Israel, it may be left out of mutually beneficial regional water projects.

4. Purchase of water from Turkey, which could be supplied to Syria, Jordan, Israel, and the PNA through a regional overland or undersea pipeline system or, alternatively, by sea transport, with special large plastic bag tankers called Medusa bags. Turkey might supply 1,000 MCM/Yr or more to the area through such projects. Of course a project involving Syrian cooperation would require that Turkey, Syria, and Iraq reach an accommodation over their long-standing disputes over the Tigris and Euphrates Rivers. The concept of an undersea pipeline from Turkey is not as far-fetched technically as might appear at first hand since there are numerous successful examples of such sea bottom pipelines. Such a pipeline would pass through international waters and overcome most of the geopolitical objections to such a project.

While estimates of the engineering feasibility and price of piping water from the Litani and Awali are encouraging, the geopolitical aspects and economics of the other three projects are less clear and require further study.[47] While these projects will undoubtedly be more expensive, they may still possibly prove to be less expensive than desalination.

Thus, when parties to a water dispute can become convinced to begin to think in more concrete economic terms, far removed from the usual emotional rhetoric of debate and from fervent pressure from the agricultural or water lobby, there is hope that conflicts can be resolved using more rational and pragmatic considerations of optimizing benefits for all. Water wars will not be fought so easily when it can be shown that the monetary size of the dispute is relatively small, and that conflict can be resolved not only to the benefit of all sides, but also with fair compensation for all. At the time of writing, the peace negotiations between Israel and Syria are stalemated over differences concerning the Golan Heights. However, if and when they are renewed, the major issues will undoubtedly remain the security arrangements, borders, and normalization of relations, with the issue of water entering the picture but not dominating it. In 1996, an authoritative source close to secretary of state Warren Christopher was reported by the press to have said that during his shuttle visits to Damascus and Jerusalem, Christopher had gained the impression that the Syrians and Israelis were prepared to accept a flexible, pragmatic approach to the water issue and would be ready to make a reasonable compromise that should not block the peace negotiations.[48] Time will tell.

NOTE

*Special thanks must be given to Professor Franklin Fisher of the Massachusetts Institute of Technology and head of HMEWP, Moshe Yizraeli of the Office of the Israel Water Commissioner, and Professor Nurit Kliot of Haifa University, for their detailed review of the manuscript and many insights and helpful suggestions.

NOTES

1. Franklin M. Fisher, "The Economics of Water Dispute Resolution, Project Evaluation and Management: An Application to the Middle East," *Water Resources Development* 11 (1995): 377-90.
2. For a few examples, see Joyce Starr, "Water Wars," *Foreign Policy* 82 (1991): 17-36; Peter H. Gleick, "Water, War, and Peace in the Middle East," *Environment* 36 (1994): 6-42; and John Bulloch and Adel Darwish, *Water Wars: Coming Conflicts in the Middle East* (London: Victor Gollancz, 1993).
3. Robert Engelman and Pamela LeRoy, *Sustaining Water: Population and the Future Renewable Water Supplies* (Washington D.C.: Population and Environment Program, Population Action International, 1993).
4. Israel sherut ha-hidrologi (Israel Hydrological Service), *Status of Water Resources: Fall 1994,* annual report (in Hebrew) (Jerusalem: Water Commission, 1995).
5. Hillel I. Shuval, "Approaches to Resolving the Water Conflicts between Israel and Her Neighbors: A Regional Water for Peace Plan," *Water International* 17 (1992): 133-43
6. Michael Brecher, *Decisions in Israel's Foreign Policy* (London: Oxford University Press, 1974), 173-224.
7. Ibid.
8. Ibid.
9. Ibid.
10. G. G. Stevens, *Jordan Water Partition* (Stanford, Calif.: Stanford University Press, 1965).
11. Of the 132 MCM/Yr allocated to Syria, 42 MCM/Yr was to come from the Banias and the mainstream of the Jordan River while 90 MCM/Yr was to come from the Yarmuk River which rises in Syria.
12. Brecher, *Decisions in Israel's Foreign Policy.*
13. David M. Wishart, "The Breakdown of the Johnston Negotiations over the Jordan Waters," *Middle Eastern Studies* 26 (1990): 536-46.
14. Brecher, *Decisions in Israel's Foreign Policy.*
15. Wishart, "Breakdown of the Johnston Negotiations."
16. Brecher, *Decisions in Israel's Foreign Policy.*
17. Thomas Naff and Ruth C. Matson, eds., *Water in the Middle East: Conflict and Cooperation* (Boulder, Colo.: Westview, 1984).
18. Miriam R. Lowi, *The Politics of Water: The Jordan River and the Riparian States,* McGill Studies in International Development, no. 35 (Montreal, Canada: Centre for Developing-Area Studies, McGill University, 1989).
19. Meron Medzini, ed., *Israel's Foreign Relations: Selected Documents* (Jerusalem: Ministry of Foreign Affairs, 1976).
20. Wishart, "Breakdown of the Johnston Negotiations."
21. Arnon Sofer, *Neharot shel esh* (Rivers of fire) (Tel Aviv: Am Oved; Haifa: Haifa University Press, 1992).
22. Naff and Matson, eds., *Water in the Middle East.*
23. Thomas Naff, "Conflict and Water in the Middle East," in *Water in the Arab World,* ed. Peter Rogers and Peter Lydon (Cambridge, Mass.: MIT Press, 1995).
24. Nurit Kliot, *Water Resources and Conflict in the Middle East* (London: Routledge, 1994).
25. Sofer, *Neharot shel esh.*
26. Ibid.
27. Ibid.
28. Ibid.

29. Fisher, "Economics of Water Dispute Resolution"; Hillel I. Shuval, "An Economic Approach to the Resolution of Water Conflicts," in *Proceedings of Workshop on Joint Management of Aquifers Shared by Israeli and Palestinians,* ed. E. Feitelson and M. Hadad (Jerusalem: Hebrew University of Jerusalem, Truman Institute for Peace, 1995).

30. Fisher, "Economics of Water Dispute Resolution."

31. Ibid.

32. Ze'ev Schiff, "The Censored Report Revealed" (in Hebrew), *Ha-aretz* (Tel Aviv) 8 October 1993. Part 2.

33. Ibid.

34. Ibid.

35. Ibid.

36. A. Ben, "USA: The Water Problems Between Israel and Syria Can Be Solved Pragmatically" (in Hebrew), *Ha-aretz* (Tel Aviv) 19 January 1996.

37. Ibid.

38. Brecher, *Decisions in Israel's Foreign Policy.*

39. Y. Amon, "A Profile of 'Mei Golan,' 1994" (in Hebrew), *Mayim v'hashkaya* (Water and irrigation) June 1994.

40. Ibid.

41. Dante Augusto Caponera, *Principles of Water Law and Administration: National and International* (Rotterdam: A. A. Balkema, 1992).

42. Fisher, "Economics of Water Dispute Resolution."

43. Ibid.

44. Peter Rogers, "The Value of Cooperation in Resolving International River Basin Disputes," *Natural Resources Forum* (May 1993).

45. Shuval, "Approaches to Resolving"; and Elisha Kally, "Costs of Inter-Regional Conveyance of Water and Cost of Sea Water Desalination," in *A Proposal for the Development of a Regional Water Master Plan,* by Karen Assaf et al. (Jerusalem: Israel Palestine Center for Research and Information, 1993), 175-92.

46. Ze'ev Schiff, "Israel and Jordan Have Agreed on the Use of Kinneret for the Storage of Water for the Jordanians" (in Hebrew), *Ha-aretz* (Tel Aviv) 5 April 1998, p. 1.

47. Assaf et al., *Proposal.*

48. Ben, "USA: The Water Problems."

PART V:
MILITARY CAPABILITIES

CHAPTER TEN

Towards the Emergence of a Common Security System in the Middle East*

YAIR EVRON

Political developments in the Arab-Israeli region have created the framework for the potential emergence of a more stable security system there.[1] For sure, the curtailment of the peace process might cause temporary setbacks and difficulties in the evolution of the said security system. However, in the longer run, the peace process appears to be robust and durable. It would require major destabilizing events to completely change the course of that process. Consequently, the emergence of a new security system is a realistic proposition. Moreover, it is likely that a stable peace in the "core" of the Middle East could endure only if it depended on various elements of stable security.

In this chapter, a general schematic outline of the main elements of a security system that could sustain and solidify peaceful inter-state political relationships in the region is presented. This presentation is preceded by a brief description of past security systems that obtained in the Arab-Israeli region from 1949; some of them collapsed, some were replaced by others.[2] Both the future security regime as well as the earlier ones could be conceptualized as different types of international security regimes.[3]

SECURITY REGIMES: AN INTRODUCTORY NOTE

International relations theory has always grappled with the problem of how states cooperate within the context of world disorder. Realists have argued that mechanisms such as balance of power and deterrence (and efficient diplomacy based on both) can stabilize interstate relations in a permanent situation of "anarchy" that prevails in the international system. Idealists have either denied that world developments are characterized by anarchy or, that if this is the case, they believe other instruments (rather than military) can transform the anarchic "rules of the game" of the international system and create a more cooperative community of states. In the past two decades, neo-realists (or structural realists) on the one hand, and neo-liberals and neo-institutionalists on the other, have continued to develop these two main intellectual traditions.[4]

The efforts to explain wide or limited international cooperation focus partly on the creation of regimes that manage various aspects of interstate behavior. Thus, even in the military-security area, which is the most difficult to manage cooperatively, due to the saliency of the self-help principle, international regimes have been identified.[5] Some realists would deny their very existence. Some neo-realists accept the existence of international regimes and explain their creation and sustainability as being rooted in the structural constraints of all international systems.[6] Neo-liberals and neo-institutionalists explain their existence as being rooted in the inherent readiness of states to cooperate in order to further their mutual interests. For them, the existence of international regimes is an obvious consequence of the inner logic of international politics.

While theoretical explanations of the current situation in the Middle East vary, and the concept of security is rightly perceived as multidimensional, the basic theoretical premises of this chapter lean more towards modified structural realist interpretations. Thus, the approach is state-centrist; military security and "high politics" issues in general hold the center stage, and the important domestic threats to security are perceived as inputs into states' policy outputs. Because of the continued saliency of political conflicts and the potential for military escalation, political stability in the Middle East depends on constraining military threats. Indeed, different types of security regimes already serve as important instruments in the management of interstate strategic interactions in the Middle East.

In analytical terms, I would separate security regimes into several categories, in ascending order of intensity of regulation of military behavior, level of political normalcy, and, ultimately, of military and political coordination and cooperation: security conventions; qualified security regimes; normal security regimes; common security regimes; cooperative security regimes. These will be defined below. The potential for some elements of a common security regime is discernible already in the Middle East, but such a comprehensive system has yet to evolve. In the European context, there exists a more advanced security regime, which could be identified as a cooperative security regime.[7]

All these regimes are based on various combinations of unilateral deterrence (by the party committed to the status quo), or mutual deterrence, coupled with Confidence and Security Building Measures (CSBM).[8] CSBM in this context could be defined as any measure that regulates military behavior over periods of time, with the objective of increasing the self-confidence of each of the parties in its own security situation.[9] Eventually, the parties come to recognize the security interests of the other side as being legitimate, and become interested in common security.

On the basis of stable deterrence and CSBM, the parties develop mechanisms and procedures designed to resolve and prevent military risks and threats. Regimes are comprised of patterns of interactions that are characterized by reciprocity and the readiness of parties to forego (when necessary) short-term interests in order to attain long-term ones. The element of reciprocity is based on the parties' mutual expectations of concessions. Within regimes, patterns of behavior are established that persist over relatively long periods of time. Regimes might affect the self-definition of the national interests of the parties. Consequently, a successful, durable regime could become a major input into the process of the foreign and security policy formulation of the parties. Some would argue that the formation of a very durable and sustainable regime might turn it into an independent variable affecting policy outcomes. Regimes can be formal and institutionalized or informal and sometimes even tacit.

Security Conventions

Security conventions are those regimes that are based on unilateral deterrence and in which only one CSBM has evolved, tailored to one specific mission. They are informal or tacit. They are formed between states that do not have diplomatic relations. For example, the demilitarization of Sinai between 1957 and 1967 is an example of a security convention. That security convention was part of a wider regime which also comprised the deployment of UN observers in some parts of the Sinai.

Qualified Regimes

Qualified regimes are those sets of understanding that are based on unilateral or mutual deterrence and in which a complex web of CSBM emerges or is agreed upon. They can be formal or informal. They are formed between states that do not have diplomatic relations and are in a conflict situation. Most of the security regimes that evolved between Israel and the Arab states belong to this category.

Normal Security Regimes

Normal security regimes are organized around a web of CSBM within the context of formal diplomatic relations between states. Following the peace treaties between Israel and Egypt and between Israel and Jordan, security regimes have emerged. While qualified regimes are also based on a complex set of CSBM, what marks out the normal regimes are the existence of formal diplomatic relations between the parties and also the greater emphasis on CSBM as compared to deterrence. Finally, they are primarily formal.

Common Security Regimes

Common security regimes are similar to the normal regimes in their greater emphasis on complex sets of CSBM and on formal institutions. What distinguishes them is that they are multilateral arrangements and, in addition, the level of cooperation among the parties is relatively high.

Cooperative Security Regimes

Cooperative security regimes are multilateral institutions encompassing complex and wide-ranging sets of CSBM with a high degree of cooperation. These are systems of states among which war is unlikely to erupt.

THE HISTORY OF SECURITY REGIMES IN THE ARAB-ISRAELI ZONE

From 1949 until the early or mid-1950s, Israel and its four immediate neighbors —Egypt, Jordan, Syria, and Lebanon—regulated their military behavior through a combination of mechanisms based on the Mixed Armistice Commissions, which were created by the armistice agreements of 1949.[10] Lebanese-Israeli relations remained tranquil until the late 1960s.[11] In the other three relationships, the parties shared a basic interest, viz., to prevent unintended escalation.[12] With that goal in mind, they tried to control and prevent border violence, to control and resolve various issues under contention and, overall, to avoid unnecessary military entanglements. In the specific Jordanian-Israeli case, the parties also had mutual or coinciding political interests.[13] Due to the convergence of dyadic, regional, and international circumstances, two of these regimes—the Egyptian-Israeli and the Syrian-Israeli—collapsed. The third, the Jordanian-Israeli regime, underwent various changes and was eventually replaced by another security regime which lasted until the 1967 war. It was then revived in 1968 and lasted until 1994, when it was superseded by the Jordanian-Israeli peace treaty.

Egyptian-Israeli conflict relations, which culminated with the 1956 war, had to be reorganized following that war. A new system of regulation of military behavior emerged in 1957, its main focus being the de facto demilitarization of Sinai. While the three systems based on the armistice agreements of 1949 were formal and resulted from direct negotiations (with the mediation of the United Nations), the demilitarization of Sinai was a tacit understanding and was based on mutual recognition of security interests.[14] Moreover, the three armistice agreements were based on combinations of deterrence, a shared interest in avoiding escalation, and a series of CSBM "organizing" military behavior, whereas the regime in the Sinai was based on one shared interest (avoidance of escalation) and one major CSBM (the mentioned demilitarization of the Sinai). In addition, UN observers had been stationed along the border and in the Straits of Sharm al-Sheikh and thus played a limited role in the regime. The system held for ten years and collapsed with the 1967 crisis.[15]

Following the 1973 war, several sets of agreements enabled the creation of two security regimes: one regularizing military behavior on the Golan (based on the cease-fire agreement of 1974); the other organizing the military relations between Egypt and Israel (Sinai I and Sinai II). Both regimes were formal and included specific mechanisms for control and verification of the various security arrangements.

In retrospect, it is clear that beyond their shared interest in avoiding hostilities, Egypt and Israel also sought to base their mutual relationship on more stable political grounds. Sinai I and Sinai II eventually led to the Camp David Accords and the Egyptian-Israeli peace treaty of 1979.[16]

A special case was the security regime that obtained between Israel and Syria in Lebanon from 1976. The fierce civil war in Lebanon which had plagued that country since 1975, created a set of de facto coinciding interests between Israel and Syria. Both parties, for different reasons, were worried about the possibility of deterioration in Lebanon. Eventually, both concluded that only strong Syrian intervention could save Lebanon from complete degeneration. Through United States mediation, the two regional powers reached a series of informal understandings that "allowed" Syria to intervene in Lebanon, but within a system of constraints limiting Syrian military behavior. In addition, active United States mediation in times of impending crisis was required. Thus, a security system that could be identified as a qualified security regime emerged in Lebanon. It collapsed with the Israeli invasion in 1982 and was renewed after the Israeli withdrawal.[17]

Finally, with Israel's peace treaties with Egypt and Jordan, two normal security regimes emerged. The qualified security regimes were based on deterrence combined with a mixture of CSBM, but existed without normal political relations between the countries. In contrast, in the normal security regimes, the political context provided the primary mechanism for conflict management and conflict resolution. Consequently, the relative roles of deterrence and CSBM changed in favor of greater emphasis on CSBM. In the case of the Jordanian-Israeli relationship, the extensive body of shared political interests provided for greater emphasis on cooperative measures. Indeed, this particular security system could gradually evolve beyond a mutual regime and attain some elements of a cooperative security regime.[18]

This brief historical background demonstrates the following: first, even during periods of fierce conflict, Israel and its neighbors succeeded in creating, over periods of time, security systems that provided a measure of stability; second, full peaceful political relations could shift the emphasis gradually from deterrence to political cooperation and CSBM.

A future common security system would consist of multilateral and bilateral CSBM, elements of deterrence, arms control, and various mechanisms and formal organizations for political and strategic coordination.

POLITICAL CONTEXT

Although the Arab-Israeli conflict has captured the attention of Middle Easterners as well as outside observers, the region is plagued by other political conflicts, both between as well as within states. Interstate conflicts persist in many parts of the Middle East. The differences between rich and poor states heighten tensions; militant Islam threatens the domestic stability of several important states and could also adversely affect interstate relations; ethnic and religious cleavages bear the potential to destabilize some states.[19] Finally, the general problem of rapid population growth and weak economies is a permanent destabilizing factor.[20] This chapter, however, while aware of these domestic and transstate destabilizing threats, will concentrate on interstate security.

Both in analytical terms as well as in practice, the Middle East comprises at least three subregions: starting from the east, the Gulf area; then the "heart," which basically comprises the Arab-Israeli region, including Egypt, Israel, and the Fertile Crescent; and the Maghrib countries.[21] Turkey, which for decades has oriented itself primarily towards Europe, has, over the past few years, become increasingly more involved in the Middle East, and its interests extend both to the heart and to the Gulf.[22] In each of these three subsets there are different dynamics in terms of threats to security and processes of cooperation and conflict, both domestic and interstate. Broadly speaking, it appears that in terms of conflicts and crises, and therefore in terms of interstate regimes designed to manage and resolve them, the Gulf and the heart are in many ways interconnected.[23] Nevertheless, when planning a regional security system, distinctions should be drawn between these two areas.

Since the beginning of the Arab-Israeli peace process, and especially since the Oslo agreement and the Jordanian-Israeli peace treaty, the likelihood of another Arab-Israeli interstate war has considerably declined. While political tensions between Egypt and Israel rise occasionally, the probability of hostilities is very low. In fact, the political relationship between the two countries is very solid and stable, having withstood several major tensions since the formal peace began.[24] A common security regime could therefore develop on the basis of stable political relations. It could further consolidate those relations and also serve as a hedge against persistent threats to stability which might arise in the heart itself, or from the Gulf.

A COMMON SECURITY REGIME

Geographic Delimitation

Because of the complexities of the Middle East system of states, it would be prudent to try to limit the geographic extent to which a security regime applies. Given the different dynamics in the various subregions of the Middle East, an attempt to create an extensive regime covering all these areas might produce a weak, ineffective system. A better approach would be to concentrate on one of the subregions while being aware of their interconnectedness. For the purpose of this chapter, the security system considered relates to the Arab-Israeli region (which is largely identified with the heart). However, because of the interconnections with the Gulf area, the security regime would have to be sufficiently flexible to manage threats from the Gulf countries.

Objectives

The objectives of the security system would be: to manage crises; to reduce the threat of escalation to war or sub-war violence; to create mechanisms that could solidify and underwrite political settlements; and, finally, to gradually diminish the centrality and saliency of the military component in interstate relations.[25]

Instruments

The first instrument would be the continuation of the peace process to the point where all the regional states have formal peace between one another.[26] Secondly, two layers of CSBM could be created—multilateral and bilateral. The CSBM are of five basic types:

1. Mechanisms designed to regulate military behavior through physical means. These include limitations on deployment of military units or weapons systems: for example, demilitarization of zones or the creation of limited deployment zones.
2. Restructuring of military forces, for example switching from predominantly standing armies—as is the case in the Arab armies—to a combination of standing army and reserves.
3. Measures designed to improve communications, create greater openness and transparency, and reduce mutual fears about the possibility of

unintended escalation or of surprise attacks. These were virtually the objectives and modes of the Conference for Security and Cooperation in Europe (CSCE) agreements in Europe, especially those in Helsinki and Stockholm in 1975 and 1987, respectively. These objectives have also been endorsed in the Treaty on Conventional Armed Forces in Europe (CFE).2727 In fact, the qualified security regimes that operated in the Arab-Israeli region, mentioned before, included several measures falling into this category.[28] Future CSBM could also include prior notification of military maneuvers and movements, dispatch of military observers to inspect military exercises of other parties, and mutual visits to specified military installations. Additional mechanisms for communication would be the establishment of direct communication links between military commanders or the creation of permanent committees to resolve outstanding issues related to military behavior. Precedents for such measures have existed in both the qualified and normal security regimes.[29]

4. Learning and socialization: these measures relate to mutual understanding of military and strategic doctrines. Seminars could be held in which the parties learn about each other's threat perceptions and about military doctrines designed to counter those threats.[30]

5. Rules of engagement: these are designed to regulate primarily air activities in which the great speed involved and the need to make instant decisions might lead to mistakes and inadvertent escalatory moves.

Bilateral and Multilateral CSBM

Some of these CSBM could be introduced on a bilateral basis, while others could be introduced on both bilateral and multilateral bases. For example, demilitarization of zones is a purely bilateral CSBM.

Several sets of bilateral CSBM that regulate military behavior between Arab states and Israel are presently in place. The Golan agreement of 1974 limits military deployment and movements in certain specified areas and allows for international inspection of these arrangements.[31] The informal and, in some respects, tacit understandings regulating Syrian and Israeli military behavior in Lebanon from 1976, have been instrumental in reducing the danger of unintended escalation between these two regional powers.[32]

The Egyptian-Israeli peace treaty of 1979 created an elaborate system of CSBM, including the demilitarization of large parts of Sinai and the formation of joint military committees to supervise some aspects of the CSBM. The multilateral force deployed in Sinai further inhibits any violation of the agreements.[33] Needless to say, the very positive experience with these CSBM contributed to the stability of the peaceful political relationship.

Because of the long-standing tradition of tacit understandings, coupled with informal contacts extending over many years between Jordan and Israel, their peace treaty rested on basic mutual confidence. There was no need, therefore, to add physical CSBM, nor to introduce third-party mechanisms for inspection and verification. In those parts of the peace treaty dealing with military issues, the two countries agreed on several important measures to increase their mutual security, such as an undertaking not to join military alliances that could be perceived as threatening the other party, and a commitment to jointly combat terrorism.[34]

In a possible future peace agreement with Syria, various CSBM of the five categories mentioned earlier, would by necessity form a central part. If the Egyptian-Israeli peace treaty serves as an approximate model, these CSBM should include the demilitarization of the Golan, the establishment of an early-warning system, the deployment of international units (with a strong United States component) on the Golan, and limitations on the size of military units deployed in areas beyond the demilitarized zone. Since Syria has a large standing army, while Israel relies primarily on reserves, it is likely that Israel would demand further CSBM designed to reduce the size of the standing Syrian army and its offensive capabilities.[35] All these measures would considerably reduce the threat of a surprise attack.

It is reasonable to assume that various CSBM designed to increase transparency and openness of military moves would be primarily multilateral in character. This is because such measures could diminish, asymmetrically, the effectiveness of military forces unless they apply to all the potential adversaries. Some limited measures of this kind could be introduced bilaterally, but once they become more elaborate, the need for multilateralism would increase. Finally, it should be noted that some regional CSBM have already been aired and discussed in the Arms Control and Regional Security (ACRS) meetings.

Deterrence

Deterrence has played an important role in stabilizing relationships in the region. However, when applied without awareness of the political context, it could not, on its own, stabilize the conflict. Thus, when the challenger suffered from fundamental grievances caused by the status quo, it was not deterred even if the expected costs were perceived by it as being very high. This happened, for example, in 1973 when Egypt and Syria, though aware of the Israeli military superiority and the expected high costs, nevertheless attacked. Furthermore, when a deterrence posture is projected imprudently, it can actually contribute to escalation. This was demonstrated in the Arab-Israeli context in two ways. First, limited military actions were taken in order to demonstrate resolve and thus enhance deterrence. This occurred when Israel applied its strategy of retaliation against Egypt in the mid-1950s, which in turn led to escalation rather than deterrence. Second, when the parties undertook firm deterring moves against each other this caused mutual anxieties and finally direct military confrontation. An example of this occurred during the 1967 crisis when Israel tried to deter Syria from its military provocation by threatening major retaliation leading, in turn, to Egypt's major military deployment in the Sinai, which initially was intended as a deterring move, but in fact led to a major Israeli mobilization and finally to war.[36]

When deterrence strategy is applied cautiously and within a context of political normalcy and interrelated CSBM, it can enhance stability.[37] The more accommodating the political relations and the more extensive the system of CSBM, the less the need for reliance on deterrence. As things stand presently, deterrence still plays an important role in the Middle East. The aim, however, is to gradually diminish the political motivations to challenge the status quo. But this will require an end to all interstate conflicts throughout the region, as well as the elimination of those domestic threats to stability that have the potential of spilling over to the interstate level.[38]

Arms Control

The quantity of armaments and the size of military establishments in the Middle East are the highest in the world relative to the size of the population and per capita income. Middle Eastern states invested in arms because of the "power dilemma" and the "security dilemma."[39] States increased their military capabilities in pursuit of political influence and in order to change the status quo in their favor (thus the power dilemma) or because they were afraid of their opponent (thus the first elementary level of the security dilemma). Overall, however, they were all caught in processes of arms build-ups that sometimes turned into arms races without, on the whole or over time, overcoming their security concerns (hence the deeper sense of the security dilemma).[40]

By and large, the process of arms build-up in the Middle East until the mid-1970s, was fueled by the Arab-Israeli conflict as well as by competition among the Arab states. During the 1980s, there was a major jump in defense expenditure in Iraq and Iran, caused by the war between them. What is significant, however, is that from the mid-1980s the level of defense expenditure in the heart of the Middle East (except for Iraq) reached a plateau. And since the end of the Iran-Iraq war, and the end of the second Gulf War, Iraq and Iran have also scaled down considerably their defense expenditures. In both countries the reductions were brought about by an end to hostilities and by enormous economic problems (especially in Iraq as a result of the international sanctions). It should be added that defense expenditures are not the only criterion to assess military build-up. Egypt, for example, received significant transfers of United States arms as gifts, thus enabling it to modernize its army.

The plateau in defense expenditures in the heart of the Middle East (as compared with continued growth in the previous years) was due to a combination of three factors: a change in threat perceptions; economic difficulties; and, finally, the need for regimes to respond positively to societal pressures for betterment of economic conditions and for welfare programs.[41]

If the peace process continues, it is therefore likely that even without agreed major cuts in defense spending, all the countries in the heart of the Middle East will not change significantly the current pattern of self-restraint in their defense build-up. Changes could come, however, if domestic conflicts and the rise of militant Islam were to spill over into interstate relations.[42]

It should be noted also that following the second Gulf War, the Gulf Cooperation Council (GCC) countries increased their defense expenditures considerably in an effort to build capabilities to counter and deter possible future threats from Iran and Iraq. This development creates, however, some concern in parts of the heart, primarily Israel, who suspects that some of the added capabilities might be transferred to hostile Arab states in time of war.

Looking ahead, if the current plateau in arms build-up in the heart is maintained, or at least does not radically change, it might be possible to gradually develop the foundation for some agreed quantitative arms control measures in the more distant future. This could hardly be done in the near future because of the basic asymmetries in military capabilities, in overall resources, in strategic doctrines and in threat perceptions. What could be expected in the short run is the gradual introduction of those CSBM that could help build sufficient confidence and mutual socialization in strategic doctrines and these in turn could form the background for future formal agreements on arms control.

Weapons of Mass Destruction (WMD)

There has been increasing interest in the possibility of introducing various measures designed to limit the proliferation of WMD and perhaps ultimately bring about their elimination. On the theoretical level, two approaches exist regarding the possible effects on stability of nuclear proliferation. The predominant approach has been that neither global nor regional proliferation can contribute to stability. The opposite approach argues that proliferation could, in fact, stabilize both the international system as a whole, and the Middle East as well.[43] It appears that most regional decision-makers consider proliferation to be, overall, a destabilizing factor.

Israel is generally regarded as a nuclear power, but it has adopted a posture of ambiguity, viz., it denies it has a nuclear capability, it conducts no nuclear tests, and it has not developed a strategic nuclear doctrine. This ambiguity somewhat reduces the concern of both the international community and parts of the Arab world over its nuclear capability.[44] Several Arab states have chemical and, possibly, biological weapons.

While the assumed Israeli nuclear capability is sometimes regarded by observers as having significantly affected the dynamics of the Arab-Israeli conflict, both as a deterrent against war and as an instrument generating peace, its actual impact on the course of the conflict appears to have been rather limited. It did not deter Egypt and Syria from launching the 1973 war, nor—most probably—was it relevant to their decision to limit the war.[45] It is doubtful whether it was a very central reason for President Anwar Sadat's decision to come to Jerusalem in 1977, and its political effect in various other ways is virtually non-existent.[46] It could basically serve only deterrent missions, first as a deterrent against an existential threat, viz., the possibility of the complete collapse of Israel in the event that an anti-Israel general Arab war coalition were to be established and eventually achieve an overwhelming military superiority. The probability that such a coalition will be formed and achieve superiority is very low, but it cannot be completely dismissed. A second deterrent mission is in the event that another regional state becomes nuclear. Finally, although with less certainty, an Israeli nuclear capability might serve as a deterrent against the use of WMD against Israel.[47] All these potential functions are loaded with major problems and dilemmas resulting from the inherently paradoxical nature of nuclear threats (i.e., deterrence), let alone their actual implementation. Nevertheless, until the region is stabilized and peace becomes permanent and solid, such potential missions cannot be considered irrational or irrelevant.

The Egyptian position vis-à-vis the Israeli capability has been rather constant, though the emphasis has changed over time. Egypt demanded, throughout the 1980s and 1990s, that Israel sign the Nuclear Non-Proliferation Treaty (NPT) and eliminate its nuclear capability. Egypt has also formulated a proposal for a WMD free zone (WMDFZ) in the Middle East.[48]

The Egyptian position appears to reflect several concerns. First, the Israeli capability provokes other regional powers to try to develop a nuclear capability. If these attempts are successful, Egypt will face grave dilemmas. Second, some Egyptian analysts, relying on certain international interpretations of the Mordechai Vanunu story, are concerned about the size of the assumed Israeli capability and have raised the argument that Israel might have developed capabilities that go far beyond deterrence against existential threats.[49] Third, Egypt is concerned that an Israel equipped with a large and extensive nuclear arsenal could gain strategic superiority in the Middle East. Finally, and related to the last concern, Egypt feels that the Israeli nuclear capability could be turned into a political instrument for gaining extensive regional influence. This last point dovetails with a larger Egyptian sense of growing uneasiness about Israel's overall political power. Israel's economic power (in relative regional terms), coupled with its close connection with the United States and its greater diplomatic maneuverability in Middle Eastern politics due to its legitimized position following the peace process and the Oslo agreements, are all perceived as creating an option for Israeli political hegemony in the region. The Egyptian position should, therefore, be interpreted not as part of an adversarial strategy vis-à-vis Israel, but as part of an attempt to maintain Egyptian centrality in a peaceful Middle East.[50]

Israel, for its part, accepted the WMDFZ proposal but argued that its implementation should begin only after the achievement of formal peace with all the regional states (including Iran). Moreover, Israel insists on mutual verification rather than international verification. The latest Israeli position was articulated by the then foreign minister Shimon Peres in a visit to Cairo in 1995, when he declared that two years after such peace had been reached Israel would be ready to begin negotiations on a WMDFZ for the Middle East.

The creation of a WMDFZ in the Middle East appears at present to be a very difficult proposition and is likely to remain so for a long time. The Israeli preconditions are likely to be firm and elaborate and the required instruments for full and credible verification are extremely difficult to develop and apply. Several Arab states, for their part, oppose WMDFZ if Israel rejects the implementation of a Nuclear Weapons Free Zone (NWFZ) in the Middle East. However, the beginning of a serious dialogue on the WMDFZ issue could come about through some version of an agreement on the proposal to "cut off" production of fissionable material advanced by the former and current United States administrations. Although not an easily digestible proposal (for both sides), it is a measure bearing a potential for success. Such an agreement would require a long period of time for deliberations, negotiations, and assessments by all the parties, since its strategic effects as well as its impact on other areas of arms control (conventional and WMD) would have to be explored and assessed.[51]

Center for Conflict Management

An important CSBM would be the creation of a center for the management of conflict. This would involve the establishment of permanent bodies of officials and analysts who would focus their activity on identifying processes that might lead to interstate conflicts, as well as on developing instruments for managing such conflicts. The definition and extent of their mandate would require extensive study and negotiations. One possible example is the Organization for Security and Cooperation in Europe (OSCE) Center for Conflict Prevention in Vienna. The proposed center will, however, have to develop its own specific identity in view of the region's special characteristics. Within the context of the dialogue between the OSCE and the Mediterranean countries, which began in 1995, the proposal to create a conflict management center for the entire Mediterranean area was raised and discussed. Such a center, if created, might be of some use. However, precisely because its mandate will have to cover the whole of the Mediterranean area, its actual utility would be very limited. A center with a mandate covering a more limited geographic area, such as the heart of the Middle East or the heart and the Gulf, in which decision-makers have already gained a better understanding of the dynamics of conflict and escalation in their own region, promises to be more effective.

Needless to say, such a center, if established, would require prior political will and readiness on the part of the parties concerned to manage their conflicts. Without that determination, the center would fail. But even if the will were there, the ability of the center to enhance stability would depend on intensive coordination and on processes of learning and socialization. The involvement of extraregional actors in the center, especially the United States, could be very useful.

Center for Crisis Management

Apart from the center for conflict management, which would be designed to identify and manage long-range processes, a crisis management center could be established to focus on the management of situations of immediate crisis. Such a center would include teams of officials and analysts, whose task would be to identify such situations at the political and strategic levels, as well as a technical unit for early warning and communications to monitor threatening military movements and establish urgent communications between parties to the crisis and other members of the center. The participation of extraregional powers would again be very useful.

It should be emphasized that it is unlikely that states will relinquish their own powers of decision-making in conflict and crisis management. The two centers should, therefore, be designed in such a way as not to replace independent decision-making, but in order to provide some coordinated long-range learning and planning, coupled with mechanisms for handling immediate flashpoints.

SYSTEMIC EFFECTS AND DILEMMAS

The creation of a common security system in the Middle East should be assessed not only in terms of the dynamics of management and resolution of the Arab-Israeli conflict and of other axes of interstate conflict, but also in terms of its interaction with various regional-systemic "rules of the game." These have to do primarily with patterns of interstate relationships in the Arab world.[52]

Following the emergence of the modern Middle Eastern state system after the Second World War, a complex balance of power mechanism emerged in the region based on a "game" of shifting coalitions among the Arab states. This game contrasted with tendencies towards pan-Arabism.[53] Overall, the game proved more important than tendencies towards unity, and in fact such tendencies were used as instruments in the competition between shifting coalitions. The coalitions and the competition for political influence had differing effects on regional stability. Mostly they aggravated regional tensions and contributed to political instability among Arab states. Indeed, at times their interaction with other axes of regional conflict generated great instability and even war. This was the case, for example, in the 1967 crisis. On the other hand, the shifting coalitions also stabilized the region to a certain extent, in that—in conjunction with other systemic mechanisms—they militated against the emergence (accompanied by violence) of any one hegemonic regional power.[54]

From the mid-1970s the Arab state system began to undergo a process of fragmentation which reached its peak in the 1990s.[55] The systemic mechanisms (with the help of external powers) still militated against the emergence of a hegemony, as demonstrated in the second Gulf War of 1991, when Iraqi ambitions were repulsed. However, the mechanism of coalition formation has declined in importance over the years. If this continues to be the case, then the possibility of creating a regional common security system will be enhanced. However, if the tendency to form meaningful competing coalitions should reemerge as a salient factor, it will become difficult to adapt this flexible and fluid system of shifting alliances to the creation of a regional security system.

Collective Security and Common Security

There is a conceptual and practical difference between collective and common security. A collective system involves undertakings to operate collectively against an aggressor inside the system or one threatening it from the outside.[56] In contrast, a common security system is designed to manage and regulate military behavior among its members and manage and resolve their conflicts. In any event, it is unlikely that states in the heart or in the heart and the Gulf will be able, in the foreseeable future, to create a genuine collective security system. A common security system could, however, lead to greater coordination among the parties.[57]

Defense Alliances and Common Security

As mentioned before, there was a tendency to create coalitions and alliances in the region, many of which took the form of defense alliances. It is certainly possible that this phenomenon might recur in the future. One possibility is that some states, which together create a common security system, might develop this into a defense alliance. Under such circumstances, the component of mutual deterrence within the new alliance would decline in importance, and mutual military coordination among the parties would increase in importance. Deterrence would then be directed against potential or actual external enemies. One of the drawbacks of such a development is that other states might feel threatened by the new development and try to form a balancing defense alliance.

There could, of course, be intermediate variants, for example, the establishment of a common security system with some elements of military coordination within it, but in which the parties limit themselves as to the extent of their military coordination. They could also refrain from creating a formal alliance in which they undertake to extend military assistance to each other in case of external threats. This modality, coupled with some wider CSBM, such as the creation of a Center for Conflict Management, in which other regional countries take part, might limit the anxieties of the other states in the region.

The Role of the United States

Since the end of the Cold War and the relative decline in the role of the Soviet Union, and later Russia, in the Middle East, the United States has assumed even greater influence than before over political and strategic developments in the region. This underlines the importance of United States participation in a common security regime, should it emerge. The role of the United States could have three dimensions: first, its ability to exert pressure and influence through diplomatic, economic, and sometimes even military means, in order to stabilize political and strategic developments; second, its potential role as a formal guarantor of various security arrangements, both on the bilateral level (as, for example, in a future Syrian-Israeli agreement on the Golan) and on the multilateral level, as in the case of participation in region-wide CSBM; and finally, its ability to compensate parties that are adversely affected by the defection of other parties from any security system or agreement. Because of these three roles, United States participation is essential for the success of major strategic agreements and the eventual establishment of a common security system.

While the United States would certainly play the leading role (as an external party) in such a system, the role of Russia as a participant in a regional security system is also relevant, as it has important political interests in the region and its influence might increase in the future.

SUMMING UP

The two main assumptions of this chapter are that the Arab-Israeli peace process will continue and that positive political developments throughout the Middle East depend on the evolvement of stable security arrangements. The paper focuses primarily on developments within the "heart" or core of the Middle East, but points out the intricate strategic relationships between the core and the Gulf. Stable security arrangements in the core would ultimately depend on the evolvement of both bilateral and multilateral CSBM and various combinations of agreements combining political and security factors. The chapter attempts to delineate and identify foci of security threats and problems and the ways in which these could be managed and controlled. This is done with the aid of conceptualizations drawn from the theoretical literature on international security regimes, CSBM, and arms control. Yet the special political-strategic context of the Middle East requires that applications of these theoretical conceptualizations to that region be nuanced and modified according to the political conditions there. Thus, the proposal for the eventual creation of a common security system is tailored to the more specific conditions of the Middle East. It also notes the specific hurdles and obstacles resulting from the structure of the Middle East state system, which could impede and complicate steps taken towards the evolvement of a regional security regime. One of the characteristics of the framework proposed here is that it has, to an extent, a modular structure and consequently there is no need for its full implementation in order to contribute to greater strategic stability in the region.

NOTE

* This paper is based on research funded by the United States Institute of Peace on "Security Regimes in the Arab Israeli Zone."

NOTES

1. The working group on Arms Control and Regional Security (ACRS) was joined within the context of the multilateral track established by the Madrid Peace Conference of October 1991. ACRS has served already and could continue to serve as a useful forum for discussions and agreements. However, it cannot be separated from the overall peace process and from other interstate developments in the Middle East.

2. For a comprehensive discussion of security systems in the Middle East and especially of the element of CSBM within them, see Yair Evron, *Emtsaim li-beniyat emun u-bitahon ba-heksher ha-yisraeli-aravi* (Confidence and security building measures in the Israel-Arab context) (Tel Aviv: Tel Aviv University, 1995).

3. On the definition of international regimes see Stephen D. Krasner, "Structural Causes and Regime Consequences," *International Organization* 36, no. 2 (spring 1982): 185.

4. For a very useful study of the differences between neo-realism and neo-liberalism see David A. Baldwin, ed., *Neorealism and Neoliberalism: The Contemporary Debate* (New York: Columbia University Press, 1993).

5. On the concept of international security regimes see Robert Jervis, "Security Regimes," *International Organization* 36, no. 2 (spring 1982).

6. See for example Charles L. Glazer "Realists as Optimists: Cooperation or Self Help," *Security Studies* 5, no. 3 (spring 1996) for a discussion of the possibilities of cooperation in the security area from the standpoint of realism.

7. The security relationships among many members of the Organization for Security and Cooperation in Europe (OSCE), and certainly among the NATO members, could be identified as a common security regime. The Western European members of NATO have created what could be characterized as a cooperative security regime.

8. The concept of Confidence Building Measures (CBM) appeared for the first time in the first half of the 1970s and was formally endorsed by the CSCE in 1975. The concept of CSBM widens the scope of CBM. It was introduced to the CSCE process for the first time by Yugoslavia and was formally endorsed by the CSCE at the Madrid Conference of 1980. For further elaboration, see, for example, Volker Rittberger et al., "Toward an East-West Security Regime: The Case of Confidence and Security-Building Measures," *Journal of Peace Research* 27, no. 1 (1990): 55.

9. This is of course a wide definition of CSBM. The narrow definition of CSBM as adopted in the European context refers primarily to measures designed to increase transparency and mutual communications in order to lessen the dangers of surprise attacks.

10. These relationships have already been partly analyzed and discussed by some authors. See, for example, Aryeh Shalev, *Shituf-peulah be-tsel imut: mishtar shevivat ha-neshek Yisrael-Suryah,* 1949-1955 (Cooperation in the shadow of conflict: the Israeli-Syrian armistice regime, 1949-1955) (Tel Aviv: Ministry of Defense, 1989); Aharon Klieman, "The Israel-Jordan Tacit Security Regime," in *Regional Security Regimes: Israel and Its Neighbors,* ed. Efraim Inbar (Albany: State University of New York Press, 1995): 127-51; Yariv Agmon, "The Israeli-Egyptian Relationship, 1949-1955, as an International Security Regime" (master's thesis, Tel Aviv University, 1994).

11. For a historical discussion of the interests and motivations that affect the formulations of Israeli policy vis-à-vis Lebanon, see Ze'ev Schiff, "Lebanon: Motivations and Interests in Israeli Policy," *Middle East Journal* 38 (spring 1984): 220-27 and Yair Evron, *War and Intervention in Lebanon: The Israeli-Syrian Deterrence Dialogue* (Baltimore: Johns Hopkins University Press, 1987). On the Maronite community's historical positions vis-à-vis Is-

rael, see Eyal Zisser, "Shattering of Illusions: Initial Contacts between the Zionist Movement and the Maronite Community in Lebanon" (in Hebrew), *Iyunim* (Ben Gurion University) 6 (1996).

12. For a theoretical discussion of the concept of "common aversion," see Arthur Stein, "Coordination and Collaboration: Regimes in an Anarchic World," *International Organization* 36, no. 2 (spring 1982): 298-323 and *Why Nations Cooperate: Circumstance and Choice in International Relations* (Ithaca, N.Y.: Cornell University Press, 1990). For a thoughtful and multifaceted application of this concept to the Israeli/Arab case, see Janice Gross Stein, "A Common Aversion to War: Regimes Creation by Egypt and Israel as a Strategy of Conflict Management," in *Conflict Management in the Middle East,* ed. Gabriel Ben-Dor and David Dewitt (Lexington, Mass.: Lexington Books, 1987), 59-77.

13. See references in note 10 above and also Evron, *Emtsaim li-beniyat emun u-bitahon.*

14. For a detailed discussion see Yair Evron, *The Demilitarization of Sinai,* 1957-1967, Jerusalem Papers on Peace Problems no. 11 (Jerusalem: Hebrew University of Jerusalem, The Leonard Davies Institute for International Relations, 1975) and "Two Periods in the Arab Israeli Strategic Relations 1957-1967, 1967 -1973," in *From June to October,* ed. Itamar Rabinovich and Haim Shaked (New Brunswick, N.J.: Transaction Books, 1978), 93-124. See also Janice Stein, "A Common Aversion to War."

15. The collapse of the regime occurred not because the parties abandoned their shared interest in war avoidance. Neither Israel nor Egypt was interested in war at that stage. Rather, it was due to a series of escalatory steps, some based on misconceptions and miscalculations. The initial Egyptian move was a deterrent. However, once the crisis unfolded, Egypt moved from a deterrent strategy to a mix of deterrence and coercive diplomacy. Israeli strategic doctrine, which considered the concentration of the Egyptian army near the border as a *casus belli,* led Israel to launch the first strike. On the 1967 crisis and war see, inter alia, Yair Evron, *The Middle East: Nations, Superpowers, and Wars* (New York: Praeger, 1973); Walter Laqueur, *The Road to Jerusalem: The Origins of the Arab-Israeli Conflict, 1967* (New York: Macmillan, 1968); Theodore Draper, *Israel and World Politics: Roots of the Third Arab-Israeli War* (New York: The Viking Press, 1968); Edgar O'Ballance, *The Third Arab-Israeli War* (London: Faber, 1972).

16. See Evron, *Emtsaim li-veniyat emun u-vitahon,* 53-57; Brian Mandell, "Anatomy of a Confidence Building Regime: Egyptian-Israeli Security Cooperation, 1973-1979," *International Journal* 45 (spring 1990): 202-23.

17. See Evron, *War and Intervention.*

18. The Israeli-Jordanian case might have led to a seeming paradox: precisely because the regime was so stable and effective there was no pressing reason to move ahead to a formal peace treaty. The reason of course was that other dimensions of Israeli-Jordanian relationships—political and economic—required such a move.

19. Lebanon is the most evident demonstration of this domestic potential for breakdown of the state resulting from different types of cleavages. But ethnic and religious cleavages with destructive potential exist in Iraq (where they exploded) and Syria as well. Even in Egypt, extreme Islamic radical groups are trying to provoke a conflict between the Muslim majority and the Copt minority

20. The growing gap between population growth and limited resources is one of the reasons for Egyptian activism in foreign policy inside the Arab world. See, for example, Gabriel Ben-Dor, "Egypt," in *Security Policies of Developing Countries,* ed. Edward Kolodziej and Robert Harkavy (Lexington, Mass.: Lexington Press, 1982): 179-202.

21. For a definition of the Middle East as a regional subsystem in international relations terms, see Evron, *The Middle East,* chap. 6.

22. Following the disintegration of the USSR, Iran increasingly diverted its foreign policy activity to the new central Asian and trans-Caucasian republics. However, it is evident that its interest in the Gulf region remains its primary concern; it also tries to maintain an active role in the whole of the Middle East.

23. Egypt has always been politically concerned with developments in the Gulf area. During the Gulf crisis of 1990-91, Egypt also demonstrated that it was ready to extend its military activity to that area if its vital political interests became involved. For this extension of Egypt's security perimeter see, inter alia, Ephraim Kam, "The Threat Perception of the Arab States," in *Arms Control and the New Middle East Security Environment,* ed. Shai Feldman and Ariel Levite (Tel Aviv: Jaffee Center for Strategic Studies, 1994), 92-93 and Abdel Monem Said Ali, "La Politique de la sécurité égyptienne," in *Perceptions de sécurité et stratégies nationales au Moyent-Orient,* ed. Bassma Kodman Darwish and May Chartouni-Dubarry (Paris: Masson, 1994).

24. At the same time, various Egyptian declarations indicate that under very extreme conditions Egypt might take threatening military action against Israel, such as renewed militarization of parts of the Sinai. Thus, Egyptian defense minister Mohamed Hussein Tantawi has recently declared that in its 1996 exercises the Egyptian army applied a military scenario of "war with a neighboring country which is armed with atomic bombs."

25. In defining these objectives, I have moved from security regimes that are designed primarily for the management of ongoing conflicts to security regimes that characterize the cooperative relationships existing, for example, among the Western European members of NATO.

26. The political problems are currently the most serious ones. Indeed, the gaps between Syria and Israel have grown tremendously since the coming to power of the new Israeli government. The likelihood of military escalation in south Lebanon has considerably increased. Even the possibility of a limited Syrian military probe on the Golan—though still unlikely—has become more realistic.

27. In the preamble to the CFE treaty, signed in 1990, three objectives are stated: (a) the establishment of a stable and secure balance of conventional forces in Europe (Atlantic to Urals) and at lower levels than existing then; (b) the elimination of gaps in capabilities which threaten stability and security; (c) the elimination of the potential for surprise attack and of large-scale military offensive.

28. See Evron, *Emtsaim li-beniyat emun u-bitahon.* The main emphasis, however, in those qualified regimes was on the preemption of limited violence along the borders. This in turn helped to avoid an escalation to a large-scale military confrontation. In addition, the de facto demilitarization of the Sinai between 1957 and 1967 contributed indirectly to transparency since it preempted the possibility of a surprise attack against Israel. The Sinai served as a major buffer zone and any major military move into it could have been detected by air surveillance, thus eliminating the possibility of a surprise attack.

29. On the importance of seminars and meetings between the parties to a conflict in order to enhance learning and understanding of the other side's interests and perceptions see, inter alia, Jervis, "Security Regimes," 61-64 and "From Balance to Concert: A Study of International Security Cooperation," *World Politics* 38, no. 1 (October 1985): 58-79. See also Emanuel Adler, "Seeds of Peaceful Change: The OSCE as a Pluralistic-Security Community-Building Institution," paper presented at the meeting of the International Studies Association, San Diego, 1996.

30. For further details see Yair Evron, "Confidence-Building in the Middle East," in *Arms Control in the Middle East,* ed. Dore Gold, JCSS study no. 15, (Boulder, Colo.: Westview; Jerusalem: Jerusalem Post, 1990), 38-48.

31. See also Aryeh Shalev, *Israel and Syria: Peace and Security on the Golan* (Boulder, Colo.: Westview; Jerusalem: Jerusalem Post, 1994).

32. See Evron, *War and Intervention.*

33. For further details concerning the elaborate system created within the peace agreement, see Itshak Lederman, *The Arab-Israeli Experience in Verification and Its Relevance to Conventional Arms Control in Europe,* CISSM occasional paper no. 2 (College Park, Md.: University of Maryland, Center for International Security Studies at Maryland, School of Public Affairs, 1989).

34. See Articles 4(4)a,b: 4(5) of *Treaty of Peace between the State of Israel and the Hashemite Kingdom of Jordan,* 26 October 1994 (Jerusalem: Israel Information Service Gopher, 1994).

35. For an elaboration and discussion of some of these measures see Shalev, *Israel and Syria.*

36. For discussion of Israeli conventional deterrence see, inter alia, Jonathan Shimshoni, *Israel and Conventional Deterrence: Border Warfare from 1953 to 1970* (Ithaca, N.Y.: Cornell University Press, 1988); Avner Yaniv, *Deterrence without the Bomb* (Lexington, Mass.: Lexington Books, 1987); Yair Evron, *Israel's Nuclear Dilemma* (Ithaca, N.Y.: Cornell University Press, 1994).

37. A good example is the Israeli general deterrence posture, which has stabilized Syrian-Israeli strategic relationships. This deterrence posture coupled with the various CSBM on the Golan combined to create a security regime there. See Janice Stein, "A Common Aversion to War."

38. Domestic threats to the stability of Arab regimes are recognized as a major security risk. See the analytical framework presented by Lenore Martin in this volume, and Mohammed Ayoob, "Unravelling the Concept: 'National Security' in the Third World," in *The Many Faces of National Security in the Arab World,* ed. Bahgat Korany, Paul Noble, and Rex Brynen (New York: Macmillan, 1993).

39. On the "power dilemma," see Barry Buzan, *People, States, and Fear: The National Security Problem in International Relations* (Chapel Hill: University of North Carolina Press, 1983).

40. On the arms races in the Middle East see Yair Evron, "Arms Races in the Middle East and Some Arms Control Measures Related to Them," in *Dynamics of a Conflict: A Re-examination of the Arab-Israeli Conflict,* ed. Gabriel Sheffer (Atlantic Highlands, N.J.: Humanities, 1975), 95-135. For details concerning defense budgets and military order of battle of different Middle Eastern states, see *The Middle East Military Balance/Jaffee Center for Strategic Studies* (Tel Aviv: Tel Aviv University, 1983-); and *The Military Balance* (London: International Institute for Strategic Studies, 1963-).

41. For detailed studies see, inter alia, Eliezer Sheffer, "The Economic Burden of the Arms Race between the Confrontational States and Israel," (in Hebrew), in *Security and Israel's Economy in the 1980s,* ed. Zvi Lenir (Tel Aviv: Ministry of Defense, 1985); Charles Perkins, *Arms to the Arabs: The Arab Military Buildup Since 1973,* AIPAC papers on U.S.-Israel Relations, no. 16 (Washington, D.C.: American Israel Public Affairs Committee, 1989); Robert Looney, "Arms Races in the Middle East: A Test of Causality," *Arms Control* 11 (September 1990): 178-90; Shmuel Ben Zvi, *Defense Expenditures and the National Economy* (in Hebrew) (Tel Aviv: Tel Aviv University, Pinhas Sapir Research Institute, 1993). For a study on the interaction between reductions in defense budgets and economic developments, see Yair Evron, "Economic Factors in the Middle East Peace Process" (unpublished manuscript prepared for the Center for International Studies, University of California, Los Angeles, December 1995).

42. For studies on the Islamic fundamentalist threat in different Arab states see, inter alia, David Menashri, ed., *Ha-Islam ha-fundamentalisti: etgar li-yetsivut ezorit* (Islamic fundamental

ism: a challenge to regional stability) (Tel Aviv: Tel Aviv University, Moshe Dayan Center, 1993).

43. See Kenneth N. Waltz, *The Spread of Nuclear Weapons: More May Be Better,* Adelphi Paper 171 (London: International Institute for Strategic Studies, 1981) and Scott D. Sagan and Kenneth N. Waltz, *The Spread of Nuclear Weapons: A Debate* (New York: W. W. Norton, 1995); Shai Feldman, *Israeli Nuclear Deterrence: A Strategy for the 1980s* (New York: Columbia University Press, 1982); Martin Van Creveld, *Nuclear Proliferation and the Future of Conflict* (New York: Free Press, 1993).

44. For an in-depth study of the policy of ambiguity see Evron, *Israel's Nuclear Dilemma.*

45. For a counter school of thought see Shlomo Aronson and Oded Brosh, *Nuclear Weapons in the Middle East* (in Hebrew) (Jerusalem: Akademon, 1994).

46. For studies on the Arab reactions to the Israeli nuclear effort, see Evron, *Israel's Nuclear Dilemma.* For a different assessment, see A. E. Levite and E. B. Landau, *Confidence and Security Building Measures in the Middle East* (Tel Aviv: Jaffee Center for Strategic Studies, 1997).

47. For an updated discussion of the proliferation of arms in the Middle East see Ian Lesser and Ashley Tellis, *Strategic Exposure: Proliferation around the Mediterranean* (Santa Monica, Calif.: RAND, 1996); see also *Middle East Military Balance.*

48. See Shai Feldman and Ariel Levite, eds., *Arms Control and the New Middle East Security Environment* (Tel Aviv: Jaffee Center for Strategic Studies, 1994) and Shai Feldman, *Nuclear Weapons and Arms Control in the Middle East* (Cambridge, Mass.: MIT Press, 1997).

49. Thus for example, Dr. 'Abd al-Munim al-Sayyid 'Ali from the Al-Ahram Center said, "There is a substantial difference between minimal nuclear deterrence and the extensive nuclear capability which Israel is assumed to have"; Ze'ev Schiff in *Ha-aretz* (Tel Aviv), 14 March 1995.

50. For such possible Egyptian suspicions see Evron, *Israel's Nuclear Dilemma.* For the Egyptian suspicions in this regard, see also Reuven Pedhatzur, "The Egyptian Suspicions," *Ha-aretz* (Tel Aviv), 25 November 1996. Pedhatzur is relying on the works of the Egyptian General Rida Fida who argued that the Israeli army's multi-year plan indicates that Israel's strategic posture extends far beyond its immediate neighbors and covers North Africa as well.

51. The literature on the proposals for cutoff of production of nuclear materials is extensive. For one example, see Frank Berkhout et al., "A Cutoff in the Production of Fissile Material," *International Security* 19, no. 3 (winter 1994-1995): 167-202.

52. On these see, for example, Yair Evron, "Gulf Crisis and War: Regional Rules of the Game and Policy and Theoretical Implications," *Security Studies* 4, no. 1 (fall 1994).

53. See ibid. and Yair Evron and Ya'acov Bar-Simantov, "Coalition in the Arab World," *Jerusalem Journal of International Relations* 1, no. 2 (winter 1975).

54. See Evron, "Gulf Crisis and War."

55. See Ghassan Salamé, "Inter-Arab Politics: The Return of Geography," in *The Middle East: Ten Years after Camp David,* ed. William B. Quandt (Washington, D.C.: Brookings Institute, 1988), 319-53; Bernard Lewis, "Rethinking the Middle East," Foreign Affairs 7, no. 2 (fall 1992): 99-119.

56. This is one of the main principles of the United Nations.

57. On the theoretical differences between "cooperation" and "coordination," see Arthur Stein, "Coordination and Collaboration," note 12 above.

CONCLUSIONS

CHAPTER ELEVEN

Crossing The "New Frontiers"

LENORE G. MARTIN

INTRODUCTION

*T*he picture of the Middle East presented by the contributors to this volume, is of a region challenged by violence, repression, and instability. Conservative Islamists challenge the legitimacy of the regime in Saudi Arabia. Autocratic governments repress freedom of the press and political participation. Authoritarian regimes resist the implementation of political reforms. In Turkey, Sunnis riot against Alevis and Kurdish radicals seek separatism. The Turkish military clashes with PKK (Kurdish Workers' Party) terrorists over the border in northern Iraq, a state whose territorial integrity and sovereignty remain in jeopardy in the aftermath of the Iraq-Kuwait war of 1990-91. Many Middle East economies are stalled in a status quo and their governments are slow to improve them either through structural reforms or international economic groupings. Water disputes interfere with the achievement of normal diplomatic relations between Syria and Israel over the Golan Heights and between Syria and Turkey over the Euphrates. The region has a high level of military expenditures devoted to the accumulation of weapons, including weapons of mass destruction, and a low level of success in implementing arms controls. This turbulent region surely serves as a significant testing ground for contending concepts of national security.

Recall that the goal of this book was to introduce readers to an "integrated approach" to the study of national security in the Middle East and to explore its implications for scholars and policymakers. The integrated approach suggests solutions to the conflicting approaches to the study of national security posed by the realist and liberal perspectives. As explained in the first chapter, the realist approach focuses on military security as the most significant determinant of national security. The liberal approach views a host of non-military factors as equally or more significant. The integrated approach selects five components of national security, including military capabilities, as essential, and treats them as variables that interact with each other. The task in this concluding chapter is to demonstrate that each of the studies of the separate variables in the paradigm inexorably leads to interlinkages with the other key variables. Moreover these linkages occur at every level of analysis. There are in this volume three levels of analysis applying the paradigm, each one focusing on one of its five variables. One level consists of country studies: Madawi Al-Rasheed on the inculcation of political legitimacy in Saudi Arabia; the Ayatas in their two chapters on the struggle for religious tolerance in Turkey and ethnic tolerance and conflict in Turkey. The second level consists of subregional studies: Mustapha Kamel Al-Sayyid on measuring political legitimacy in the Arab Middle East; Hillel I. Shuval on allocating essential water resources among Israel and its Jordan Valley neighbors; and Yair Evron on creating controls over military capabilities among Israel and the surrounding Arab states. The third level consists of full regional studies: Augustus Richard Norton and Farhad Kazemi on increasing political legitimacy through political reform; Roger Owen on increasing economic capabilities through interstate economic organizations; and Sohrab Shahabi and Farideh Farhi on the problems involved in improving the economic capabilities of the states of the region. Each study does not necessarily link all of the variables all of the time, but the linkage is comprehensive enough to be considered an "integrated" picture of national security.

INTEGRATING THE VARIABLES

Political Legitimacy

Madawi Al-Rasheed examines one of the key foundations of political legitimacy in Middle East states, namely, the inculcation of ideological support for the regime and political community through the "production" of official history. The foundations of political legitimacy in Saudi Arabia include Islam, tribal integration through intermarriage with the house of Saud, redistribution of oil wealth for social welfare, and coercion. Al-Rasheed shows how official history, as produced in school texts, is written by or for the organs of state in order to create consensual control through mystification that emphasizes Islamic history, in particular Wahhabism, as well as the Najdi origins of the al-Saud. At the same time, these texts ignore the Shi'is of Saudi Arabia, and reject tribal traditions of other regions of the kingdom, Arab nationalism, and Westernization. Al-Rasheed demonstrates that this creates serious challenges for the legitimacy of the regime and invites some of its political opponents to promulgate alternative versions of this history. Thus the Shi'is write their own history, and the more radical Islamist opponents accuse the regime of financial corruption and diverging from the true path of Islam.

Al-Rasheed also demonstrates how the legitimacy of the regime and political community in Saudi Arabia interplays to different degrees with three other variables in the national security paradigm: economic capabilities, religious tolerance, and military capabilities. In order for the regime to propagate the principles of Wahhabism and post-tribal national identity that support its legitimacy through official, historical texts, it needed a state-wide educational system. That was enabled by the state's economic capabilities, fueled by revenues from the kingdom's wealth from gas and oil exports (an essential natural resource in abundance in the kingdom). The use of religion to support the legitimacy of the regime creates problems for religious tolerance in the society. The conservative Islamists, as Al-Rasheed discusses, are grossly dissatisfied with the lack of orthodoxy in the regime and question its legitimacy. The Shi'is, who represent a sizable minority and who have settled in the oil-rich Eastern Province, resent their exclusion from the political community by a regime that is intolerant of religious differences. Extreme reactions to the lack of orthodoxy of the regime have, in the past, led to violence and the diversion of military capabilities—and possibly could do so in the future. Al-Rasheed mentions briefly the Ikhwan revolt that challenged King Saud in the 1920s, and the siege of the Great Mosque in 1979. She dwells more on the dissatisfaction with the importation of Western forces to repel the Iraqis from Kuwait in 1990-91, which has allegedly incited acts of terror within the kingdom. In sum, one cannot comprehend the development of consensual political legitimacy in Saudi Arabia without taking into consideration the other variables of economic capabilities, religious tolerance, and military capabilities, and by implication the essential natural resources of oil and gas that contribute to the kingdom's economic and military capabilities.

Mustapha Kamel Al-Sayyid seeks to measure political legitimacy and security in the Arab Middle East by ranking five representative states (Saudi Arabia, Egypt, Iraq, Libya, and Algeria) along various scales in the period from approximately 1989 to 1996. To measure the legitimacy of regimes, Al-Sayyid examines the numbers of political prisoners, numbers of people killed in political conflicts (including civil wars and terrorist acts), repression of freedom of expression (such as freedom of the press and of association) and political participation, orderly or violent changes of government, and numbers of economic and political migrants. For security, which he defines as both state, in the sense of the regime and government, and societal or personal in the liberal tradition,

Al-Sayyid examines the management of external military threats, the management of external economic threats (economic sanctions such as trade embargoes), ratios of governmental military and welfare spending, and crime rates.

Al-Sayyid's approach to measuring political legitimacy in turn integrates at least three of the variables in the national security paradigm: military capabilities, religious and ethnic tolerance, and economic capabilities. Al-Sayyid's first group of criteria involves government generated violence or repression through the use of force, i.e., military or police capabilities, in order to maintain the authority of the Arab regimes under study. He measures the effects of the use of such violence, namely, political imprisonment and deaths in political conflicts. Indeed, if one were to explore beyond the statistics of political violence in the Arab countries used in Al-Sayyid's study, one would find many instances of extreme effects of the lack of religious and ethnic tolerance. Thus Iraq scores highly in this category because of the violence involving Kurds in the north and Shi'is in the south. Algeria scores next highest because of the violence involving the radical religious revolutionaries after the aborted election of 1991. Al-Sayyid's last measure of political legitimacy involves accounting for economic migrants. Clearly, the failure of the state's economic capabilities to provide employment or welfare increases the numbers of economic migrants.

Farhad Kazemi and *Augustus Richard Norton* examine the possibilities for the achievement of political reforms in the predominantly authoritarian regimes of the Middle East. Reforms mean creating governments that are honest, efficacious, and accountable to their populations. They result from liberalization of the economies, institution of the type of associational life that is present in civil society, meaningful political participation in the government process, as well as separation of church and state. Kazemi and Norton point out that Middle Eastern regimes, particularly in the oil-rich rentier states, erect barriers to reform by maintaining control over the economies of their states. Governments of rentier states need not be responsible to their populations because most of their revenues are not provided through taxation. They also point out that in many states of the region elections are not meaningful indicators of political participation. Authoritarian rule is pervasive and does not tolerate political opposition. Therefore the regimes restrain private organizations and restrict freedom of speech and the press. Kazemi and Norton emphasize that so-called Islamic governments and Islamic political groups are often illiberal, particularly in terms of minority rights, religious freedom, and the rights of women. The authors state, however, that when Islamists "obey the rules of the game," they should be included in the political process. This, they hope, will lead the Islamists to become more moderate and pragmatic.

In discussing the processes and obstacles to achieving political reforms in the Middle East, Kazemi and Norton focus on the problems of political legitimacy in the region. They link political legitimacy issues to three variables in the paradigm: military capabilities, economic capabilities, and religious tolerance. The authoritarian regimes require military capabilities to maintain their restraints and restrictions on the political community and deploy force when popular protests turn violent (such as in the Egyptian bread riots of 1977, riots in Algeria in 1988, the violent responses to structural reforms in Jordan in 1989, and protests in Bahrain in 1994-96). The rentier states avoid political reform by using their economic capabilities to provide public welfare and subsidization of commercial enterprise. By contrast, lack of economic capabilities has created political crises, and movement towards political reform, as in Jordan. And the informal economies of many Middle East states, which deny regimes resources for taxation, constitute subtle forms of political protest. Furthermore, extreme Islamization threatens the religious tolerance that might enable associational life to thrive and become the precursors to "civil society" in these states.

Religious and Ethnic Tolerance

In the first of their two chapters, *Sencer Ayata* and *Ayşe Güneş-Ayata* analyze the interrelationships of religious groups and the political ramifications of the growth of religious identity in Turkey since the 1950s. In particular they examine the relationship with the state of more radical Islamists and the Alevis, who represent significant sectors of Turkish society. Although officially a secular regime, Turkish governments have supported the Sunni religious education in the Schools for Chaplains and Preachers and operated the country's mosques through the Directorate of Religious Affairs. Since the 1980s the Islamist Welfare Party (WP) has attracted diverse support ranging from students, white-and blue-collar workers and small shopkeepers to members of the business, professional, and intellectual elite. The WP briefly took power in a coalition government in 1996-97, but a confrontation with the military led to the suppression of the party. Although the WP has been reincarnated in the form of the Virtue Party, Islamic fundamentalism remains under siege. The rise of Islamic fundamentalism has produced a secularist backlash in Turkey among broad sectors of society, particularly women's groups and big business. It has also exacerbated social conflict with the Alevis, a more liberal Islamic sect which claims approximately 20 percent of the population. Alevis tend to support more secularist, left-wing political parties, and because of their tendency to cluster in urban settings they have become vulnerable to mob violence from radical Islamists. In response the Alevis have taken on a more public identity and some of their youth have become more radical.

The work of Ayata and Güneş-Ayata on the regime's earlier support for religion and then rejection of the Islamization of Turkish society involves an understanding of the roles of at least three other national security variables in that process: political legitimacy, economic capabilities, and military capabilities. Clearly, the suppression of the WP and the Turkish military's other anti-fundamentalist actions were in response to the perceived threats to the political legitimacy of a regime based on Ataturk's secularist principles. The substantial changes in the Turkish economy produced social dislocations that gave popular support to the WP. The government's inability to deploy economic capabilities to provide welfare supports to the larger population contributed to the growth of the WP. The government has deployed military (including police) capabilities to respond to mob violence against the Alevis, and also warn against the risks of religious fundamentalism when it sent tanks into Sincan.

In their second chapter, *Ayşe Güneş-Ayata* and *Sencer Ayata* examine the "Kurdish issue" that arises for Turkish society because of the Kemalist ideological resistance to the recognition of separate ethnic identities in Turkey's multiethnic society. Kurds in Turkey are segmented into different religious, linguistic, and tribal groups. Large numbers have assimilated into Turkish culture, particularly in Turkish cities, and many have emigrated to escape the harshness of the Southeast Anatolia region, with its high unemployment, continuing feudal social structure, and violence. The Kurds have also sought recognition of their separate cultural identity through the use of the Kurdish language, schools, television, radio, and newspapers, and outside of the Southeast they maintain ethnic networks in metropolitan areas. However, the government has not developed a coherent response to the Kurds' demands for cultural rights. Different national parties espouse different positions on whether to recognize Kurdish cultural autonomy. Even so, the Kurdish nationalist party, Halkin Demokrasi Partisi (HADEP), has gained only a small percentage of the vote. The more radical reaction to their economic plight in the Southeast and lack of cultural identity has been evident in the growth since the mid-1980s of the separatist, originally Marxist, PKK guerrilla group. The regime has responded militarily by trying to crush the PKK. It has formed an anti-PKK militia known as the Village Guards; it has sent large-scale military forces against the PKK across the border into Iraq; and it has formed an alliance with an Iraqi Kurdish faction, the Kurdish Democratic Party. Still the regime claims that the PKK receives considerable international support from Kurdish émigrés and Turkey's neighbors, Iraq, Iran, and Syria. The regime has also tried to alleviate the adverse economic conditions in the Southeast by development of the Southeastern Anatolia Project (GAP) which aims to reverse unemployment through more efficient irrigation and economic development generally. The authors look to the growth of a new entrepreneurial class in the Southeast as providing new solutions to the ethnic conflict in that area.

The discussion by Güneş-Ayata and Ayata of the threats to the Turkish regime and political community from Kurdish ethnic separatism involves all four of the other variables in the paradigm: political legitimacy, military capabilities, economic capabilities, and essential natural resources. The regime opposes demands for a Kurdish cultural identity as contravening the legitimating principle of a single "Turkish" national identity for the political community. Terrorist attacks by the radical PKK are intended to shake popular confidence in the regime, and hence its legitimacy. The regime responded with military force to earlier Kurdish revolts in 1924, 1926, and 1936-38, and continues to respond to the PKK by deploying military capabilities in its attempt to eliminate it and its demands for Kurdish separatism. The power vacuum in northern Iraq after the Gulf War of 1990-91 has enabled the PKK to create safe havens there and has also led to incursions by Turkish troops seeking to deny them those havens. The operations of the Turkish military in the Southeast has also disrupted local village life and has led to the evacuation of villages. The Kurdish refugees streaming into the cities of the Southeast and other metropolitan centers have in turn created additional strains for the Turkish economy. The regime also uses economic measures to combat the economic plight of the Kurds in the Southeast. The GAP project is intended to improve the economy of the Southeast which worsened with the Gulf War of 1990-91 and loss of Iraqi cross-border trade. The GAP project also seeks to better manage a significant essential natural resource, water. The project, which involves construction of dams on the Euphrates and Tigris Rivers, has raised fears on the part of Turkey's downstream neighbors, Iraq and Syria, concerning their loss of access to water.

Economic Capabilities

Sohrab Shahabi and *Farideh Farhi* discuss the effects of the end of the Cold War and the initiation of the Arab-Israeli peace process on the stimulation of demands for economic reforms in the Middle East region. They outline three main sets of reforms to release more funds for economic improvement: structural adjustments, attraction of foreign capital, and arms control and confidence building measures. Structural adjustments are essentially governmental actions to liberalize economies through such means as privatization and creation of free markets. The problem for Middle Eastern regimes is that governmental implementation of structural adjustments requires strong action, and possibly greater degrees of political legitimacy than the regimes can muster, or greater political participation than the authoritarian regimes are willing to tolerate. As a result there is stiff resistance to such economic reforms from governmental bureaucracies and private sector monopolies. Shahabi and Farhi see the problem of attracting foreign capital in the Middle East as directly related to the problem of inadequate political legitimacy and security for investors. The same problem stimulates substantial outflows of capital from the states of the region. Shahabi and Farhi see similar impediments to the implementation of arms control, because of vested interests in Middle East military-industrial sectors as well as those involved in the arms trade. They identify the general problem of achieving economic improvements in the states of the region as the absence of political reform that can create civil societies and change the status quo that currently favors certain economic elites.

Shahabi and Farhi's examination of the preconditions for improving Middle East economies very clearly depends upon the interplay between economic capabilities and two other variables: political legitimacy as well as military capabilities. In their discussion of the need for structural adjustments and an influx of foreign capital (or stemming the outflow of domestic capital), the authors underscore their point that such economic reforms are impossible without increasing political legitimacy through political reforms. They make a similar point with respect to achieving reductions in defense expenditures and arms controls. Those with vested economic interests in maintaining the economic status quo resist such measures as threatening to their political and economic interests.

Roger Owen takes a different approach from Shahabi and Farhi to the process of improving the economies of the Middle East states. Owen looks at the region as a whole and detects both centrifugal and centripetal forces at work that affect the formation and longevity of international economic groupings. Historically, regional economies sought independence from their colonial status through "defensive" economic development, for example, the erection of trade barriers and economic controls to achieve food security. There were also politically motivated Arab economic groupings, such as the Gulf Cooperation Council (GCC) and the Maghrib Union, as well as the now defunct Arab Cooperation Council. However, in the post-Cold War world and peace process environment, it is possible to ask if other groupings are possible. Owen examines six major options: (a) a region-wide Middle East Economic Union modeled on the European Union (EU), which he believes is highly unlikely; (b) subregional groupings such as the GCC and an Arab Free Trade Zone, as well as a new Israel-Jordan-Palestinian group, all of which are experiencing coordination problems; (c) joining a larger economic union, such as the Euro-Mediterranean Free Trade Area, a rather complex process hampered by competition in agricultural products and the lack of political cooperation; (d) bilateral economic arrangements such as sharing water, oil, and electricity—another process subject to serious political obstacles; (e) joining global economic organizations such as the World Trade Organization (WTO), which is problematic because of the need to implement structural adjustments; and (f) combinations of the above, i.e., multiple memberships in economic organizations. Owen predicts that the EU will control whether and which Middle East states join it and that the subregional groups will be difficult to coordinate. He concludes that in the absence of Middle Eastern institutional forums, extra-regional leadership, such as from the EU, will be needed to overcome the difficult domestic political obstacles to the larger economic groupings.

Owen's chapter uses a region-wide macro-level analysis that deals with the considerable diversity in both political and economic systems within the region. At that macro level there are the fewest linkages between economic capabilities and the other variables in the paradigm. Owen is of course very much aware of the issue facing the many states in the region lacking adequate essential natural resources, both of water and of food. His analysis is less concerned, however, with the national security of individual states and more concerned with the economic security of the region as a whole. Nonetheless, in explaining the well-springs of many of the economic policies of the states in the region, he does need to recall their concerns for post-colonial political legitimacy. And in considering the options for the future, like Shahabi and Farhi, Owen notes the considerable domestic political obstacles to the coordination of regional economic groupings. These obstacles implicitly include challenges to the legitimacy of the regime arising from opposition to the implementation of economically painful structural reforms.

Essential Natural Resources

Hillel I. Shuval traces the history of the Israeli-Syrian confrontations over the waters of the Jordan River since the founding of the Israeli state. He describes the approach taken by the United States mediator, Eric Johnston, in developing a plan for sharing water based upon usage and needs. However, conflicting political interests prevented the adoption of the Johnston plan. He also examines the international legal approach to resolving water claims. The approach favored by Shuval is the proposal of the Harvard Middle East Water Project to monetize water and treat it like any other commodity. The real value of water has an upper limit in the cost of desalination. The water needy states can therefore pay the water supplier states a calculated amount, which Shuval believes is readily affordable. He recognizes that adoption of this proposal requires a regional approach, because Syrian water claims affect the Palestinian community, as well as Israel and Jordan, and are in turn affected by Turkey's water claims.

Shuval's work links the essential natural resource of water to at least three of the variables in the paradigm: economic capabilities, military capabilities, and political legitimacy. Clearly the availability of water is closely connected to the economic capabilities of Israel and its Jordan Valley neighbors: Syria, Lebanon, Jordan, and the Palestinian West Bank. Even though Shuval disputes the claim that the June 1967 war between Israel and the Arab coalition was a "water war," there is sufficient evidence from the low level of conflict among Israel, Lebanon, and Syria prior to 1967 that those states expended military capabilities to try to secure their Jordan Valley water sources. The negotiation of the boundary lines between Israel and Syria at the Golan Heights is very much influenced by differing perceptions as to the need to secure the Golan water sources. Shuval proposes an economic solution to this issue which, if adopted, would involve expenditure of economic capabilities. Interestingly, in discussing the context of these negotiations, Shuval reveals that secure water sources are more than an economic or military security issue. They are part of the national identity, particularly for the Jewish state with its agricultural, Zionist origins. In other words, the legitimacy of the political community is related to its ability to work the land and hence secure water, an essential natural resource, for this purpose. A regime that conceded these water sources to its Arab neighbors might therefore risk losing its legitimacy at least for some segments of the Israeli population. We must also recognize that the reverse of Shuval's point is also true, that the legitimacy of the Syrian regime might be enhanced by regaining Golan territory.

Military Capabilities

Yair Evron has taken the position of a "modified structural realist." He examines the various forms of tacit and explicit, bilateral cooperation and unilateral confidence building and security building measures that Middle Eastern states have adopted to deter the outbreak of hostilities in the region during the interwar periods since the formation of the state of Israel in 1948. Evron sees the possibility for the creation of a security regime of informal norms that could be respected by the states of the Middle East, even though this regime would not achieve the level of cooperation evident in post-Cold War Europe. He advocates the adoption of a number of measures to manage interstate crises, deter escalation, support arms control efforts, and reduce military threats generally. These include creation of demilitarized zones, imposing limitations on military deployments, improving communications to avoid fears of surprise attacks, socialization of military cultures through joint seminars, and adoption of rules of air combat engagement. Evron sees the mid-1990s plateau in military defense expenditures and continuation of the peace process as potential foundations for arms control negotiations even over the difficult issue of controlling weapons of mass destruction. To encourage such negotiations, he advocates the creation of a Center for Conflict Management and a Center for Crisis Management in the style of the Organization for Security and Cooperation in Europe (OSCE) and points to the need for United States support for such efforts.

Evron's discussion of the possibility of restraints and controls over the use and build-up of military capabilities in the "heartland" of the region touches only briefly upon three of the variables in the paradigm: economic capabilities, religious tolerance, and, implicitly, political legitimacy. In explaining the plateau of defense expenditures in the region after the 1990-91 Gulf War, two of his three grounds were economic: economic difficulties and pressure for greater welfare expenditures. Furthermore, when Evron considers what might interrupt the trend towards cooperation and cause a resumption of increased defense spending, he reaches for other variables that could create interstate conflict. In his words, "Changes could come, however, if domestic conflicts and the rise of militant Islam were to spill over into interstate relations."[1] The point that Evron makes is that the predictability of arms build-ups requires consideration of the variables of religious (and probably ethnic) tolerance that would create intrastate conflict, and of political legitimacy that could be challenged by militant Islam.

IMPLICATIONS FOR SCHOLARS AND POLICYMAKERS

There are two general conclusions that derive from the policy solutions offered both implicitly and explicitly in this volume. Both underscore the validity of the integrated approach to national security posited here. The first is that there is no single variable solution to any Middle East state's security problems. The second is that there are both single state and multi-state solutions.

As stated in chapter 1, the most often proposed single variable solution to national security issues, the realist focus on military capabilities, is too limited. Even the policy prescriptions of Yair Evron, the author closest to the realist perspective, recognize the need to address other sources of conflict than purely external threats to Middle Eastern states. These include ethnic and religious conflicts and civil wars. Yet such conflicts, when examined closely, originate from various causes linked to breakdowns in political legitimacy, religious and ethnic tolerance, and economic capabilities.

Moreover, it is equally obvious from the other contributions to this volume, all of which focus on non-military variables of the paradigm, that there are no single variable solutions to the problems of national security. In studying and designing security policies for their states, Middle Eastern scholars and statesmen must clearly concern themselves with what Al-Rasheed, Al-Sayyid, Kazemi and Norton warn of endemic challenges to political legitimacy; what Ayata and Güneş-Ayata describe as the perils of breakdowns of religious and ethnic tolerance; what Shahabi and Farhi foretell of internal economic strains and instability; what Owen predicts as the problems of achieving external economic cooperation; what Shuval advocates as solutions to potential conflict over valuable water resources as well as what Evron proposes for arms controls and confidence and security building measures.

Moreover, in seeking these integrated solutions, statesmen would likely explore the possibility of multi-state solutions to national security problems. Three of the chapters in this volume, for example, focus specifically on such multilateral solutions. Roger Owen prescribes methods for increasing the economic capabilities of all the Middle East states through international economic groupings.

Yair Evron advocates a security regime for Israel and the surrounding states. The same approach could also be taken to the other locus of military conflict in the region, the Gulf. Hillel I. Shuval proposes economic solutions to the potential conflicts between Israel and its Jordan Valley neighbors. The same proposal could also be made for the other intractable water dispute in the region, among Turkey, Syria, and Iraq. Moreover, even proposed solutions for single variable security issues, whether explicit or implicit, could benefit from multi-state solutions. For example, Turkey's ability to resist the radical Islamization of its society might be assisted if it had better relations with the external sources of support of the Islamic groups emanating from Iran and the Gulf states. These states could impose restrictions on the export of radicalism by government or private groups within their control. Turkey's responses to the PKK and ethnic Kurdish separatism could be assisted if it could solve its water issues with Syria, thereby gaining Syria's help in denying safe havens for the PKK fighters.

The work presented in this volume is compelling evidence of the value of the integrated approach to the understanding of national security. I hope it will convince security studies scholars, both realists and liberals, of the greater explanatory power of this interrelated set of military and non-military variables. I also hope it will convince policymakers of the need to take into consideration the interconnectedness of policy choices in all five areas of the conceptual framework. Recognition of this interconnectedness should help in more accurate assessment of the outcomes of their policy choices.

NOTE

1. See p. 330 above.

Bibliography

'Abd al-Raziq, Husayn. *Misr fi 18 wa-19 yanayir: dirasa siyasiyya watha'iqiyya.* Beirut: Dar al-kalim, 1979.

Abdelnasser, Walid. *The Islamic Movement in Egypt: Perceptions of International Relations, 1967-1981.* London: Kegan Paul, 1994.

Abells Z. and A. Arbit. *The City of David Water Systems.* Jerusalem: Abells, 1995.

Adler, Emanuel. "Seeds of Peaceful Change: The OSCE as a Pluralistic-Security Community-Building Institution." Paper presented at the meeting of the International Studies Association, San Diego, 1996.

Afkami, Mahnaz and Erika Friedl, eds. *In the Eye of the Storm: Women in Post-Revolutionary Iran.* London: I. B. Tauris, 1994.

Akşit, Bahattin. *Köy, Kasaba ve Kentlerde Toplumsal Değişme.* Ankara: Turhan Yayınevi, 1985.

Ali, Abdel Monem Said. "La Politique de la sécurité égyptienne." In *Perceptions de sécurité et stratégies nationales au Moyent-Orient,* edited by Bassma Kodman Darwish and May Chartouni-Dubarry. Paris: Masson, 1994.

Al-Rasheed, Madawi. "Saudi Arabia's Islamic Opposition." *Current History* 95, no. 597 (January 1996): 16-22.

——. *Politics in an Arabian Oasis: The Rashidi Tribal Dynasty.* London: I. B. Tauris, 1991.

—— and Loulouwa Al-Rasheed. "The Politics of Encapsulation: Saudi Policy towards Tribal and Religious Opposition." *Middle Eastern Studies* 32, no. 1 (January 1996): 96-119.

Al-Sayyid, Mustapha Kamel. "Slow Thaw in the Arab World." *World Policy Journal* (autumn 1991).

Amon, Y. "A Profile of 'Mei Golan'1994." In Hebrew. *Mayim v'hashkaya,* June 1994.

Anderson, Lisa. "Liberalism, Islam, and the Arab State." *Dissent* (fall 1994): 439-44.

——. "The Tunisian National Pact of 1988." *Government and Opposition* 26, no. 2 (spring 1991): 244-60.

Andrews, Peter Alford, ed. *Ethnic Groups in the Republic of Turkey.* Weisbaden: Reichart, 1989.

Arjomand, Said Amir. "Traditionalism in Twentieth-Century Iran." In *From Nationalism to Revolutionary Islam,* edited by Said Amir Arjomand, 195-232. London: Macmillan, 1984.

Aron, Raymond. *Main Currents in Sociological Thought.* Vol. 2. Harmondsworth, U.K.: Penguin, 1982.

Aronson, Shlomo and Oded Brosh. *Nuclear Weapons in the Middle East.* In Hebrew. Jerusalem: Akademon, 1994.

Ashraf, Ahmad. "Bazaar-Mosque Alliance: The Social Bases of Revolts and Revolutions." *Politics, Culture, and Society* 1 (summer 1988): 538-67.

Assaf, K., N. Al-Khatib, E. Kally, and H. Shuval. *A Proposal for the Development of a Regional Water Master Plan.* Israel Palestine Center for Research and Information: Jerusalem, 1993.

Avcıoğlu, Doğan. *Türklerin Tarihi I.Cilt.* Istanbul: Tekin Yayınevi, 1989.

Aykan, Balı Mahmut. "Turkey's Policy in Northern Iraq, 1991-95." *Middle Eastern Studies* 32, no. 4 (October 1996): 343-66.

Ayoob, Mohammed. *The Third World Security Predicament: State Making, Regional Conflict and the International System.* Boulder, Colo.: Lynne Rienner, 1995.

———. "Unravelling the Concept: 'National Security' in the Third World." In *The Many Faces of National Security in the Arab World,* edited by Bahgat Korany, Paul Noble, and Rex Brynen. New York: Macmillan, 1993.

Ayubi, Nazih. *Over-Stating the Arab State: Politics and Society in the Middle East.* London: I. B. Tauris, 1995.

Azar, Edward E. and Chung-in Moon, eds. *National Security in the Third World: The Management of Internal and External Threats.* Aldershot, U.K.: Edward Elgar, 1988.

al-Azmeh, Aziz. "Populism Contra Democracy: Recent Democratist Discourse in the Arab World." In *Democracy without Democrats? The Renewal of Politics in the Muslim World,* edited by Ghassan Salamé, 112-29. New York: I. B. Tauris, 1994.

Baldwin, David A. "Security Studies and the End of the Cold War." World Politics 48 (1995): 117-41.

———, ed. *Neorealism and Neoliberalism: The Contemporary Debate.* New York: Columbia University Press, 1993.

Banuazizi, Ali. "Social Psychological Approaches to Political Development." In *Understanding Political Development,* edited by Myron Weiner and Samuel Huntington. Boston: Little, Brown, 1987.

Barkey, Henri. "Turkey, Islamic Politics, and the Kurdish Question." *World Policy Journal* 13, no. 1 (spring 1996): 43-52.

———. *The State and the Industrialization Crisis in Turkey.* Boulder, Colo.: Westview Press, 1990.

———, ed. *The Politics of Economic Reform in the Middle East.* New York: St. Martin's Press, 1992.

——— and Graham Fuller. *Turkey's Kurdish Question.* Lanham, Md.: Rowman and Littlefield, 1998.

Beblawi, Hazem and Giacomo Luciani, eds. *The Arab State.* London: Routledge, 1990.

———. *The Rentier State.* London: Croom Helm, 1987.

Bellin, Eva. "Civil Society in Formation: Tunisia." In *Civil Society in the Middle East,* edited by Augustus Richard Norton. Vol. 1. New York: E. J. Brill, 1995.

Ben, A. "USA: The Water Problems between Israel and Syria Can Be Solved Pragmatically." In Hebrew. *Ha-aretz* (Tel Aviv) 19 January 1996.

Ben-Dor, Gabriel. "Egypt." In *Security Policies of Developing Countries,* edited by Edward Kolodziej and Robert Harkavy, 179-202. Lexington, Mass.: Lexington Books, 1982.

Bennet, D. "Security Bargaining and the End of Laterstate Rivalry." *International Studies Quarterly* 40, no. 2 (1996): 157-84.

Benyounes, Lakhdar. " Le Cercle des morts anonymes." *Le Monde Diplomatique.* March 1996.

Berkhout, Frank et al. "A Cutoff in the Production of Fissile Material." *International Security* 19, no. 3 (winter 1994-95): 167-202.

Betts, Richard K., ed. *Conflict after the Cold War: Arguments on Causes of War and Peace.* New York: Macmillan, 1994.

Bilgili, Ahmet and Feramuz Aydoğan. "Doğu Anadolu Bölgesinde Zorunlu Göç Olgusunun Sosyolojik Çözümlemesi: Van Örneği." In Sosyoloji Derneği ve T.C. Başbakanlık Devlet İstatistik Enstitüsü, *II Ulusal Sosyoloji Kongresi: Toplum ve Göç.* Ankara: Sosyoloji Derneği Yayın no.5, DİE Yayın no.2046, 1997.

Bird, Jerine. "Revolution for Children in Saudi Arabia." In *Children in the Muslim Middle East,* edited by Elizabeth Fernea, 276-94. Austin: University of Texas Press, 1995.

Birtek, Faruk and Binnaz Toprak. "The Conflictual Agendas of Neo-Liberal Reconstruction and the Rise of Islamic Politics in Turkey." *Praxis International* 13, no. 2 (1993): 192-212.

Bobrow, B. "Complex Insecurity: Implications of a Sobering Metaphor." *International Studies Quarterly* 40, no. 4 (1996): 435-50.

Booth, Ken and Peter Vale. "Security in Southern Africa: After Apartheid, beyond Realism." *International Affairs* 71, no. 2 (1995): 285-304.

Bouazid, Ali. "A la recherche des 'disparus'." *Le Monde Diplomatique.* March 1996.

Brand, Laurie. "'In the Beginning was the State . . .': The Quest for Civil Society in Jordan." In *Civil Society in the Middle East,* edited by Augustus Richard Norton. Vol. 1. New York: E. J. Brill, 1995.

Braverman A. *Israel Water Study for the World Bank.* Beersheba: Ben Gurion University of the Negev and Tahal Consulting Engineers Ltd., August 1994.

Brecher, Michael. *Decisions in Israel's Foreign Policy.* London: Oxford University Press, 1974.

Brian, Mandell S. "Anatomy of a Confidence Building Regime: Egyptian-Israeli Security Cooperation, 1973-1979." *International Journal* 45 (spring 1990): 202-23.

Brown, J. "The Turkish Imbroglio: Its Kurds," American Academy of Social and Political Science, *Annals* (September 1995): 541.

Bruinessen, Martin van. "Gerilla Savaşı ve Siyasi Cinayet Arasında: Kürdistan İşçi Partisi." In *Kürdistan Üzerine Yazılar,* 361. Istanbul: İletişim, 1992.

———. *Agha, Shaikh, and State: On the Social and Political Organization of Kurdistan.* Utrecht: University of Utrecht, 1978.

Brynen, Rex. "Economic Crisis and Post-Rentier Jordan." *Canadian Journal of Political Science* 15 (March 1992).

Bulloch, John and Adel Darwish. *Water Wars: Coming Conflicts in the Middle East.* London: Victor Gollancz, 1993.

Bumpke, P. J. "The Kurdish Alevis: Boundaries and Perceptions." In *Ethnic Groups in the Republic of Turkey,* edited by Peter Alford Andrews. Weisbaden: Reichart, 1989.

Button S. "Turkey Struggles With Kurdish Separatism." *Military Review* (1995): 70-79.

Buzan, Barry. *People, States, and Fear: An Agenda for International Security Studies in the Post-Cold War Era.* 2d. ed. Boulder, Colo.: Lynne Rienner, 1991.

———. "People, States and Fear: The National Security Dilemma in the Third World." In *National Security in the Third World: The Management of Internal and External Threats,* edited by Edward E. Azar and Chung-in Moon, 14-43. Aldershot, U.K.: Edward Elgar, 1988.

———. *People, States, and Fear: The National Security Problem in International Relations.* Chapel Hill: University of North Carolina Press, 1983.

———, Charles Jones, and Richard Little. *The Logic of Anarchy: Neorealism to Structural Realism.* New York: Columbia University Press, 1993.

Çakır, Ruşen. *Ne şeriat ne Demokrasi.* Istanbul: Metis Yayınları, 1994.

Calabrese, John. *Revolutionary Horizons: Regional Foreign Policy in Post-Khomeini Iran.* New York: St. Martin's Press, 1994.

Cantori, Louis J. and Steven L. Spiegel. *The International Politics of Regions: A Comparative Approach.* Englewood Cliffs, N.J.: Prentice-Hall, 1970.

Caponera, Dante Augustus *Principles of Water Law and Administration: National and International.* Rotterdam: A. A. Balkema, 1992.

Carapico, Sheila. "Yemen between Civility and Civil War." In *Civil Society in the Middle East,* edited by Augustus Richard Norton. Vol. 2. New York: E. J. Brill, 1996.

Carr, E. H. *The Twenty Years' Crisis, 1919-1939: An Introduction to the Study of International Relations.* London: Macmillan and Co., 1939.

Celil, Celile. *XIX Yüzyıl Osmanlı İmparatorluğunda Kürtler.* Ankara: Öz-Ge Yayınları, 1992.

Chaliand, Gerard. "Introduction." In *A People without a Country: The Kurds and Kurdistan,* edited by Gerard Chaliand. New York: Olive Branch Press, 1993.

Chaudhry, Kiren Aziz. "Economic Liberalization and the Lineages of the Rentier State." *Comparative Politics* 27 (October 1994).

Connor, Walter. "Ethno-nationalism." In *Understanding Political Development,* edited by Myron Weiner and Samuel Huntington, 196-220. Boston: Little, Brown, 1987.

Cottam, Richard. *Nationalism in Iran.* Pittsburgh: University of Pittsburgh Press, 1964.

Criss, Nur Bilge. "The Nature of PKK Terrorism in Turkey." *Studies in Conflict and Terrorism* 18 (1995): 17-37.

Crystal, Jill. "Civil Society in the Arabian Gulf." In *Civil Society in the Middle East,* edited by Augustus Richard Norton. Vol. 2. New York: E. J. Brill, 1996.

———. "Authoritarianism and Its Adversaries in the Arab World." *World Politics* 46, no. 2 (January 1994): 262-89.

———. *Oil and Politics in the Gulf: Rulers and Merchants in Kuwait and Qatar.* Cambridge: Cambridge University Press, 1990, reprinted 1995.

Davis, Eric. "History of the Many or History for the Few? The Historiography of the Iraqi Working Class" In *Workers and Working Classes in the Middle East: Struggles, Histories, Historiographies,* edited by Zachary Lockman. New York: State University of New York Press, 1994.

———. "Theorizing Statecraft and Social Change in Arab Oil-Producing Countries." In *Statecraft in the Middle East: Oil, Historical Memory and Popular Culture,* edited by Eric Davis and Nicolas Gavrielides. Miami: Florida International University Press, 1991.

Davis, John. *Libyan Politics: Tribe and Revolution.* London: I. B. Tauris, 1987.

Dekmejian, Hrair. "The Rise of Political Islamism in Saudi Arabia." *Middle East Journal* 48, no. 4 (autumn 1994).

Demokratik Sol Parti. *Demokratik Sol Parti Program.* Ankara: Sistem Ofset, n.d.

Department of Defense Office of International Security Affairs. *United States Security Strategy for the Middle East.* Washington, D.C., May 1995.

Dessouki, Ali E. Hillal. "Globalization and the Two Spheres of Security." *Washington Quarterly* 16, no. 4 (1993): 109-17.

———. "Dilemmas of Security and Development in the Arab World: Aspects of the Linkage." In *The Many Faces of National Security in the Arab World,* edited by Bahgat Korany, Paul Noble, and Rex Brynen. London: Macmillan, 1993.

Draper, Theodore. *Israel and World Politics: Roots of the Third Arab-Israeli War.* New York: Viking, 1968.

Dresch, Paul. *Tribes, Government, and History in Yemen.* Oxford: Clarendon Press, 1989.

Dwyer, Kevin. *Arab Voices: The Human Rights Debate in the Middle East.* Los Angeles: University of California Press, 1991.

Easton, David. *A Systems Analysis of Political Life.* New York: Wiley, 1965.

Engelman, Robert and Pamela LeRoy. *Sustaining Water: Population and the Future Renewable Water Supplies.* Washington D.C.: Population and Environment Program, Population Action International,1993.

Enloe, Cynthia H. *Ethnic Soldiers: State Security in Divided Societies.* Harmondsworth, U.K.: Penguin, 1980.

Entelis, John. "Civil Society and the Authoritarian Temptation in Algerian Politics: Islamic Democracy vs. the Centralized State." In *Civil Society in the Middle East,* edited by Augustus Richard Norton. Vol. 2, 45-86. New York: E. J. Brill, 1996.

Esman, Milton J. *Ethnic Politics.* 2d ed. Ithaca, N.Y.: Cornell University Press, 1995.

——— and Itamar Rabinovich. *Ethnicity, Pluralism, and the State in the Middle East.* Ithaca, N.Y.: Cornell University Press, 1991.

Evron, Yair. *Emtsaim li-beniyat emun u-bitahon ba-heksher ha-yisraeli-aravi* (Confidence and security building measures in the Israel-Arab context). Tel Aviv: Tel Aviv University, 1995.

———. "Economic Factors in the Middle East Peace Process." Unpublished manuscript prepared for the Center for International Studies, University of California, Los Angeles, December 1995.

———. *Israel's Nuclear Dilemma.* Ithaca, N.Y.: Cornell University Press, 1994.

———. "Gulf Crisis and War: Regional Rules of the Game and Policy and Theoretical Implications." *Security Studies* 4, no. 1 (fall 1994).

———. "Confidence-Building in the Middle East." In *Arms Control In The Middle East,* edited by Dore Gold, 38-48. JCSS study no. 15. Boulder, Colo.: Westview Press; Jerusalem: Jerusalem Post, 1990.

———. *War and Intervention in Lebanon: The Israeli-Syrian Deterrence Dialogue.* Baltimore: Johns Hopkins University Press, 1987.

———. "Two Periods in the Arab Israeli Strategic Relations, 1957-1967; 1967-1973." In *From June to October,* edited by Itamar Rabinovich and Haim Shaked, 93-124. New Brunswick, N.J.: Transaction Books, 1978.

———. *The Demilitarization of Sinai, 1957-1967.* Jerusalem Papers on Peace Problems no. 11. Jerusalem: Hebrew University of Jerusalem, The Leonard Davies Institute for International Relations, 1975.

———. "Arms Races in the Middle East and Some Arms Control Measures Related to Them." In *Dynamics of a Conflict: A Re-examination of the Arab-Israeli Conflict,* edited by Gabriel Sheffer, 95-135. Atlantic Highlands, N.J.: Humanities, 1975.

———. *The Middle East: Nations, Superpowers, and Wars.* New York: Praeger, 1973.

——— and Ya'acov Bar-Simantov. "Coalition in the Arab World." *Jerusalem Journal of International Relations* 1, no. 2 (winter 1975).

Feldman, Shai. *Nuclear Weapons and Arms Control in the Middle East.* Cambridge, Mass.: MIT Press, 1997.

———. *Israeli Nuclear Deterrence: A Strategy for the 1980s.* New York: Columbia University Press, 1982.

——— and Ariel Levite, eds. *Arms Control and the New Middle East Security Environment.* Tel Aviv: Jaffee Center for Strategic Studies, 1994.

Fabietti, Ugo. "Control and Alienation of Territory among the Bedouin of Saudi Arabia." *Nomadic Peoples* (1986).

Field, Michael. *The Merchants: The Big Business Families of Saudi Arabia and the Gulf States.* New York: Overlook, 1985.

Fischer, Dietrich. *Nonmilitary Aspects of Security: A Systems Approach.* Brookfield, Vt.: Dartmouth Publishing, 1993.

Fischer, S., L. Hausman, A. Karasik, and T. C. Schelling, eds. *Securing Peace in the Middle East: Project on Economic Transition.* Cambridge, Mass.: MIT Press, 1994.

Fisher, Franklin M. "The Economics of Water Dispute Resolution, Project Evaluation and Management: An Application to the Middle East." *Water Resources Development* 11 (1995): 377-90.

Fishman, Robert M. "Rethinking State and Regime: Southern Europe's Transition to Democracy." *World Politics* 62, no. 3 (April 1990).

Fouad, Ashraf. "Gulf Arabs Move Closer to Unity." Reuters quoted in Beirut *Daily Star,* 18 December 1997.

Freitag, Ulrike. "Writing Arab History: The Search for the Nation." *British Journal of Middle Eastern Studies* 21, no. 1 (1994): 19-37.

Fritz, Dr. *Kürtlerin Tarihi.* Istanbul: Hasat Yayınları, 1992.

Gaddis, John Lewis. "International Relations Theory and the End of the Cold War." *International Security* 17, no. 3 (1992-93): 5-58.

Gause, F. Gregory, III. *Oil Monarchies: Domestic and Security Challenges in the Arab Gulf States.* New York: Council on Foreign Relations, 1994.

Ghareeb, Edmund. *The Kurdish Question in Iraq.* Syracuse: Syracuse University Press, 1981.

Giddens, Anthony. *Durkheim on Politics and the State.* Cambridge: Polity Press, 1986.

Glazer, Charles L. "Realists as Optimists: Cooperation or Self Help." *Security Studies* 5, no. 3 (spring 1996).

Gleick, P. H. "Water, War, and Peace in the Middle East." *Environment* 36 (1994): 6-42.

Glubb, Faris. "The GCC: Important Steps Forward." *Middle East International,* 5 December 1997.

Godelier, Maurice. "Mirror, Mirror on the Wall . . . The Once and Future Role of Anthropology: A Tentative Assessment." In *Assessing Cultural Anthropology,* edited by Robert Borofsky, 97-112. New York: McGraw Hill, 1994.

Gökçe, Birsen. "Doğu ve Güneydoğu Anadolu'da Göç Konusunda Yapılmışç Çalışmaların Metod Açısından Değerlendirilmesi." In Sosyoloji Derneği ve T.C. Başbakanlık Devlet İstatistik Enstitüsü, *II Ulusal Sosyoloji Kongresi: Toplum ve Göç.* Ankara: Sosyoloji Derneği Yayın no.5, DİE Yayın no.2046, 1997.

Göktürk, Atilla. "Zorunlu Göç ve bir Kent: Van." In Sosyoloji Derneği ve T.C. Başbakanlık Devlet İstatistik Enstitüsü, *II Ulusal Sosyoloji Kongresi: Toplum ve Göç.* Ankara: Sosyoloji Derneği Yayın no.5, DİE Yayın no.2046, 1997.

Graham, Norman A., ed. *Seeking Security and Development.* Boulder, Colo.: Lynne Rienner, 1994.

Gramsci, Antonio. *Selections from the Prison Notebooks of Antonio Gramsci,* edited and translated by Quentin Hoare and Geoffrey Nowell Smith. New York: International Publishers, 1971.

Günay Anadolu Projesi (GAP) Research Team. *Population Movements in the Southeastern Anatolia Project Region.* Ankara: Middle East Technical University, Department of Sociology, 1994.

Güneş-Ayata, Ayşe. "Geleneksel ve Modern Dayanışma." In T.C. Başbakanlık Kadın ve Sosyal Hizmetler Müsteşarlığı, *Gecekondularda Ailelerarası Geleneksel Dayanışmanın Çağdaş Organizasyonlara Dönüşümü.* Ankara: T.C. Başbakanlık Kadın ve Sosyal Hizmetler Müsteşarlığı Yayınları no. 75, 1993.

Gunter, Michael M. *The Kurds in Turkey: A Political Dilemma.* Boulder, Colo.: Westview, 1990.

Gurr, Ted Robert and Barbara Harff. *Ethnic Conflict in World Politics.* Boulder, Colo.: Westview, 1994.

Gwertzman, Bernard and Michael T. Kaufman, eds. *The Collapse of Communism.* New York: Times Books, 1990.

Haeri, Shahla. *Law of Desire: Temporary Marriage in Shi'i Iran.* Syracuse, N.Y.: Syracuse University Press, 1989.

Haftendorn, Helga. "The Security Puzzle: Theory-Building and Discipline-Building in International Security." *International Studies* 35 (1991): 3-17.

Halliday, Fred. "State and Society in International Relations: A Second Agenda." *Millennium: Journal of International Studies* 16, no. 2 (1987): 215-29.

Harik, Iliya and Denis J. Sullivan, eds. *Privatization and Liberalization in the Middle East.* Bloomington: Indiana University Press, 1992.

al-Hassan, Hamza. *Al-shi'a fi al-mamlaka al-'arabiyya al-sa'udiyya.* Vols. 1 and 2. Beirut: Mu'assasat al-baqi li ihya' al-turath, 1993.

Hatipoğlu, Ömer Vehbi. *Bir Başka Açıdan Kürt Sorunu.* Ankara: Mesaj Yayın, 1992.

Havel, Vaclav. "Transcending the Clash of Cultures." *Journal of Democracy* 6, no. 2 (April 1995): 9.

al-Hawali, Safar. *Kashf al-ghamma 'an 'ulama' al-umma.* N.p.: Dar al-hikma, 1991.

Henze, Paul B. *Turkey toward the Twenty-First Century.* Santa Monica, Calif.: Rand, 1992.

Heydemann, Steven. "Taxation without Representation: Authoritarianism and Economic Liberalization in Syria." In *Rules and Rights in the Middle East: Democracy, Law, and Society,* edited by Ellis Goldberg, Resat Kesaba, and Joel Migdal. Seattle: University of Washington Press, 1993.

Holsti, Ole R. "Theories of International Relations and Foreign Policy: Realism and Its Challengers." In *Controversies in International Relations Theory: Realism and the Neoliberal Challenge,* edited by Charles W. Kegley, Jr. New York: St. Martin's Press, 1995.

Hudson, Michael C. *Arab Politics: The Search for Legitimacy.* New Haven: Yale University Press, 1977.

Huntington, Samuel P. "What Cost Freedom? Democracy and/or Economic Reform." *Harvard International Review* 15, no. 2 (winter 1992/93).

İmset, İ. *PKK: Ayrılıkçı Şiddetin 20 Yılı (1973-1992).* Ankara: Turkish Daily News Publications, 1993.

Ibrahim, Hassan. "The Arab Common Market." *Newsletter of the Economic Research Forum for the Arab Countries, Iran, and Turkey* (Cairo) 3, no. 4 (December 1997-January 1998).

Ibrahim, Sa'd al-Din. *Al-milal wa-al-nihal wa-al-'araq: humum al-aqalliyyat fi al-watan al-'arabi* (Religions, sects, and races: concerns of minorities in the Arab motherland). Cairo: Markaz Ibn-Khaldun li-al-dirasat al-inma'iyya, 1989.

———. "Masadir al-shar'iyya fi al-anzima al-'arabiyya" (Sources of legitimacy in Arab political systems). In *Azmat al-dimuqratiyya fi al-watan al-'arabi* (Crisis of democracy in the Arab motherland), by Sa'ad al-Din Ibrahim et al., 403-30. Beirut: Markaz dirasat al-wahda al-'arabiyya, 1984.

International Criminal Police Organization (Interpol). *Statistiques criminelles internationales. International Crime Statistics. Saint-Cloud,* France: Secretariat générale de l'O.I.P.C, 1950/52-.

International Institute for Strategic Studies. *The Military Balance, 1995-1996.* London: Oxford University Press, 1995.

Islam, Shada. "Santer Slams Israel." *Middle East International,* 27 February 1998, 13.

Israel sherut ha-hidrologi (Israel Hydrological Service). *Status of Water Resources: Fall 1994.* Annual Report. In Hebrew. Jerusalem: Water Commission, 1995.

Izady, Mehrdad R. *The Kurds.* Washington, D.C.: Taylor and Francis, 1992.

Jervis, Robert. "Security Regimes." *International Organization* 36, no. 2 (spring 1982).

Kally, Elisha. "Costs of Inter-Regional Conveyance of Water and Cost of Sea Water Desalination." In *A Proposal for the Development of a Regional Water Master Plan,* by Karen Assaf et al, 175-92. Jerusalem: Israel Palestine Center for Research and Information, 1993).

Kam, Ephraim. "The Threat Perception of the Arab States." In *Arms Control and the New Middle East Security Environment,* edited by Shai Feldman and Ariel Levite, 92-93. Tel Aviv: Jaffee Center for Strategic Studies, 1994.

Kazemi, Farhad. "Civil Society and Iranian Politics." In *Civil Society in the Middle East,* edited by Augustus Richard Norton. Vol. 2, 139-40. New York: E. J. Brill, 1996.

——— and Augustus Richard Norton, "Civil Society, Political Reform, and Authoritarianism in the Middle East." *Contention: Debates in Society, Culture, and Science* 5, no. 2 (winter 1996): 107-19.

Kegley, Charles W., Jr., ed. *Controversies in International Relations Theory: Realism and the Neoliberal Challenge.* New York: St. Martin's Press, 1995.

Kelman, Herbert C. "Social-Psychological Dimensions of International Conflict." In *Peacemaking in International Conflict: Methods and Techniques,* edited by I. W. Zartman and J. L. Rasmussen. Washington D.C.: U.S. Institute of Peace, 1996.

Keohane, Robert O., ed. *Neorealism and Its Critics.* New York: Columbia University Press, 1986.

——— and Joseph S. Nye. *Power and Interdependence.* 1st ed. Boston: Little, Brown, 1977; 2d ed. New York: Harper Collins, 1989.

Kepel, Gilles. *The Prophet and the Pharaoh: Muslim Extremism in Egypt.* London: Al Saqi Books, 1985.

Kertzer, David. *Ritual, Politics, and Power.* New Haven: Yale University Press, 1988.

Kışlalı, M. A. *Güneydoğu Düşük Yoğunlu Çatışma.* Ankara: Ümit Yayıncılık, 1996.

Kirişçi, Kemal and Gareth M. Winrow. *Kürt Sorunu; Kökeni ve Gelişimi.* Istanbul: Tarih Vakfı Yurt Yayınları, 1997.

Klieman, Aharon. "The Israel-Jordan Tacit Security Regime." In *Regional Security Regimes: Israel and Its Neighbors,* edited by Efraim Inbar, 127-51. Albany: State University of New York Press, 1995.

Kliot, Nurit. *Water Resources and Conflict in the Middle East.* London: Routledge, 1994.

Koch-Weser, Caio. "Economic Performance and Regional Cooperation: A Development Agenda for the Middle East and North Africa." *Middle East Policy* 2, no. 2 (1993).

Kolodziej, Edward A. "Renaissance in Security Studies? Caveat Lector." *International Security Studies* 36 (1992): 421-38.

Korany, Bahgat, Paul Noble, and Rex Brynen, eds. *The Many Faces of National Security in the Arab World.* New York: St. Martin's Press, 1993.

Krasner, Stephen D. "Structural Causes and Regime Consequences." *International Organization* 36, no. 2 (spring 1982): 185.

Krause, Keith and Michael C. Williams. "Broadening the Agenda of Security Studies: Politics and Methods." *Mershon International Studies Review* 40 (1996): 229-54.

Kut, Gün. "Burning Waters: The Hydropolitics of the Euphrates and Tigris." *New Perspectives on Turkey* 9 (fall 1993): 1-19.

Laqueur, Walter. *The Road to Jerusalem: The Origins of the Arab-Israeli Conflict, 1967.* New York: Macmillan, 1968.

Lawson, Fred. "Neglected Aspects of the Security Dilemma in the Arab World." In *National Security in the Third World: The Management of Internal and External Threats,* edited by Edward E. Azar and Chung-in Moon, 100-26. Aldershot, U.K.: Edward Elgar Publishing, 1988.

Lederman, Itshak. *The Arab-Israeli Experience in Verification and Its Relevance to Conventional Arms Control in Europe.* CISSM occasional paper no. 2. College Park, Md.: University of Maryland, Center for International Security Studies at Maryland, School of Public Affairs, 1989.

Leonard, James et al. *National Threat Perceptions in the Middle East.* United Nations Institute for Disarmament Research, research paper no. 37. New York: United Nations, September 1995.

Lesser, Ian and Ashley Tellis. *Strategic Exposure: Proliferation around the Mediterranean.* Santa Monica, Calif.: RAND, 1996.

Levite, A. E. and E. B. Landau. *Confidence and Security Building Measures in the Middle East.* Tel Aviv: Jaffee Center for Strategic Studies, 1997.

Levy, Marc A. "Is the Environment a National Security Issue?" *International Security* 20, no. 2 (fall 1995): 35-62

Levy, Marion J., Jr. *Modernization and the Structure of Societies: A Setting for International Affairs.* Princeton: Princeton University Press, 1966.

Lewis, Bernard. "Rethinking the Middle East." *Foreign Affairs* 7, no. 2 (fall 1992): 99-119.

——. *The Emergence of Modern Turkey.* New York: Oxford University Press, 1961.

Libiszewski, Stephan. *Water Disputes in the Jordan River Basin Region and Their Role in the Resolution of the Arab-Israeli Conflict.* Environment and Conflicts Project occasional paper no. 13. Zurich: Center for Security Studies and Conflict Research, 1995.

Looney, Robert. "Arms Races in the Middle East: A Test of Causality." *Arms Control* 11 (September 1990): 178-90.

Lowi, Miriam R. *The Politics of Water: The Jordan River and the Riparian States.* McGill Studies in International Development, no. 35. Montreal, Canada: Centre for Developing-Area Studies, McGill University, 1989.

Luciani, Giacomo. "The Oil Rent, the Fiscal Crisis of the State and Democratization," In *Democracy without Democrats? The Renewal of Politics in the Muslim World,* edited by Ghassan Salamé. New York: I. B. Tauris, 1994.

——. "Allocation vs. Production States: A Theoretical Framework." In *The Rentier State,* edited by Hazem Beblawi and Giacomo Luciani, 63-82. London: Croom Helm, 1987.

Lustick, Ian S. "The Absence of Middle Eastern Great Powers: Political 'Backwardness' in Historical Perspective." *International Organization* 51, no. 4 (autumn 1997): 653-83.

Macleod, Arlene. *Accommodating Protest: Working Women, the New Veiling and the Change in Cairo.* New York: Columbia University Press, 1991.

McDowall, David. *A Modern History of the Kurds.* London: I. B. Tauris, 1996.

McNaugher, Thomas L. "Arms Sales and Arms Embargoes in the Persian Gulf: The Real Dilemmas of Dual Containment." In *The Powder Keg in the Middle East: The Struggle for Gulf Security,* edited by Geoffrey Kemp and Janice Gross Stein. Lanham, Md.: Rowman and Littlefield, 1995.

Makiya, Kanan. "A Turning Point in Arab Politics?" *Journal of Democracy* 6, no. 1 (January 1995): 90-103.

Mastanduno, Michael, David A. Lake, and G. John Ikenberry. "Toward a Realist Theory of State Action." *International Studies Quarterly* 33 (1989): 457-74.

Mathews, Jessica Tuchman. "Redefining Security." *Foreign Affairs* (spring 1989): 162-77.

Mayer, Ann. "Universal versus Islamic Human Rights: A Clash of Cultures or a Clash with a Construct?" *Michigan Journal of International Law* 15 (winter 1994).

Mayhew, Leon H. "Society." In *International Encyclopedia of the Social Sciences,* edited by David L. Sills. Vol. 14, 577-85. New York: Macmillan, 1968.

Medzini, Meron, ed. *Israel's Foreign Relations: Selected Documents.* Jerusalem: Ministry of Foreign Affairs, 1976.

Menashri, David, ed. *Ha-Islam ha-fundamentalisti: etgar li-yetsivut ezorit* (Islamic fundamentalism: a challenge to regional stability). Tel Aviv: Tel Aviv University, Moshe Dayan Center, 1993.

Morgenthau, Hans J. *Politics among Nations: The Struggle for Power and Peace.* New York: Alfred Knopf, 1948 and other editions to 1985.

Moussalli, Ahmad S. "Modern Islamic Fundamentalist Discourses on Civil Society, Pluralism, and Democracy." In *Civil Society in the Middle East,* edited by Augustus Richard Norton. Vol. 1, 70-119. New York: E. J. Brill, 1995.

Mumcu, Uğur. *Kürt Islam Ayaklanması.* Ankara: Tekin Yayınevi, 1991.

Munazzama al-'arabiyya li-huquq al-insan (Arab Organization for Human Rights). *Huquq al-insan fi al-watan al-'arabi* (Human rights in the Arab world). Cairo, 1989-96.

Naff, Thomas. "Conflict and Water in the Middle East." In *Water in the Arab World,* edited by Peter Rogers and Peter Lydon. Cambridge, Mass.: MIT Press, 1995.

—— and Ruth C. Matson, eds. *Water in the Middle East: Conflict and Cooperation.* Boulder, Colo. : Westview, 1984.

National Democratic Institute for International Affairs. *Promoting Participation in Yemen's 1993 Elections.* Washington, D.C.: National Democratic Institute for International Affairs, 1994.

Niblock, Tim. "Economic Liberalisation in the Arab World: The Social and Political Significance." RUSEL working paper 1. Exeter: University of Exeter, Research Unit for the International Study of Economic Liberalisation and its Social and Political Effects, 1991.

Nonneman, Gerd. "Economic Liberalisation in the Developing World: The State of the Debate, and the Case of the Middle East." RUSEL working paper 12. Exeter: University of Exeter, Research Unit for the International Study of Economic Liberalisation and its Social and Political Effects, 1993.

Nye, Joseph S., Jr. *Understanding International Conflicts.* New York: Harper Collins, 1993.

O'Ballance, Edgar. *The Third Arab-Israeli War.* London: Faber, 1972.

O'Brien, Patrick. *Revolution in Egypt's Economic System: From Private Enterprise to Socialism.* New York: Issued under the auspices of the Royal Society for International Affairs by Oxford University Press, 1966.

O'Donnell, Guillermo and Philippe C. Schmitter. *Transitions from Authoritarian Rule: Tentative Conclusions about Uncertain Democracies.* Baltimore: Johns Hopkins University Press, 1986.

Olzak, Susan. *The Dynamics of Ethnic Competition and Conflict.* Stanford, Calif.: Stanford University Press, 1992.

Öniş, Ziya. "The Political Economy of Islamic Resurgence in Turkey: The Rise of the Welfare Party in Perspective." *Third World Quarterly* 18, no. 4 (1997): 743-66.

Özdağ, Ü. *Güneydoğu Anadolu Bölgesi'nde Doğu ve Güneydoğu Anadolu'dan Batı'ya Göç Edenlerde Kültürel Yapı ve Kültürel Kimlik Sorunu.* Ankara: Türk Metal-İş Sendikası Yayınları, 1995.

Paul, James A. *Human Rights in Syria: A Middle East Watch Report.* Washington, D.C.: Human Rights Watch, 1990.

Perkins, Charles. *Arms to the Arabs: The Arab Military Buildup since 1973*. AIPAC Papers on U.S.-Israel Relations, no. 16. Washington, D.C.: American Israel Public Affairs Committee, 1989.

Przeworski, Adam. *Democracy and the Market*. Cambridge: Cambridge University Press, 1991.

Putnam, Robert D. *Making Democracy Work: Civic Traditions in Modern Italy*. Princeton: Princeton University Press, 1993.

———. "Diplomacy and Domestic Politics: The Logic of Two-Level Games." *International Organization* 42, no. 3 (summer 1988): 427- 60.

Pye, Lucian W. "The Legitimacy Crisis." In *Crises and Sequences of Political Development*, edited by Leonard Binder, 135-158. Princeton, N.J.: Princeton University Press, 1971.

Qutb, Sayyid. *Milestones*. Kuwait: Islamic International Unity, 1978.

Ransome, Paul. *Antonio Gramsci: A New Introduction*. London: Harvester Wheatsheaf, 1992.

Razi, G. Hossein. "Legitimacy, Religion, and Nationalism in the Middle East." *American Political Science Review* 84, no. 1 (March 1990).

Refah Partisi. *14 Aralık 1995*. Ankara: Seçimleri Beyannamesi, 1995.

Richards, Alan. "Beyond Islamic Extremism: The True Causes of Instability in the Middle East." Paper presented at the Center for Strategic and International Studies, Georgetown University, Washington, D.C., 7 September 1995.

Rittberger, Volker et al. "Toward an East-West Security Regime: The Case of Confidence and Security-Building Measures." *Journal of Peace Research* 27, no. 1 (1990): 55.

Robins, Philip. "The Overland State: Turkish Policy and The Kurdish Issue." *International Affairs* 69, no. 3 (1993): 657-76.

Rogers, P. "The Value of Cooperation in Resolving International River Basin Disputes." *Natural Resources Forum*, May 1993.

Rouleau, Eric. "Turkey: Beyond Ataturk." *Foreign Policy* 103 (1996): 76.

Roy, Delwin. "Saudi Arabian Education: Development Policy." *Middle Eastern Studies* 28, no. 3 (July 1992): 477-508.

Rustow, Dankwart. "Transitions to Democracy." *Comparative Politics* 2, no. 3 (1970): 337-63.

Saffari, Said. "The Islamic Financial Sector in Iran: Locating the Informal-Organized Qarz al-Hasseneh Institution." Paper presented at the conference on "State and Informal Economies." Harvard University, 22-23 February 1996.

Sagan, Scott D. and Kenneth N. Waltz. *The Spread of Nuclear Weapons: A Debate*. New York: W. W. Norton, 1995.

Saktanber, Ayşe. "Formation of a Middle-Class Ethos and its Quotidian: Revitalizing Islam in Urban Turkey." In *Space, Culture, and Power*, edited by Ayşe Öncü and Petra Weyland. London: Zed Books, 1997.

Salamé, Ghassan. "Small is Pluralistic: Democracy as an Instrument of Civil Peace." In *Democracy without Democrats? The Renewal of Politics in the Muslim World,* edited by Ghassan Salamé, 85-111. New York: I. B. Tauris, 1994.

———. "Political Power and the Saudi State." In *Power and Stability in the Middle East,* edited by Berch Berborglu. London: Zed Books, 1989.

———. "Inter-Arab Politics: The Return of Geography." In *The Middle East: Ten Years after Camp David,* edited by William B. Quandt, 319-53. Washington, D.C.: Brookings Institute, 1988.

Sarnevaz, Bahar. *Guardians of Thought: Limits on Freedom of Expression in Iran.* New York: Middle East Watch, 1993.

Saudi Arabia, Ministry of Education. *Al-sira al-nabawiyya wa-tarikh al-dawlat al-islamiyya.* Textbook for secondary schools, vol. 1. Saudi Arabia: Wizarat al-ma'arif, 1993.

Saudi Arabia, Ministry of Education. *Tarikh al-mamlaka al-'arabiyya al-sa'udiyya.* Textbook for secondary schools, vol. 3. Saudi Arabia: Wizarat al-ma'arif, 1993.

Saudi Arabia, Monetary Agency. *Annual Report.* Saudi Arabia, 1994.

Schiff, Ze'ev. *Peace with Security: Israel's Minimal Security Requirements in Negotiations with Syria.* The Washington Institute for Near East Policy Paper no. 34. Washington D.C.: Washington Institute for Near East Policy, 1993.

———. "The Censored Report Revealed." In Hebrew. *Ha-aretz,* (Tel Aviv) 8 October 1993.

———. "Lebanon: Motivations and Interests in Israeli Policy." *Middle East Journal* 38 (spring 1984): 220-27.

Schroeder, Paul. "Historical Reality and Neo-Realist Theory." *International Security* 19, no. 1 (1994): 108-48.

Segal, Aaron, comp. and ed. An Atlas of International Migration. London: Hans Zell, 1993.

Seufert, Günter. "Between Religion and Ethnicity: A Kurdish-Alevi Tribe in Globalizing Istanbul." In *Space, Culture, and Power,* edited by Ayşe Öncü and Petra Weyland. London: Zed Books, 1997.

Sever, Metin. *Kürt Sorunu: Aydınlarımız ne Düşünüyor.* Istanbul: Cem Yayınevi, 1992.

Shahabi, Sohrab. "Investment Policy in Iran." *Iranian Journal of International Affairs* 7, no. 4 (winter 1996).

Shalev, Aryeh. *Israel and Syria: Peace and Security on the Golan.* Boulder, Colo.: Westview Press; Jerusalem: Jerusalem Post, 1994.

———. *Shituf-peulah be-tsel imut: mishtar shevivat ha-neshek Yisrael-Suryah, 1949-1955* (Co-operation in the shadow of conflict: the Israeli-Syrian armistice regime, 1949-1955). Tel Aviv: Ministry of Defense, 1989.

Shambayati, Hootan. "The Rentier State, Interest Groups, and the Paradox of Autonomy: State and Business in Turkey and Iran." *Comparative Politics* 26, no. 3 (April 1994).

Sheffer, Eliezer. "The Economic Burden of the Arms Race between the Confrontational States and Israel." In Hebrew. In *Security and Israel's Economy in the 1980s,* edited by Zvi Lenir. Tel Aviv: Ministry of Defense, 1985.

Shimshoni, Jonathan. *Israel and Conventional Deterrence: Border Warfare from 1953 to 1970.* Ithaca, N.Y.: Cornell University Press, 1988.

Shultz, Richard. "Introduction to International Security?" In *Security Studies for the 1990s,* edited by Richard Shultz, Roy Godson, and Ted Greenwood. Washington: Brassey's, 1993.

Shuval, Hillel I. "An Economic Approach to the Resolution of Water Conflicts." In *Proceedings of Workshop on Joint Management of Aquifers Shared by Israeli and Palestinians,* edited by E. Feitelson and M. Hadad. Jerusalem: Hebrew University of Jerusalem, Truman Institute for Peace, 1995.

———. "Approaches to Resolving the Water Conflicts between Israel and Her Neighbors: A Regional Water for Peace Plan." *Water International* 17 (1992):133-43.

Sigmund, Paul E. *The United States and Democracy in Chile.* Baltimore, Md.: Johns Hopkins University Press, 1993.

Singer, Hans W. "Are the Structural Adjustment Programmes Successful?" *Pakistan Journal of Applied Economics* 11 (summer and winter 1995).

Singerman, Diane. *Avenues of Participation: Family, Politics, and Networks in Urban Quarters of Cairo.* Princeton: Princeton University Press, 1995.

———. "Civil Society in the Shadow of the Egyptian State: The Role of Informal Networks in the Constitution of Public Life." Paper presented at the conference on "Civil Society Debate and Middle Eastern Studies." University of California, Los Angeles, 29 January 1996.

Soffer, Arnon. "The Relevance of the Johnston Plan to the Reality of 1993 and Beyond." In *Water and Peace in the Middle East,* edited by J. Isaac and H. I. Shuval, 107-122. Amsterdam: Elsevier Press, 1994.

———. *Neharot shel esh* (Rivers of fire). Tel Aviv: Am Oved, 1992.

Sönmez, Mustafa. *Doğu Anadolu'nun Hikayesi: Ekonomik ve Sosyal Tarih.* Ankara: ArkadaşYayınevi, 1992.

Sosyaldemokrat Halkçı Parti. *Güneydoğu Raporu.* Ankara: Sosyaldemokrat Halkçı Parti, 1989.

Soysal, Yasemin Nuhoğlu. *Limits of Citizenship: Migrants and Postnational Membership in Europe.* Chicago: University of Chicago Press, 1994.

Springborg, Robert. "The President and the Field Marshal: Civil Military Relations in Egypt Today." *Middle East Report* 17 (July-August 1987): 8-16.

Stack, John F. *Ethnic Identities in a Transnational World.* Westport, Connecticut: Greenwood Press, 1981.

Starr, Joyce. "Water Wars." *Foreign Policy* 82 (1991): 17-36.

Stein, Arthur. *Why Nations Cooperate: Circumstance and Choice in International Relations.* Ithaca, N.Y.: Cornell University Press, 1990.

———. "Coordination and Collaboration: Regimes in an Anarchic World." *International Organization* 36, no. 2 (spring 1982): 298-323.

Stein, Janice Gross. "A Common Aversion to War: Regimes Creation by Egypt and Israel as a Strategy of Conflict Management." In *Conflict Management in the Middle East,* edited by Gabriel Ben-Dor and David Dewitt, 59-77. Lexington, Mass.: Lexington Books, 1987.

Stevens, G. G. Jordan *Water Partition.* Stanford, Calif.: Stanford University Press, 1965.

Stockholm International Peace Research Institute. *SIPRI Yearbook 1995: Armaments, Disarmament and International Security.* Oxford: Oxford University Press, 1995.

Sullivan, Denis J. *Private Voluntary Organizations in Egypt: Islamic Development, Private Initiative, and State Control.* Gainesville: University Press of Florida, 1994.

Sunar, İlkay and Binnaz Toprak. "Islam in Politics: The Case of Turkey." *Government and Opposition* 18, no. 4 (1983): 421-41.

Şeker, Murat. "Survey on Ethnic and Religious Identity in Turkey." Unpublished mimeo. 1998.

Tarhanlı,İstar. *Müslüman Toplum "Laik" Devlet.* Istanbul: AFA Yayınları, 1993.

Task Force on Multilateral Development Banks. "Serving a Changing World." *World Report.* Washington, D.C.: 15 March 1996.

Tetzlaff, Rainer. "Good Governance and Structural Adjustment Programs: The World Bank's Experience in Africa South of Sahara." *Pakistan Journal of Applied Economics* 11 (summer and winter 1995).

Tilly, Charles. "Where do Rights Come From?" Paper prepared for the Vilhelm Aubert Memorial Symposium, University of Oslo, August 1990.

Treaty of Peace between the State of Israel and the Hashemite Kingdom of Jordan, 26 October 1994. Jerusalem: Israel Information Service Gopher, 1994.

Türkdoğan, Orhan. *Alevi Bektaşi Kimliği.* Istanbul: Timaş Yayınları, 1995.

Türkiye Odalar ve Borsalar Birliği (TOBB). *Doğu Sorunu: Teşhisler ve Tesbitler, Özel Araştırma Raporu.* Stratejik Araştırmalar Dizisi 1. Ankara: TOBB, 1995.

Türk Mühendis ve Mimar Odaları Birliği (TMMOB). *Bölgeiçi Zorunlu Göçten Kaynaklanan Toplumsal Sorunların Diyarbakır Kenti Öçeğinde Araştırılması.* Ankara: TMMOB, 1996.

Ullman, Richard H. "Redefining Security." *International Security* 8, no. 1 (summer 1983): 129-53.

United Nations Development Program. *Human Development Report.* Oxford: Oxford University Press, 1990-96.

United Nations High Commissioner for Refugees. *Facts and Figures.* UNHCR, 1996.

Van Creveld, Martin. *Nuclear Proliferation and the Future of Conflict.* New York: Free Press, 1993.

Voll, John. "Renewal and Reform in Islamic History: Tajdid and Islah." In *Voices of Resurgent Islam,* edited by John Esposito, 32-47. New York: Oxford University Press, 1983.

Waltz, Kenneth N. "The Emerging Structure of International Politics." *International Security* 18, no. 2 (1993): 44-45.

———. *The Spread of Nuclear Weapons: More May Be Better.* Adelphi paper 171. London: International Institute for Strategic Studies, 1981.

———. *Theory of International Politics.* Reading: Addison-Wesley, 1979.

———. *Man, the State, and War: A Theoretical Analysis.* New York: Columbia University Press, 1959.

Waltz, Susan E. *Human Rights and Reform: Changing the Face of North African Politics.* Los Angeles: University of California Press, 1995.

Waterbury, John. "Democracy without Democrats?: The Potential for Political Liberalization in the Middle East." In *Democracy without Democrats? The Renewal of Politics in the Muslim World,* edited by Ghassan Salamé. New York: I. B. Tauris, 1994.

Weber, Max. "Politics as a Vocation." In *From Max Weber: Essays in Sociology,* translated and edited by H. H. Gerth and C. Wright Mills. New York: Oxford University Press, 1958.

Weiner, Myron. "A Security Perspective on International Migration." *The Fletcher Forum of World Affairs* 20, no. 2 (summer/fall 1996): 17-34.

White, Jenny B. "Civic Culture and Islam in Urban Turkey." In *Civil Society: Challenging Western Models,* edited by Chris Hann and Elizabeth Dunn, 143-54. London: Routledge, 1996.

Williams, Frances. "Palestine Trade Hit by Stalemate in Mideast." *Financial Times* (London), 13 March 1998.

Wilson, Peter and Douglas Graham. *Saudi Arabia: The Coming Storm.* New York: M. E. Sharpe, 1994.

Wilson, Rodney. "The Economic Relations of the Middle East towards Europe or within the Region?" *Middle East Journal* 48, no. 2 (spring 1994).

Wishart, D. M. "The Breakdown of the Johnston Negotiations over the Jordan Waters." *Middle Eastern Studies* 26 (1990): 536-46.

Wolf, A. "A Hydropolitical History of the Nile, Jordan, and Euphrates River Basins." In *International Water of the Middle East,* edited by A. K. Biswas, 5-43. New York: Oxford University Press, 1994.

World Bank. *World Development Report.* London: Oxford University Press, 1989-96.

———. *Claiming the Future: Choosing Prosperity in the Middle East and North Africa.* Washington D.C., 1995.

———. *International Economics Department, Analysis and Prospects Division.* "The World Economy and Implications for the Middle East and North Africa Region, 1995-2010." By E. Mick Riordan et al. Unpublished. Washington D.C., June 1995.

Yalçın-Heckmann, L. "Kurdish Tribal Organization and Local Political Processes." In *Turkish State, Turkish Society,* edited by Andrew Finkel and Nükhet Sirman. London: Routledge, 1990.

Yaniv, Avner. *Deterrence without the Bomb.* Lexington, Mass.: Lexington Books, 1987.

Yariv, Agmon. "The Israeli-Egyptian Relationship, 1949-1955, as an International Security Regime." Master's thesis, Tel Aviv University, 1994.

Yeğen, M. "The Turkish State Discourse and the Exclusion of Kurdish Identity." *Middle Eastern Studies* 32, no.2 (April 1996).

Zacher, Mark W. and Richard A. Matthew. "Liberal International Theory: Common Threads, Divergent Strands." In Charles W. Kegley, Jr., ed. *Controversies in International Relations Theory: Realism and the Neoliberal Challenge*. New York: St. Martin's Press, 1995.

Zanoyan, Vahan. "After the Oil Boom." *Foreign Affairs* 74, no. 6 (November/December 1993).

Zisser, Eyal. "Shattering of Illusions: Initial Contacts between the Zionist Movement and the Maronite Community in Lebanon." In Hebrew. *Iyunim* (Ben Gurion University) 6 (1996).

Zvi, Shmuel Ben. *Defense Expenditures and the National Economy*. In Hebrew. Tel Aviv: Tel Aviv University, Published for the Pinhas Sapir Research Institute, 1993.

Index